Families Facing Death

Revised Edition

Elliott J. Rosen

Families Facing Death
Revised Edition

A Guide for Healthcare

Professionals and Volunteers

Jossey-Bass Publishers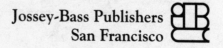
San Francisco

THE ORIGINAL EDITION OF THIS BOOK WAS PUBLISHED BY LEXINGTON BOOKS IN 1990.

Substantial discounts on bulk quantities of Jossey-Bass books are available to corporations, professional associations, and other organizations. For details and discount information, contact the special sales department at Jossey-Bass Inc., Publishers (415) 433–1740; Fax (800) 605–2665.

For sales outside the United States, please contact your local Simon & Schuster International Office.

Jossey-Bass Web address: http://www.josseybass.com

 Manufactured in the United States of America on Lyons Falls Turin Book. This paper is acid-free and 100 percent totally chlorine-free.

Library of Congress Cataloging-in-Publication Data

Rosen, Elliott J.
    Families facing death : a guide for healthcare professionals and volunteers / Elliott J. Rosen. — Rev. ed., Updated ed.
      p.   cm.
    Includes bibliographical references and index.
    ISBN 0-7879-4050-X
    1. Death—Social aspects. 2. Terminally ill—Family relationships. 3. Terminal care. 4. Family psychotherapy.
    I. Title.
HQ1073.R65   1998
306.87—dc21   97-42590

UPDATED EDITION
PB Printing 10 9 8 7 6 5 4 3 2 1

This book is dedicated to the memory of my father,
Leonard Rosen,
who taught me respect for work and zeal for living.

Contents

Preface

My experience as a clinician and teacher of family therapy preceded my interest in death and dying. When I began clinical work and teaching about families and their adjustment to the crises of illness and loss, I discovered that although everyone talked about families and was concerned for their welfare, a coherent framework that shed light on how families actually functioned at this crucial time was missing. It was apparent that the melding of these two fields—family therapy and death and dying—was not only possible but necessary. *Families Facing Death* is a product of that union.

I have struggled with how best to present this material. The thanatology, care-of-the-dying, and grief literature fall roughly into two categories: inspirational and academic. In the former category are those books that reflect an author's personal experience with suffering and loss; the search for meaning in a cruel and chaotic universe; a religious, spiritual, or humanistic journey in quest of the right way to live and die; or a philosophical discourse on death and suffering in the scheme of human life. Academic literature, by contrast, includes those texts that present well-researched and scholarly data, edited compilations of essays or articles, or clinical material based on systematic investigation and replete with data and statistics. To my knowledge, there are no books in either the inspirational or the academic category that comprehensively address the family as a system and how it is affected by terminal illness and loss.

Families Facing Death does not fit into either the inspirational or the academic category. The reader will find little mention of what beliefs are right or wrong, how people ought to feel, or why things go "bump" in the night. Nor does this book offer tables, graphs, data, or statistics that prove or disprove any theory or dramatically break new ground. This book, as its subtitle suggests, is a guide for those people who are trying to help families through the struggle of living with dying. Rather than offer inspiration, I have suggested principles for understanding why families behave as they do and how they can be helped. Instead of presenting academic research, I have included examples of real families who have confronted loss—some successfully and some not so well. Both inspiration and intellectual stimulation are part of the work I do every day, and I have tried to make that reality a part of *Families Facing Death*.

Once, the family gathered around the bed of their dying loved one, supported by the wise family doctor who, knowing the limits of his healing powers, informed them that "it's now in God's hands." He has been replaced by a team of highly trained specialists, and the family is being challenged to participate in the decisions of life and death in unprecedented ways. The healthcare establishment, threatened by a litigious society and weakened by myriad legal, moral, and societal constraints, has no choice but to look to the patient's family to play an active role in medical care. Increasingly, patients are not dying "natural deaths," a fact well known within the medical community but generally not discussed in society at large. Patients are routinely removed from life-support machinery or aided in the dying process, because merely staying alive is no longer deemed adequate. The decisions to take such action, which may at one time have been solely in the province of the physician, now nearly always involve the family. Thus understanding families and how they function is not a luxury but a necessity. *Families Facing Death* can help healthcare personnel develop that understanding.

This book also presents an approach for those working in less dramatic situations, where people really do die natural deaths. The healthcare setting serving the terminally ill in which the needs of families are most comprehensively addressed is hospice. A basic tenet of hospice is "the family as the unit of care," and this philosophy is reflected in the commitment of hospice personnel to join in partnership with families as they care for their dying loved ones. Patients are encouraged to remain at home, and family members are supported so that they can provide both physical and emotional care for the patient. Hospice professionals may provide primary nursing care, medication, palliative treatment, and pain control, while nonprofessionals—paid paraprofessionals as well as unpaid volunteers—offer assistance with bathing, feeding, and other daily needs. In all of these areas, however, family members take active roles. Hospice also attends to the family's psychosocial needs, and the support does not end at the time of death but continues through the bereavement period and with long-term follow-up.

However, although many hospices provide the highest quality of care to families, even in the finest of hospice settings the care of the patient and family remains understandably rooted in a traditional medical model. This means that the subtle shift of patienthood from the individual to the family is lacking. That shift to consideration of the family as the unit of care is the underlying theme of this book.

In other healthcare settings as well, an emphasis on the family as the systemic whole and the unit of care is beneficial: in oncology, intensive care, or coronary care units of acute care hospitals, where families are confronted with the harsh and imminent specter of death; in nursing homes, where elderly residents may soon be separated from their families by death; and in private medical practice, where patients and their families look to the doctor not only for physical care but for support in times of crisis. The concepts presented in this book will also be meaningful to laypersons who interact with families with dying members. Indeed, paraprofessionals and volunteers who may have no formal training in medicine or psychology serve important roles in the care of families facing death.

Although nurses in acute and chronic care units are often intimately conversant with patients' families, they seldom consider the information they have in a systematic way, nor do they share it with their colleagues. A unified approach is rarely taken toward family members. When the nursing staff is not trained to consider treatment of a patient's family, the likelihood of family discontent with nursing care is virtually guaranteed. Complaints by families that they are treated poorly by some nurses may reflect a failure of psychosocial planning rather than the personality of individual nurses.

In the hospital setting, particularly in units where patients are terminally ill, psychosocial planning should be based on a family systems model. Daily conferences ought to include a psychosocial component that addresses the needs of the patient's family. For example, certain family members may need to be taught and encouraged to provide physical care for the patient; another relative might be urged to speak with the physician to get a clear understanding of the patient's condition; and yet another family member may need help in talking with the patient. The staff must understand the impact of the patient's condition on the family as a whole. Some attention might be paid to helping families begin the tasks necessary to facilitating anticipatory grief, an important palliative in the family's healing.

Although personnel in nursing homes have frequent contact with patients' families, a unified, carefully planned program of psychosocial intervention is unheard of in most nursing home settings. The operational isolation of staff members from each other discourages exchange of information among them. Because nurses oversee entire floors with many patients, they may not be present when patients and their families are together. Practical nurses and nurses' aides are more likely to watch patient-family interaction, but they usually represent the least consulted stratum of the staff. Social workers interface with families, and in some settings they may be the only staff formally permitted to do so. But they, like physicians, may not be available to share this information with the staff as a whole.

Nursing homes would be well advised to establish a forum for the sharing of psychosocial information about patients and their families. Such a program may best be implemented by a social worker who has been trained in a family systems approach to gerontologic care. In many facilities, this would be a revolutionary innovation; for, rather than including families as part of the unit of care, the attitude toward families has traditionally been defensive. Family members may be seen at best as adversaries to be avoided, or at worst as snoops who need to be waylaid so as not to interfere with the smooth running of the institution.

I have had occasion to be part of an outreach program in a progressive nursing home, where families are invited to attend meetings along with staff. Besides going to lectures, small group discussions, staff presentations, and relevant movies, family members are encouraged to voice their fears and concerns about the prospective loss of a loved one. This public forum has had a powerful impact on the staff, who have become more attuned to the needs of families. A serious focus on families as valuable allies in the care of patients, and as persons themselves in need of attention by staff, enhances the quality of care in the nursing home setting.

The caretaker who is usually most isolated from colleagues is the physician in a solo practice. The private practitioner who is concerned with the physical needs of the patient does not necessarily think of the larger system when encountering families facing death. Nor are opportunities usually available to the private physician to consult with others regarding psychosocial issues in the lives of patients. When the physician does share his or her impressions of the family with peers, they may together be able to develop strategies for treating the entire family as the unit of care. Alas, few physicians seem inclined to avail themselves of such opportunities. Moreover, medical education does not characteristically encourage young doctors to think in terms of family systems.

Occasionally, a physician may employ a social worker or psychologist to handle the psychosocial issues that arise in patients' lives, and this is indeed admirable. The person invited to join the practice in this capacity must be attuned not only to the psycho-dynamic of the patient but also to the particular needs of the family.

It is my hope that this book will provide guidance to the wide range of disciplines that interact with families facing death. The family as the unit of care is not a novel concept, nor are family systems theory and practice considered an innovation in psychotherapy. However, the joining of these two approaches can provide an effective addition to the clinician's arsenal. In the following chapters, I will explore in greater depth those aspects of family systems theory that are relevant to professionals working with dying patients and their families. I will present, with identities altered, many families with whom I have worked over the years as a private practitioner and consultant. These representative families illustrate the intricate dynamics of families as systems. The more caregivers understand the dynamics of families, the better equipped they will be to help families grow and survive the loss of people they love.

PREFACE TO THE REVISED EDITION

It is a privilege to have the opportunity to create this revised edition of *Families Facing Death*. The experience of these past eight years has reinforced my belief that we best serve the needs of the dying by meeting the needs of their families. Unquestionably, the many people who have told me they were able to use the ideas in this book in their work and in their personal lives have made this effort more deeply gratifying than I could ever have imagined.

In this edition, aside from generally updating sources and available resources, I have added a chapter (Chapter Eight, "Ethical Dilemmas") that addresses many issues that had just begun to surface publicly in 1990. In my continuing work with families, and as chair of a hospice bioethics committee, I have been struck by the degree to which families must grapple quietly with the difficult questions that occupy the front pages of our newspapers. The ethical dilemmas created by burgeoning medical technology, managed care, and increased litigiousness now occupy a more central place in the drama of families facing death. In one respect, this is deeply disturbing, in that we have created yet another obstacle to the peaceful death most of us wish for. Yet these ethical dilemmas also create opportunities for families, and the caregivers who serve them, to deepen their relationships and find creative avenues for managing the end of life.

I can only hope that this new edition of *Families Facing Death* will prove as valuable as the first. I remain grateful to the families and the patients who make this work so satisfying.

Scarsdale, New York   Elliott J. Rosen
November 1997

Acknowledgments

In the late summer of 1973, as a newly appointed professor, I was surprised to learn that I was scheduled to teach an undergraduate course called "Psychology of Death and Dying." I knew little about this subject and could not imagine why anyone would register for the course. Even now, it seems incomprehensible that seventeen years later, I am putting the finishing touches on a book about families confronting death. What began as a frantic search for information on the subject of death has evolved over the years into a deep interest in, and commitment to, working with families and teaching the personnel who serve them.

My academic interest in death and dying and my clinical work with families were soon augmented by real-life contact with families facing death, when I was asked to teach professionals and volunteers as part of the Cancer Support Team program in Rye, New York. I remain grateful to them and have been pleased to remain associated with that program over the years.

I began to see more families with terminally ill members in my private practice and started examining the clinical issues related to grief and mourning and to families caring for the fatally ill. In 1983, I delivered my first lecture to the volunteers and staff of the newly created Jansen Memorial Hospice in Tuckahoe, New York, which was the beginning of a fruitful professional relationship. My gratitude to Jansen's first director, Judy Donovan, for her encouragement and her friendship is beyond words. To be a part of the Jansen interdisciplinary team was a joy and a privilege. As I complete the second edition of this book, I have begun work with a new hospice team, and I look forward to as rich a future with them.

My involvement with the Family Institute of Westchester (FIW) has long provided the primary pillar of support in my professional life. It is there that I have had the opportunity to work with and learn from colleagues and to be a participant in the training of the next generation of family therapists. Since the publication of the first edition of *Families Facing Death*, I have been named director of FIW. I am particularly grateful to Betty Carter, FIW's founder, who has been my mentor and teacher since the very beginning. Everything in this volume that is "right" about families I learned from her; the errors are mine. In addition, my faculty colleagues have consistently provided an atmosphere of friendship and intellectual ferment within which I have learned and grown. I thank them for that. I specifically want to mention the work of my colleagues Monica McGoldrick and Fredda Herz Brown, whose ideas I have drawn on extensively throughout this book.

I am also grateful to the National Hospice Organization, which for several years has given me a forum for presenting my perspective on families. My thanks, as well, to Diodato Villamena, a hospice medical director par excellence; Sugar Genereaux, who knows how to make it all work; and Karyn Feiden, a talented editor.

My family is wonderfully supportive of my work, and I especially thank my wife, Phyllis, for her good humor and her toleration of my excesses and anxiety as I struggled through the revision of this book. My daughters, Aliza and Ariel, have been launched into careers that have afforded us great joy, and I continue to take great pride in their intellectual curiosity, psychological insight, and loving support.

Finally, my deepest gratitude goes to the patients and families whose stories form the guts of this book and my professional life. I have learned more from them than I have learned in any book, and I thank them for entrusting themselves to me in the most painful moments of their lives. I am forever grateful.

Families Facing Death
Revised Edition

1

Focus on the Family

Death ends a life,
but it does not end a relationship,
which struggles on in the survivor's mind,
toward some resolution which it may never find.

Robert Anderson
I Never Sang for My Father

Alice Berg is sixty-one years old, and she is dying of cancer. Alice and her family are no strangers to illness, having lost many of their family members to cancer through the years. Alice's first husband, her father, and her aunt all succumbed to malignancies.

Alice lives with her ninety-three-year-old mother, Barbara, and her thirty-year-old daughter, Susan. The three women have lived as a family ever since Susan's father died in her infancy. The atmosphere in their home is characterized by friction and bickering, and they are constantly criticizing each other. While they are each quite charming with outsiders, displaying wit, intelligence, and civility, their behavior with each other is frequently cruel and cutting, and they seem oblivious to how hurtful they can be. Health-care workers wonder how the three have managed to survive with each other over the years.

Barbara, Alice, and Susan are all that remains of what was once a fairly large, extended family (see Figure 1.1). Barbara lost her father

Figure 1.1. Genogram of the Berg Family, 1997.

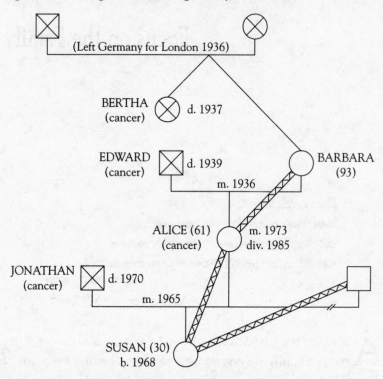

Note: The genogram or diagrammatic family tree, such as that shown in Figure 1.1, is a visual presentation of a family across three generations. The genogram is a practical tool for assessment, education, and the sharing of data. An explanation of the symbols, and guidelines for constructing genograms, can be found in Chapter Two, on pages 40–42. The dates of births and deaths, and information on how and where deaths occur, create a natural guide for tracking the family's history and also for planning appropriate interventions. For clarity, the dating of all genograms in this book has been organized with 1997 as the present year.

when she was a young child, and her mother died in the early 1930s. Shortly thereafter, sensing the growing threat to Jews in their native Germany, Barbara and her twin sister, Bertha—her only sibling—fled to distant relatives in London. Within a few months, Barbara met and married Edward, an older friend of the family. A few months after their marriage, Barbara became pregnant, and almost simultaneously her sister Bertha was diagnosed with cancer. Alice was born just months before Bertha's death. Two years later, Edward fell ill with cancer; he died two weeks short of his daughter's third birthday. Barbara was left to raise her daughter alone with few family or friendship supports. Virtually their entire family remained in Germany and perished in the Holocaust, adding to the overwhelming loss that is a prominent theme for these three women.

Barbara boasts that she is a "tough survivor." Alice also speaks of her mother's toughness, saying that she feels it prevented both of them from showing much affection. "I was never sure," says Alice, "whether Mom loved me or simply saw me as another burden in her difficult life."

Alice grew to young adulthood and married Jonathan, an American who was working in England, and soon afterward, along with Barbara, they moved to the United States. Two years later, Alice became pregnant with Susan, and during her pregnancy Jonathan was diagnosed with cancer; he died before Susan's second birthday. Several years later, Alice remarried, and this marriage ended in divorce after twelve years.

Alice is now stricken with cancer. Barbara, too, is in failing health, and for the first time in her life, she feels unable to cope with daily living. As Alice weakens, Barbara and Susan are incapable of fully managing her care, and the family has turned to the community hospice program for assistance. All three members of the family form an immediate bond with Ruth, an elderly hospice volunteer, herself a Holocaust survivor. Ruth is distressed by the tension in the household and frequently urges the three women to "be nice to each other," but to no avail.

Frustrated, Ruth takes counsel with the hospice team. As the family therapist consulting with the team, I observe how difficult it must be for the three women to be close to each other, for surely their family history has taught them that loving means suffering loss. As a result, these women have made a supreme effort *not* to get close, constructing invisible walls of arguing and unpleasantness to ensure their mutual goal of a safe emotional distance.

At my suggestion, the volunteer writes Barbara, Alice, and Susan a long letter. Recounting the many losses this family has suffered over the years, Ruth concludes: "You have done very well by separating yourselves from each other in order to survive. Closeness would have suffocated you. Independence, however, gives you strength and courage to go on. I congratulate you on having been able to do that."

The women are baffled by the letter and wonder why Ruth is now congratulating them for the very behavior she had criticized. Nevertheless, the letter seems to change the emotional tenor of the household, as the more visible displays of anger and hostility subside. The women do not become affectionate, but they are less prone to incessant bickering. Susan, in fact, hears for the first time stories about her grandmother's and mother's lives in England and about the family that perished in Europe.

When Alice dies not long afterward, Susan and her grandmother are able to settle her affairs with little antagonism. One evening, as they are sorting some of Alice's belongings, Barbara, whose own health is deteriorating, tells her granddaughter that she has decided to enter a nursing home. Susan accepts the decision, although she had always insisted that she would never put her mother or grandmother in a home.

Why did something so seemingly trivial as a volunteer's letter have such an enormous impact on the Bergs? What was it about this letter that triggered a subtle shift in their heretofore hostile patterns of interaction? At this vulnerable point in the family's life, the volunteer's letter seemed to have granted the women permission to accept their attitudes toward each other. They were now able to see themselves as three persons coping with a painful past. The "reframing" of their behavior, describing it not as hostility but as an effective way of coping with the losses of the past and the pain of the present illness, helped relieve the Berg family of guilt about their attitudes toward each other. It further resulted in their being able to address topics that had been taboo for many years.

Although the suggestions contained in a single letter are not sufficient to bring about permanent changes in any family structure, the response of the Bergs demonstrates the profound impact that appropriate interventions can have on families at times of life-threatening illness. Given the limited amount of time usually available, any technique used with such families ought to have some immediate impact, even if the effects are relatively short-term. Ideally, work done with a family at this critical juncture of its life might also have a longer-term effect. Thus it is important to examine the potential shifts that interventions might set in motion at some later time.

The case of the Bergs highlights how terminal illness affects all members of the family, a fact that anyone who has worked with the fatally ill cannot fail to know. The delicate emotional balance of the family is threatened by a terminal diagnosis, and the prospect of death and the concomitant loss of family integrity becomes manifest in shifting patterns of interaction among family members. Often overwhelmed by the uncertainties of terminal care and shattered by the realization that they are going to lose someone they love, family members struggle to find ways to cope better with the loss.

All healthcare personnel are accustomed to frequent and sometimes difficult involvement with patients' families. They may not realize that the family in the present is also a powerful representation of its history across previous generations.

Alice Berg's family wonderfully illustrates this notion, as the interactions between its members were profoundly influenced by their painful and unresolved past. As seen in their genogram, a joyful event—the birth of a child—was consistently coupled in the family's history with the loss of a significant person. Repeatedly through the years, this family had experienced the untimely loss of loved ones: the death of Barbara's twin sister at the prime of her life, closely followed by the death of Edward (Alice's father); the destruction of the extended family in the Holocaust; the death of Jonathan (Susan's father) shortly after his child's birth; and now the imminent death of Alice. For this family, closeness and love were fraught with the prospect of tragic loss. And the sheer number and propinquity of their losses made adequate resolution impossible. A part of this family's legacy was the unspoken belief that survival in the face of tragedy and loss was of greater importance than expressions of love and affection. The death of a loved one was so painful that it was better to avoid love—or at least the demonstrative expression of love. Warmth and affection were replaced by bickering and antagonism, and oddly, such negative interaction became a covert manifestation of intimacy and caring.

The Bergs' story—in particular, the mechanisms they developed for coping with crises such as Alice's illness—illustrates how families function as a system. Anyone who has worked with patients and their families has observed that some families respond to the greatest of tragedies with calm and equanimity, while others, faced with lesser difficulties, fail to function and nearly disintegrate. The diagnosis of life-threatening illness is not in itself sufficient to explain the upheaval of domestic life in such cases. Another, more complex, factor is surely at work, and this is the nature of the larger family system. Chapter Two will explore the family as a system in which the whole (family) is monumentally greater than the sum of its parts (family members). All families operate according to certain fundamental rules, the most significant being that the action of any one part of the system will have an effect on the system as a whole.

Another "rule" is that families act purposefully, although for the most part family members are not aware of the antecedents or reasons for their behavior and interaction. The tendency of family systems to act purposefully is not consistently evident to the observer, since acting purposefully is not always identical to acting productively. Such was the case with the Bergs, whose sarcasm and conflict may have appeared to be cruel and destructive. But the motivation and purpose for their behavior made sense in the larger context of their multigenerational history.

For families do not exist merely in the present; relics of the past embellish and enrich the family picture. Appreciating the influences of the past will help families make the changes necessary to cope with the present.[1] The more those who provide healthcare understand this concept, the better prepared they will be to truly help—and positively change—those whom they serve. Part of the responsibility of the healthcare provider, regardless of professional discipline, is to be attuned to these historical forces and to work with the family systems dynamic to effect desirable change. The hospice volunteer's efforts with the Bergs illustrate the importance of this historical framework. Ruth's attempt to make the three women kinder to each other met with firm resistance until she addressed the underlying motivation for behavior; only then did change begin to take place.

Although each family member reacts idiosyncratically to the prospect of loss, the focus in this book will be on the family as a whole. Its patterns of interaction shift in such a way that it will never again be what it once was. Families facing death must adjust to more than the loss of a loved one. The fundamental reorganization resonates with the history of previous generations and will resound into generations yet to come. This book will provide insight into the ways families are affected by illness, the historical antecedents of the family's reaction to the prospect of loss, and the assistance that personnel in many disciplines may offer that can make a difference in the family's life, now and in the future.

A NEW DEFINITION OF FAMILY

Since *family* is the key concept in this book, it is appropriate to examine exactly what the word means. While an individual's family background contributes to his or her concept of what families are and how they function, the influences of culture are also powerful determinants in that thinking. For each person, the word *family* evokes different images. For those whose formative years spanned the forties and fifties, family is perhaps best depicted in the portrait of Mother, Father, Dick, Jane, and Spot lovingly gathered in their yard, surrounded by a neat picket fence that protects them from all misfortune. For those who came of age a bit later, family is represented by the idyllic life of the Andersons, headed by the all-knowing father, portrayed by Robert Young, whose children are adoringly regarded as "Princess" or "Kitten," and whose problems are solved sensitively and kindly—and within a mere half-hour![2] For children of the past three decades, however, "family" takes on a more complicated cast: picket fences do not seem to offer protection; fathers are often absent and mothers overburdened; and blended and reconstituted families may contribute to, and be unable to solve, the complexities of modern life.

All of these images, and many others that are part of our cultural baggage, are inadequate to describe the family. True, families often do consist of spouses, parents, children, and siblings; but in today's world of divorce and remarriage, step-relatives also enter the family portrait. In other instances, people unrelated by blood or marriage may function as a family. Such "families" include couples who have chosen to cohabit and not marry or bear children; elderly persons who, having outlived their spouses and children, form tight kinship bonds with other senior citizens; and homosexuals who enter into emotional relationships nearly identical to those of married couples.[3]

Healthcare providers, particularly those who care for acutely ill or dying patients, frequently encounter elderly persons who seem to be the sole survivors of their families. It has been my experience, however, that few people have *no* family; rather, family members may be estranged from each other as a result of earlier emotional upheaval. A poignant example of this was an elderly patient who claimed to have no family whatsoever and whose hospital records attested to this fact. However, during an informal chat designed to learn something about this woman and to make an informal evaluation of why she seemed particularly depressed, she accidentally revealed that she had a daughter who lived in the same town and to whom she had not spoken for more than ten years. I urged the social worker to speak with the patient about the cause of the emotional cutoff and, if possible, to obtain her permission to contact her daughter. This resulted in a rapprochement between mother and daughter shortly before the woman's death.

Thus the definition of *family* must be expanded. Family is not merely an assemblage of individuals; it is those same individuals inextricably intertwined in ways that are constantly interactive and mutually reinforcing. And family, in the fullest sense of the word, embraces all generations—those living, those dead, and those yet to be born.

Is the inclusion of the "ghosts" of previous generations helpful in understanding family dynamics? To answer this question, one need only look at the Bergs. Barbara's dead twin sister, her husband (Alice's father), Alice's first husband (Susan's father), and the stepfather who helped raise Susan—all were an integral part of the family despite no longer being physically present. Their influence was actively felt in the lives of the three women, who struggled on with those past relationships toward a resolution that they could not seem to find. And these same players will have significant roles in the not-yet-written script of Susan's future family.

A NEW PERSPECTIVE FOR CAREGIVERS

This expanded definition of the family as a system will provide the framework for this book and its exploration of death and loss in the family context. Most healthcare professionals, and most texts in the field, are rooted in the traditional medical model, which stresses the pathologic condition and the commitment to "do no harm." This approach differs from a family systems perspective, which stresses normal family development, as well as a mandate to effect change and growth in the group as a whole. The medical model concerns itself with the dying patient's basic needs for comfort, pain control, and palliation; the family systems model, on the other hand, addresses the effects of the illness on the entire family.

Healthcare providers have made a commitment to serve families, and the notion of the family as the primary unit of care has become increasingly popular. In practice, however, the family is viewed as a group of individuals who can either prove helpful or resist efforts to deliver care. An adequate grasp of the inner workings of the family—that is, the properties of the family as a system—eludes most healthcare professionals. Although they may speak of the family as the unit of care, in most cases this is no more than a pro forma acknowledgment that patients do indeed have families. They may further concede that families play a role in the patient's physical and emotional well-being. But this is often where it ends; the meaning of the illness in the context of the family is seldom understood and rarely addressed.

The questions posed by healthcare providers who operate from a family systems perspective are different from those asked by providers who practice within a strictly medical model. The latter typically ask questions such as: What is the status of the patient today? What are his symptoms? Who is overseeing medication? Are her emotional needs being met? Are family members following the doctor's orders? Is the family cooperating with nurses and other care providers? Personnel anchored in a family systems approach are certainly going to ask these same questions, for the care of the patient is of great importance to all caregivers, whatever their philosophical orientation, but such providers will likely ask an additional set of equally important questions: How is the daily function of the family being affected by this illness? What coping skills are family members using to care for themselves and the patient? Who is assuming the patient's functions in the family—not only the visible functions, such as providing income or preparing meals, but also the more subtle, emotional functions? Does anything in this family's behavior suggest the possibility of a complicated bereavement?

The family systems perspective on illness itself also differs from the view of the traditional medical model. The healthcare provider whose thinking is rooted in the medical model is likely to focus on the phases through which the patient passes as the illness progresses. Nonprofessional laypersons also view illness as an array of symptoms that worsen over time, bringing the patient closer to death. Although the systems-trained person considers the progression of the patient's illness and symptoms, no less important is the notion that families themselves pass through stages of adaptation that, though related to the physical course of the illness, do not proceed in lockstep with that illness. As Chapter Four will show, making the family the unit of care demands a broader recognition of the phases through which the family and patient pass as they live and cope with illness.

In the final scene of Robert Anderson's extraordinary drama, *I Never Sang for My Father*, Gene, a man who has struggled for many years to achieve some relationship with his now aging and feeble father, screams, "You really think your door was always open to me?" His father replies, "Is that my fault if you never came through it?" Anderson is correct; the complex dynamic of the parent-child relationship cuts in both directions, as do all relationships among family members. If sophisticated, quality care is to be provided, caregivers need to understand how these relationships work and that a multitude of factors combine to make families what they are.

Notes

1. The influences of previous generations on the family is a major theme of this book. The reader who wishes to pursue this concept further is referred to Augustus Y. Napier and Carl A. Whitaker, *The Family Crucible* (New York: HarperCollins, 1978). This readable, popular depiction of the underpinnings of the notion of

intergenerational reciprocity can be enormously helpful in deepening understanding of what makes families behave as they do.

2. Stephanie Coontz's book *The Way We Never Were: American Families and the Nostalgia Trap* (New York: Basic Books, 1992) presents a fascinating perspective on the idealization of family life in previous generations and suggests that we continue to harbor many myths about how families functioned in the past.

3. The shifts in family and marriage patterns from 1970 through 1995 reinforce the magnitude of the changes in what family means. The number of families with children under eighteen with a single male head-of-household rose by nearly 50 percent in those years, and families headed by a single woman rose by even more. In 1960, there were 2.2 divorces per thousand in the population; by 1985, the figure had more than doubled to 5 per thousand, and in 1990 had stabilized at about 4.7. Presently, it is estimated that one-half of all first marriages will end in divorce, with an even higher divorce rate for subsequent marriages. Ken Bryson, author of the 1995 Commerce Department's census report, says: "The increasing diversity of household types continues to challenge our efforts to measure and describe American society. The 'typical household' is an illusion" (U.S. Bureau of the Census, *Household and Family Characteristics*, [Washington, D.C.: U.S. Government Printing Office, 1995], p. 24.).

2

The Family as a System

Happy families are all the same.
Every unhappy family is unhappy in its own way.
                                        Leo Tolstoy
                                        Anna Karenina

Richard Marsh, forty-three, is a successful lawyer and avid tennis player. His wife, Char, runs a prospering mail-order business from an office in their home and, when not attending community or organization meetings, can usually be found with their two teenagers, Richard Jr. (Richie), sixteen, and Andrea, fourteen (see Figure 2.1). Until a few weeks before I first met the Marshes, Char emphasized, their lives were "just perfect."

But then Richie was summarily thrown out of soccer camp for punching a counselor and tearing up the cabin he shared with five other boys. Such uncharacteristic behavior, coupled with a similarly unprecedented drop in grades in the last quarter of his sophomore year, disturbed his parents and prompted them to seek professional guidance. In our first session, the Marshes revealed that Andrea had become withdrawn and depressed in recent months and was no longer her ebullient self. The parents had attributed their two teenagers' changing behavior to normal adolescent rebellion. Richie's outburst at camp forced them to consider other possibilities.

During this first meeting, Richard seemed somewhat distant. Char anxiously reassured both me and her family that they were

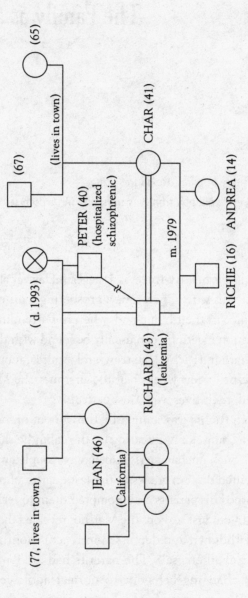

Figure 2.1. Genogram of the Marsh Family, 1997.

"just going through a difficult time." Exactly what was difficult about this time remained unclear, despite my probing.

The Marshes are a white, Protestant family. Both Richard and Char are products of private secondary schools and prestigious East Coast colleges. Char is an only child, and although her parents live just a few miles away, she does not see or speak with them frequently. Richard's mother died four years ago, and his father continues to live in the family house, some twenty miles away. Richard has two siblings: an elder sister, Jean, who lives in California with her husband and three children; and a brother, Peter, about whom Richard seemed reluctant to speak. When pressed, he stated that Peter was "hopelessly schizophrenic" and had been hospitalized since he was nineteen. It was at the initial session with me that Richie and Andrea learned for the first time the specifics about their uncle, who had begun showing signs of mental illness in his midteens. As the early signs were extreme anger and belligerence, both Richard and Char were worried that Richie's behavior might indicate that he, too, was becoming mentally ill.

I was feeling increasingly sure that there were bigger problems in the marriage than either Richard or Char was willing to admit. Richard was emotionally disconnected from his wife and children. In light of his behavior, I tentatively (and erroneously) concluded that he was having an extramarital affair.

I decided to meet alone with Richard and Char. Before the couple's second session, without the children, Char called to say that Richard was going to be out of town. I suggested that she come to see me alone, as it seemed like an ideal opportunity to explore my intuitions about their marriage. When she entered my office, she seemed particularly anxious, and within moments she was in tears. But what Char told me was not what I had expected. Richard had leukemia, diagnosed some four years before. Aggressive chemotherapy had led to a remission, but the previous spring—just before the children started acting out—blood work indicated that the disease had recurred, and the doctors had made a grim prognosis: Richard would likely be dead in less than two years.

Char feared that Richard would be angry with her for telling me this. No one knew about the illness—not their parents, not the children, not a single friend. From the moment of diagnosis, Richard and Char had agreed that they would contain the secret and not burden anyone. Telling me, Char felt, was a betrayal of Richard, but she was no longer able to carry this secret and felt that it was time she and her husband reconsidered their silence.

Richard was, indeed, enraged with Char, refusing to see any reason for revealing that he was fatally ill. It took some time for him to acknowledge that the children's behavior might be related to the keeping from them of this terrible fact. Only reluctantly did he admit that his own determination to guard the secret had begun to weaken when he realized that the disease was not going to go away.

Eventually, Richard and Char began to share the information with their children, parents, close friends, and other relatives—with some remarkable results. Richie, instead of becoming more angry, as his parents had feared, seemed to calm down. Andrea no longer shut herself in her room for hours; she resumed her more characteristic warm, social behavior. Richard and his father had grown somewhat distant from each other after his mother's death; the disclosure about Richard's illness drew father and son closer together. Char's parents became more involved with the Marshes, taking the children on a trip during midsemester break so that Richard and Char could spend a long-awaited week alone together.

In what were to be the last fourteen months of his life, Richard became closer to his family, sharing with his wife, children, and father his feelings about dying, about living, and about his hopes for them in the future. Thanks to a quality medical team, devoted family, and close friends, Richard remained at home through his illness, and at his death he was surrounded by those he loved.

The symptoms that first compelled the Marshes to seek the aid of a family therapist were not, as they had assumed, typical expressions of adolescence but rather a reaction to a secret that had insidiously invaded the life of the family. Richard and Char had become expert at hiding Richard's illness and, indeed, no one suspected that he was fatally ill. However, both children knew that something had happened to upset the emotional balance in their family's life. Although neither youngster could define that "something," or was aware that his or her behavior had changed in response to it, Richie's belligerence and Andrea's withdrawal were unconscious adjustments to the subtle change that occurred when their parents learned of the unfavorable prognosis. The Marshes' story illustrates how a change in any one part of the family system can shake up the entire structure.

There is no more emotionally connected system than the family, if for no other reason than because no one can ever truly leave it. Because of these strong emotional connections, the behavior of any one individual is likely to have an effect on the behavior of all other members of the family. The responses of all members of the family system have likely achieved some balanced, predictable pattern over time. In other words, the behavior of A, responded to predictably by B, will impact on C, which will in turn reinforce the behavior of B, ensuring the continued behavior of A, and so on.

Westerners are accustomed to thinking of cause and effect in a simple, linear relationship; how or why things happen is expressed as "A causes B." When a child behaves unacceptably—for example, when Richie hit the camp counselor—the first impulse is to seek some specific event or person that caused that behavior. However, families do not behave in this linear fashion but rather in mutually reinforcing ways that can best be viewed as circular. This circular view of causality suggests a no-fault approach that focuses on the ongoing sequences of interaction among family members.

The observation of two young children who are playing together provides a graphic illustration of how this process works. To get some attention from Mommy, who is talking on the telephone, little Bobby pokes his sister Mary; she, in turn, kicks him; he screams and pokes her again; she calls him a jerk; when he runs off to tell Mommy, Mary trips him, and he kicks her. Mommy, irritated by the disruption, scolds Mary for not acting her age. Mary sulks and withdraws, Bobby clings to Mommy, and she responds to Daddy's lunchtime phone call with curt remarks about "his" children. At the end of the day, Daddy returns home, hoping for his wife's warm welcome but anticipating her anger and frustration. Bobby's anxiety about Mommy turning her attention from him to Daddy makes him cranky. While Daddy pours himself a stiff drink to unwind, Mommy rails that he has no appreciation of how difficult her day has been. Repetition of these events has wider ramifications: Mommy begins to worry that she's married to someone just like her father, and Daddy begins to avoid his wife and kids so that he doesn't get "eaten alive" by them the way his father was. Neither parent feels comfortable with these thoughts, but rather than working on their interaction as a couple, they start to worry about daughter Mary, convinced she's an unhappy, immature child. The most common result of this not-atypical family interaction is to blame someone as the cause of the difficulties.

When families first seek psychotherapy, they are likely to identify one person—usually a child—as the patient. The Marshes, by identifying Richie as the patient, were able to ignore the powerful subterranean forces that were eating at the family. Each member of the family displayed aberrant or disturbing behavior: Richard was emotionally withdrawn from his wife and children; Char was jumpy and nervous; Richie was aggressive; Andrea was depressed. Richard's leukemia had profoundly upset the emotional balance of the Marsh family. His decision to keep the illness a secret, though a workable coping strategy at the beginning, began to break down as time passed and the disease recurred. Each family member reacted to the strain of that decision, creating the potential of malfunction in the family as a whole as it sought balance and stability in the face of imminent catastrophe.

A primary goal of all family systems, though it is seldom, if ever, articulated, is to maintain a balance that ensures a reasonable degree of function and comfort for everyone. This tendency to seek equilibrium is referred to in the family therapy literature as the family's need to maintain homeostasis.[1] *Homeostasis* means, literally, "staying the same," although in the family it takes on a more complex meaning, for homeostasis in a family systems context is not a static concept but rather quite a dynamic one. Families are capable of change in response to challenges to their integrity. Internal forces, such as the normative passages of the life cycle, and external forces, such as a lost job or an untimely illness or death, are constantly challenging the family to adjust. The paradox inherent in the notion of homeostasis, then, is that although it is a process for maintaining sameness, it is also a process that allows for adaptation and change.

TWO METAPHORS FOR THE FAMILY SYSTEM

Two helpful metaphors may enhance understanding of the family as a system—in particular, of how the whole is greater than the sum of its parts. One metaphor sees the family as a machine. The other metaphor suggests a human comparison and incorporates the concepts of homeostasis and compensation.

In certain respects, one may imagine the family as a complicated machine consisting of a series of complex, interlocking gears, which correspond to individual family members. Some gears are small, others large; some seem to serve a more important function than others, some seem less vital. When properly assembled, the machine operates beautifully, each gear interlocking with its companion in elegant precision. The machine purrs along, accomplishing whatever it was designed to do. Periodically the gears may need oil, and on occasion they may need some minor maintenance as a result of the normal wear and tear to which machines are prone. But a break in a single tooth, in even a minor gear, may have a crippling effect on all the other gears, and the machine may completely lose its ability to function and grind to a halt. The machine will remain inoperative until all the damaged gears have been repaired, and then it will not operate at high efficiency unless the entire mechanism is rebuilt and recalibrated.

The machine has no ability to compensate for a malfunction in its component parts; it either works or it doesn't. This is the fallacy in the mechanistic metaphor: families, unlike machines, do not entirely cease operation when one member breaks down. Rather, they continue to function, albeit in a different way, and one mechanism that makes this possible is homeostasis.

This suggests a second metaphor. Imagine that a man slips on a patch of ice and severely sprains his left ankle. Barely able to walk, he hobbles along, scrupulously avoiding placing weight on the vulnerable ankle and putting most of his weight on his right leg. After limping around like this for a while, he notices discomfort in his right hip. Not long after, he complains of neck and shoulder pain on his left side, and within a few days his back is out. By this time, the pain in his ankle has eased somewhat, but his right hip, his left shoulder, and his back are hurting.

This metaphor expands on the description of the family as a machine by introducing two additional notions: compensation and homeostasis. Just as an individual with a sprained ankle does anything possible to get around, families do everything in their power to continue operating, even in the face of catastrophe. Thus they compensate for the damage to the system while simultaneously trying to keep themselves in balance. Homeostasis is central to the purposeful and meaningful movement of the family system, even though family members do not declare, "Today we are going to achieve a new state of equilibrium." The systemic comfort achieved via homeostasis should not be confused with happiness or even feeling good. Recall the Berg family in Chapter One. They were in balance and had achieved a level of equilibrium, but they were miserable!

The Marsh family demonstrates the parallel between the anatomic compensation for an ankle sprain and compensation within the family system. Originally, the couple had managed to maintain balance by withholding information and keeping the illness a secret. The compensatory mechanisms consisted of maintaining distance from extended family members and creating a facade of normalcy. This had worked in the short run, but recurrence of the disease produced a strain that was no longer containable. Richie's provocative behavior and Andrea's depression were attempts at compensation that proved too damaging for the family anatomy, and the equilibrium was disturbed. Only when the parents revealed the secret that had caused the initial injury to the system was the family able to achieve a functional level of balance, even though they then had to deal with a mortal blow to their future.

BOUNDARIES AND THE RANGE OF FAMILY EMOTIONAL FUNCTION

The overall emotional tenor of family life is determined by the fluidity or rigidity of its boundaries. All systems have boundaries; external boundaries separate the system from all other systems, whereas internal boundaries create functional divisions within the system itself. These boundaries can be rigid and unyielding; more often, they are permeable or semipermeable.

External boundaries define the unique character of the family in relation to the outside world. A family may be Italian or Chinese, big or small, Democrat or Republican. Some families consist of multiple generations in one house; others are just a single parent with one child. Some families are deeply religious, others proudly secular.

Internal boundaries help members define themselves within the family itself. Individuals may belong simultaneously to various subsystems of the family: spousal subsystem, parental subsystem, child subsystem, female subsystem, sports-loving subsystem, artistically creative subsystem, and so on.

In general, healthy families are ones in which boundaries are well defined without being too rigid. This means that each individual can move freely from the family to the outside world, and that individuals can also move freely among the family's subsystems. For example, brother Joe won't feel uncomfortable if he goes shopping with Mom and sister Peg, and Dad can invite Peg to a ball game with him and Joe.

The boundaries established by a family, both to differentiate itself from external systems and to define where each member belongs within the family system, form the framework of the family's emotional functioning.[2] A particular family system can be categorized by its placement along various continua of emotional function. The terms *happy* and *sad*, for example, define the extremes of emotion on a continuum called "mood." We shall now explore three continua of family emotional function that describe different family types: open-closed, enmeshed-disengaged, underfunctioning-overfunctioning. These terms are intended to suggest extremes of family behavior; in reality, no family is entirely closed, disengaged, or underfunctioning.

The Open Versus Closed Family System

The open-closed continuum represents the degree to which family members are permitted to communicate on any subject without fear of reproach or censure. In families classified as open, individuals are free to express their thoughts and emotions, whereas closed family systems discourage and invalidate members' attempts to express unacceptable ideas or feelings. This continuum also reflects how easy it is to enter and leave the system. An open family system allows for uncomplicated comings and goings, and thus is likely to experience minimum stress at times of life when entrances and exits are common, such as at the birth of an infant or the marriage of a child. A relatively closed system, however, has difficulty with members' entering and leaving and is thus likely to be distressed at these times.

No family is wholly open or closed, as each would represent an unlikely extreme. It is more correct to speak of relative openness or closedness. Where a family falls on the spectrum will be directly related to its boundaries. A family with rigid external boundaries will experience difficulty allowing individuals to leave and will therefore lie toward the closed end of the continuum. For instance, families that fret over children going off to school are likely to operate in relatively closed systems. So are families that worry about prospective in-laws or the effects of a child's marriage. One couple became anguished when their son decided to marry a woman who lived in another state; they were convinced that he would never return to visit them, and they were shocked that he decided to marry someone who lived so far away. Similarly, families with rigid internal boundaries have enormous difficulty when individual members behave in an "unacceptable" manner. I treated a man who was livid with his wife for contributing to a political candidate who supported the right to abortion. He was incapable of accepting that she could use "his" money to support a view that he opposed. Families with rigid gender roles and prescriptions for what men or women should or should not do are also categorized as relatively closed systems.[3]

Open systems, of course, have more fluid boundaries. Families with flexible external boundaries are likely to tolerate more easily the entrance of new people, such as in-laws, or the exit of children who are ready to live independently. Because of their rather resilient internal boundaries, open systems can manage a wide variety of viewpoints on sensitive subjects. Members are encouraged to develop independent interests, opinions, and friendships, which are tolerated by other members even if they disagree with the viewpoint or dislike the friend. No family can achieve total openness, nor would it wish to, since privacy would be violated, resulting in a complete and unhealthy breakdown of boundaries.

Another measure of the open-closed continuum is the degree to which a family harbors secrets or reacts to "toxic" issues—that is, subjects tacitly barred from discussion. It is not unusual for people to discover astounding information about their families late in their lives. One man of forty-five discovered his adoption papers while going through his mother's belongings after her death; he had no inkling until that moment that he had been adopted. In an initial interview I was conducting with another family, the children were shocked to discover that their father had been married before and that his first wife had died. The Marshes not only kept Richard's leukemia a secret but also never discussed his brother's mental illness. Typical taboo subjects are alcoholism, extramarital affairs, and criminal wrongdoing. The toxicity of these issues is implicitly understood by the family, and thus they are seldom, if ever, addressed and are usually denied. Talking about such issues invites censure or anger.

In families characterized as closed, the discussion of serious illness and the prospect of death is predictably difficult. These families often resist acknowledging the gravity of illness and also fail to comply with treatment regimens.

Some years ago, I had an opportunity to work with a family that, for me, represents the epitome of openness. The mother, Jackie, had been through surgery and radiation therapy for a malignant melanoma, but the disease had not been cured. Jackie, her husband Merle, and their four daughters allowed me to videotape seven hours of wide-ranging interviews, which touched on all aspects of their lives, her life-threatening illness, her plans for the family after her death, and the way in which each person was dealing with the prospect of that death. The family members were enormously open to one another, and no one seemed to shy away from what in other families would be forbidden subjects, such as cancer, funerals, and obituaries. One aspect of the family's openness was their use of humor, which was often quite morbid. Merle joked with his wife that she shouldn't go to the dentist; he'd have her teeth straightened during the autopsy. Jackie claimed that she was going to interview candidates to be Merle's new wife.

In my teaching, I use excerpts from the videotaped interviews of Jackie and her family to demonstrate some of the qualities of the open system. I am always fascinated by the reaction of audiences who watch these tapes.[4] Nearly everyone is taken with the family's candor, humor, and willingness to face painful subjects head-on. But many people are disturbed by an openness that goes beyond their own level of comfort. Viewers often comment on the appropriateness of speaking about such sensitive subjects in front of young children. The reactions of these audiences demonstrate the wide spectrum of comfort that exists in working with extremely open systems. Furthermore, it would be difficult to define either an open or a closed system in absolute terms.

The Enmeshed Versus Disengaged Family System

The level of intensity with which a family responds to crisis often depends on the degree to which family members are emotionally connected with each other. My private practice is in an affluent suburb where parents tend to be highly focused on their children's happiness and success. Frequently, such enmeshed families come to me grimly concerned about a child who has received a B– on a report card or who does not seem as happy and carefree in high school as in junior high. An off day on the football field can send certain families into paroxysms of grief. But I have also seen disengaged families who have never sought professional help for their obviously disturbed adolescents, although encouraged to do so for years. Even when an adolescent develops the most disturbing symptoms, the problem may appear to have little impact on other family members. It sometimes takes a dramatic crisis, such as a criminal arrest or a suicide gesture, for the family to acknowledge that the child's behavior is problematic. When such a family discusses the past,

I am astounded at the behavior and events—involving all family members, not just the youngster who "has the problem"—that have been allowed to pass without reaction. Other families would certainly have run for help.

In the enmeshed family system, where family members are often deeply involved in each other's affairs, the difficulties experienced by one person are likely to impact deeply on the emotional well-being of others. Internal boundaries are overly permeable in the enmeshed family, and often one member cannot clearly discern where he or she stops and another person begins. The pain of one is the pain of all. A common manifestation of the "we-ness" that characterizes enmeshed families is mind-reading—everyone claims to know what everyone else is thinking and feeling. This obliteration of internal boundaries prevents individuals from developing a sense of autonomy and makes it difficult for children to establish separate identities.

The Harlans were an enmeshed family. The sudden death of their adult daughter left the survivors unable to move forward in their own lives. Some eight years after the death, the parents were still demanding that their two remaining children keep in constant contact with them; they would become enraged when even a few days went by without hearing from their son and daughter. Despite the extreme shakiness of her marriage, the daughter was obsessed with getting pregnant; this would be the family's first grandchild. The son had turned down a prestigious position in a distant state, fearing that his father would suffer a heart attack and his mother a nervous breakdown if he moved away. Like his sister, he was having enormous marital difficulty. Although neither sibling denied the connection, they did not feel comfortable acknowledging continued enmeshment with their parents as an important reason for their inability to function well in their marriages.

Enmeshed families tend to overreact to serious illness and other significant crises, creating much emotional upheaval and, frequently, troubling behavioral symptoms. The younger child in the Charles family was diagnosed with Lyme disease, a serious but not life-threatening illness. Within six months, the father, who had been abstinent for seven years, returned to active drinking, and the mother began an extramarital affair with their housepainter. The elder child, meanwhile, experienced a serious exacerbation of asthma after having been virtually asymptomatic for two years. The Charleses were incredulous when I suggested that the diagnosis of Lyme disease might have played some role in their subsequent difficulties. Not surprisingly, both parents came from families where crises in previous generations had been followed by dramatic upheavals, such as alcoholism, marital breakups, and illness.

If enmeshed families overreact, disengaged families are likely to underreact or seem not to be reacting at all. Thus a disengaged family may appear, on the surface, to be handling a crisis with great equanimity. For example, as Louise Pritchett's father returned from walking the dog one evening, he found his eighteen-year-old daughter huddled beside the shrubbery, vomiting. The car was idling in the garage, and Louise wailed that she had wanted to kill herself but had become ill from the fumes. Mr. Pritchett telephoned his family doctor, who suggested that he call me. I told him that I would squeeze in a short appointment for him, his wife, and daughter early the next morning. Later, remembering that he had an important meeting in the morning, he told his wife and Louise to keep the appointment and explain why he was unable to come. I met briefly with Louise and her mother and asked them to return in the early afternoon, when I would have more time. The two women were fifteen minutes late for their second appointment, explaining that they had gone to a local shopping mall and lost track of the time. I asked Louise what her mother had said about her suicide attempt, and she replied, "We didn't really discuss it. We just went shopping."

Boundaries, instead of being fluid and permeable, are rigid and unyielding in disengaged families. It may take extraordinary events to compel people to react. Louise's father was motivated to do *something*, but what he did was to enlist his wife. The rigid boundaries in this family not only prevented much expression of emotion but also defined gender roles.

Within days of Jim McGrath's death, everyone had returned to work, and there seemed to be no change in his family's routine or interruption of its life. When interviewed individually by hospice bereavement volunteers, however, Jim's wife, mother, and three children all expressed enormous grief and loss, and each of the five survivors commented how little the other four seemed to be suffering. His mother, son, and younger daughter indicated that they had been unable to stop crying, but they wept in their own rooms behind closed doors so as not to upset anyone. Both Jim's wife and his elder daughter were taking long, solitary walks during which they cried copiously. The hospice social worker and bereavement team helped the McGraths emotionally engage as a family so that they could be supportive in their grief. This was extremely difficult; the McGrath family truly believed that sharing the sorrow would make things worse.

The Underfunctioning Versus Overfunctioning Family System

Families that contend with endless series of crises, major and minor, are often underfunctioning and characteristically find themselves unable to cope and to navigate the environment. Underfunctioning families frequently contain alcoholic or chemically dependent members, and they may be no strangers to chronic illness.

The underfunctioning Dombarski family was referred to me by the employee assistance counselor at the company where Edna Dombarski worked. Her twenty-year-old daughter, Marilyn—the middle child—was very depressed, had quit her job, refused to leave home during the day, and was talking about suicide. The five Dombarskis all seemed quite willing to see me. Stanley explained that he was on long-term disability because of a chronic back problem. His son, Nicky, a high-school senior, guffawed at his father's description, muttering, "Yeah, you never get off it." Nicky, I learned, always seemed to be in trouble with school authorities, although he proudly stated that he'd "never been busted." The eldest child, twenty-two-year-old Marsha, had worked her way through the two-year community college and held a job as an executive secretary. She had been engaged a number of times and went through two or three serious relationships every year. Marsha barely spoke at all but appeared to be fighting back tears throughout this first session.

The family had never been able to accumulate enough money to do much more than keep themselves afloat. They had always lived with Stanley's mother, and he had inherited the house from her when she died five years before. Stanley had been an active alcoholic until serious diabetes was diagnosed in his early forties, and Edna had suffered from severe migraine headaches since adolescence.

Marilyn, the identified patient, gave few details about how she was feeling except to say that she was depressed, and that the only good thing about life was going out with her friends to a local bar every night and "getting pretty wasted." With much hesitancy, Edna volunteered that Marilyn and her father "had kind of been involved with each other" when she was in the seventh grade. Further questioning, which no one, including Stanley, objected to, revealed that there had been two or three incidents of sexual molestation when Stanley was drinking. Marilyn told her mother, who warned Stanley that another such incident would result in his arrest and her leaving with the children; this ended the abuse. Shortly after this, Edna decided to get a job over Stanley's objection, and she had been the family's primary breadwinner ever since, with Marsha becoming a major contributor in recent years.

Much like their family history, my work with the Dombarskis had ups and downs. Sometimes they tried quite hard to change family patterns. During one such period, Marilyn finally talked with her father about the abuse; at another time, Edna demanded that the children do their own laundry, and she and Stanley agreed to go away for a weekend without calling home repeatedly. But these periods were interrupted by behavior characteristic of this family: Marsha became engaged and pregnant and had an abortion; Nicky was finally arrested for drunk and disorderly conduct; on a less serious note, but equally important in this family's story, Edna found it impossible to avoid cleaning the children's rooms.

Therapy with the Dombarskis eventually ground to a halt. They canceled a few sessions; I called them several times; they promised to get back to me; and then we all gave up the pretense of working on their problems.

The Dombarskis functioned only adequately enough to survive; they were not entirely nonfunctioning, but they were underfunctioning. In such families, the characteristics of closed, enmeshed systems are prominent. External boundaries are rigid, keeping the family insulated from any positive impact of the outside environment, and internal boundaries are so inappropriate that every person's behavior seems to rattle every other member and to cause gross dysfunction.

Whereas underfunctioning families present the therapist with a formidable challenge, psychotherapists rarely have trouble with overfunctioning families—because we seldom see them! When they do seek help, it is usually at times of serious, undeniable crisis, and then they are prone to understate their difficulties. These families see themselves as capable of handling their problems through hard work and rational thinking.

I saw the Farnhams only because the school authorities demanded it. The only child, Ty, had always been a model student; he was popular, got good grades, played two varsity sports, and was involved in many other school activities. Suddenly, early in his senior year, he turned sullen and started to do poorly in classes. In his counselor's words, Ty appeared to have become "a totally different kid." When the counselor called Marlene Farnham, she was genuinely shocked, saying she had no sense that Ty had changed in any way and was incredulous that anyone at school should think he had a problem. In my first interview with Ty and his parents, they repeated this claim: they saw no change in behavior at home and were bewildered by the school's report.

When I inquired about their respective families, both adults reported the deaths during the previous summer of their parents. Roy Farnham's father, widowed for five years, had died suddenly of a heart attack, and two weeks later, Marlene's parents perished in a fire that demolished her childhood home. Although naturally saddened by the losses, neither Roy nor Marlene had been raised to dwell on the negative. Ty learned his parents' lessons well and acted accordingly in their presence. But the sudden deaths of three important persons in his life within less than a month had left him bereft. The expression of grief was implicitly forbidden at home, and since Ty had never learned how to show such feelings appropriately, his grief was expressed symptomatically, but only outside the home.

Extreme denial can be an earmark of the overfunctioning family. When questioned individually about their emotional states only a few months after the deaths, all three Farnhams admitted to suffering more than a little stress. But unaccustomed to acknowledging the severity of difficulties, families like the Farnhams are prone to camouflage their anxiety or pain and carry on as if there were no problem. In one respect, they are like the underfunctioning family: they are likely to have fairly rigid external boundaries, which prevent them from accepting any help from the outside. But unlike the Dombarskis, the Farnhams had internal boundaries that were rigid in the extreme, walling off each of the three people from the pain felt by the others.

Therapy with the Farnhams was short-term. Within a few sessions, given permission and encouragement to talk more openly with each other and, most important, understanding why this would be helpful for Ty, the family was able to break down some of its rigid walls. Soon Ty was back to his old self, and the Farnhams quickly terminated therapy.

PREDICTORS OF FAMILY
EMOTIONAL RESPONSE

Families and individuals respond to crisis characteristically—that is, they respond in the present much the same way they have responded in the past. In fact, history is the best predictor of how families will react to crisis. The nuclear family's experience with the stressors of family life, together with the response of previous generations to stress, gives a comprehensive picture of a family's emotional style.

To view this principle graphically, consider the family's reaction to stress along two dimensions (see Figure 2.2). Responses to events in the nuclear family are charted along the horizontal axis. The patterns of emotional response inherited from previous generations are plotted on the vertical axis. The point at which these two axes intersect represents the family as it is presently functioning. Armed with this knowledge, caregivers are better able to find ways of helping families cope with troubles.

Crises in the Nuclear Family:
Horizontal Stressors

Life without stress is nearly impossible to imagine. Some stressful developmental events, while not necessarily universal, are relatively normative: birth, death, marriage, divorce, work-related problems, financial difficulties, separations. All of these events fall somewhere along the horizontal axis in Figure 2.2, which plots events in the nuclear family. But not all horizontal events are normative. Some are external rather than developmental: a fire or tornado that destroys the family home, or the death of a mother and her young child due to a drunk driver. These unanticipated external events are also plotted along the horizontal axis. A basic tenet of family systems theory is that just as individuals react to stressful events, so does the larger family system. The circular view of causality presented earlier suggests that the way each individual copes with stress

Figure 2.2. The Intersect of Vertical and Horizontal Stressors.

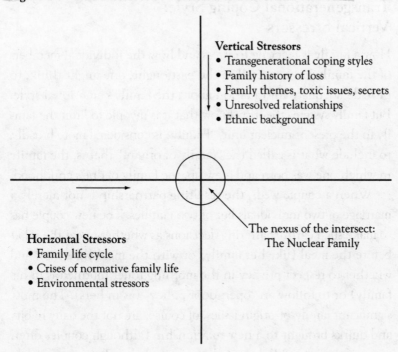

Vertical Stressors
- Transgenerational coping styles
- Family history of loss
- Family themes, toxic issues, secrets
- Unresolved relationships
- Ethnic background

The nexus of the intersect:
The Nuclear Family

Horizontal Stressors
- Family life cycle
- Crises of normative family life
- Environmental stressors

Source: Adapted from B. Carter and M. McGoldrick (eds.). *The Family Life Cycle: A Framework for Family Therapy* (Lake Worth, Fla.: Gardner Press, 1980), p. 10.

will be greatly influenced by the way other parts of the family system cope.

Over time, the nuclear family develops a characteristic style of responding to upset. An enmeshed or disengaged system and an open or closed system reflect coping styles that have been displayed in critical periods of the nuclear family's history. In all likelihood, a family's response to a current stressor will reflect its past performance. Thus knowledge of the family's functioning during earlier stressful events will be a valuable aid in predicting how the family will meet a present crisis.

Transgenerational Coping Style:
Vertical Stressors

How a family is reacting to stress and how the individual members of the family have reacted in the past ought, one might think, to provide adequate information about the family's emotional style. But family systems theorists know that it is myopic to limit the family to the present nuclear unit. "Family" is considered more broadly, to include what is called the "family of origin," that is, the family in which one was born and grew up, the family of one's childhood.

When a couple weds, the resulting partnership is not merely a marriage of two individuals but of two families. The new couple has to make such earth-shattering decisions as whether to eat the salad before the meal (like her family) or with the meal (like his), and whether to respect privacy in the morning toilet routine (as in his family) or to follow an "open-door policy" (as in hers). The most significant family-of-origin issues, of course, are not the daily habits and quirks brought to a new relationship (although couples often act as if they were) but the beliefs, attitudes, and emotional style that are deeply imbedded in each individual from childhood. This cross-generational transmission of family patterns, emotions, and behaviors is of paramount importance in the way families function. The product that results from the joining of two families in marriage is both predictable, given the way two emotional styles are likely to fit with each other, and random, as there is always an element of surprise when two different entities are combined. Recall the maxim: the whole of the family is greater than the sum of its parts.

The extent of the influence of vertical stressors—an individual's emotional inheritance from the family of origin—is greatly dependent on whether issues have been resolved or are carried intact into the next generation. Resolution does not imply total solution. No one ever fully escapes from his or her family, and this ought not to be a goal, because much of what is valuable in life comes from the family. When I speak of the necessity of resolving issues from the family of origin, I am focusing on the task of individuation. A person who has effectively individuated has established appropriate boundaries between self and others. Decisions about politics, religion, morality, or when to eat the salad are based on a mature self-perception that has integrated relevant childhood experiences into an adult independence.

The resolution of family-of-origin issues necessitates addressing the beliefs, attitudes, and emotional style of the family of origin and putting relationships with family members in order. The Marshes' inclination to keep secrets and their reluctance to discuss sensitive issues were powerful legacies that both adults brought to their relationship. In the Berg family of Chapter One, the toxic issue of loss, implicitly proscribed from discussion, created aggression and hostility among members. Unresolved conflicts with parents and siblings will be perpetuated in the families that later form. Rage at her husband for being an "inadequate" breadwinner may reflect a woman's unresolved relationship with her father, on whom she formerly depended for every need. A man's frustration with his wife for being emotionally unavailable—whether or not she really is— may have its roots in his relationship with his mother, who he felt was cold and withholding. Competition between two recently married young adults often reflects unresolved relationships with their respective siblings. These family-of-origin issues are not merely historical artifacts but are actively present in current lives.

Without clarification and resolution, issues and relationships in the family of origin will impede individuation. When I see this in people with whom I work, I urge them to make contact with their parents, siblings, and other family members to clarify the issues and conflicts that remain from the past. Sometimes this is done together in the context of family therapy; more often, I send people off on their own to work with family members, using a method called "coaching" that will be described more fully in Chapter Six.

The Interaction of Horizontal and Vertical Stressors

The emotional flow or behavior in the family can best be seen as the simultaneous effects of the horizontal and vertical axes just described. The horizontal flow is the reaction of the family to the stresses experienced in the usual passages of family life, as well as the reaction to stresses that are external, circumstantial, or unexpected at a particular stage of life. The vertical emotional flow reflects the patterns of interaction transmitted historically from generation to generation. The interaction of the emotional currents from these two directions predicts with uncanny precision how the family will respond at times of crisis.

For the sake of simplicity, horizontal and vertical stressors can be plotted as two axes of a two-by-two matrix (see Table 2.1).

Two types of horizontal stressors are shown: predictable life cycle events on the left and extraordinary psychosocial stressors on the right. Vertical stressors—that is, family-of-origin emotional issues—are shown as either resolved (top) or unresolved (bottom). Together, these axes form a grid divided into four quadrants, which essentially describe four different types of nuclear families:

Quadrant I   The family experiencing predictable life events
                 (such as a child leaving home for college), where
                 emotional issues in the families of origin have
                 been adequately resolved.

Quadrant II   The family experiencing extraordinary psycho-
                 social stressors (such as the death of a young
                 parent) and in which emotional issues in the
                 families of origin have been adequately resolved.

Quadrant III   The family experiencing predictable life events
                 (such as the birth of a child) but hampered by
                 much unresolved emotional baggage from past
                 generations.

Table 2.1. Stressors in the Family.

Vertical Stressors	Horizontal Stressors	
	Predictable Unremarkable Life Cycle Events	Extraordinary Psychosocial Stressors
	I	II
Emotional issues in family of origin resolved	*Function* Good; normative reaction to occasional stressors	*Function* Intense but normative reaction to stressors
	Tractability Able to change; moves in positive direction	*Tractability* Able to change; acts to remove stressor
	Duration Short-term; normative time frame for problem solving	*Duration* Normative time frame for problem solving
	III	IV
Emotional issues in family of origin unresolved	*Function* Chronic anxiety and low-level dysfunction	*Function* Intense reaction to most stressors
	Tractability Resistant to change and movement in any direction; tends to recycle anxiety	*Tractability* Strongly and consistently resistant to change and movement in any direction
	Duration Occasional short-term resolution; long-term repetitive difficulty resolving anxiety	*Duration* Chronic, repetitive patterns; short-term and long-term resolution seldom occurs

Levels of stress measured on three dimensions:
    Function—behavior of family in present
    Tractability—openness of family to change or movement
    Duration—length of time needed to resolve stress

 Quadrant IV   The family experiencing extraordinary psycho-social stressors (such as bankruptcy and the simultaneous diagnosis of a chronic illness) and burdened by unresolved emotional issues from previous generations.

I have found it helpful to measure the level of stress experienced in each of these four family prototypes in three dimensions: function, tractability, and duration. The function dimension assesses how well the family operates under the stress of the present crisis. The tractability dimension measures how open the family might be to changing its patterns of behavior. The duration dimension predicts how long the family is likely to suffer from the emotional impact of the stress. The family's emotional makeup often affects the length of recovery more than does the nature of the stressor.

The four prototype families can now be examined on the basis of how well they function, how open they are to change, and how long it will take them to recover from stress. Bear in mind that families in quadrants I and II are well differentiated—that is, the individuals have managed to establish separate and mature distinctions between themselves and the families from which they came. Families in quadrants III and IV, however, are poorly differentiated. Their members have not clearly defined themselves in relation to the past or resolved the emotional issues from their families of origin.[5]

Quadrant I

Every family meets predictable difficulties as it moves through life. In families where individuals are well differentiated from their families of origin and have resolved most relationship issues with parents and siblings, the reaction to these predictable crises will be mild and asymptomatic. These families continue to function well, though not necessarily as efficiently as they normally do, because some emotional energy will be expended in coping with the crisis. In addition, these families are likely to be alert to ways they can accommodate themselves to the crisis, and the changes they make are usually positive, ameliorating difficulties rather than exacerbating them. Temporal norms for how long it "should" take to recover from certain psychosocial stressors (for example, twelve to eighteen months is presumed to be a normal period of grief over death of a loved one) are established through observation of better functioning families, such as those in this quadrant.

Quadrant II

Even though a family has achieved good resolution of family-of-origin issues, it will nevertheless have difficulty when confronted with extraordinary psychosocial stressors. The family will function well, although its reaction will be intense, in keeping with the extreme stress of the event. This type of family is able to change, and it will attempt to cope with or remove the stressor in a purposeful and efficient way. In such families, then, the time required to recover from the crisis will depend on the nature of the event.

Quadrant III

Families in this quadrant have yet to resolve issues in their families of origin—that is, the adult members have not achieved individuation from their parents. When faced with the expected and predictable setbacks of life, this type of family, which tends to be in a chronic state of anxiety, is unlikely to function at an optimum level. Such a family is seldom tractable and will resist change in any direction, even when a shift in behavior would help them cope better. The most minor stresses become major traumatic events. The family may occasionally achieve short-term resolution of problems but will continue in its characteristic state of perpetual crisis.

Quadrant IV

This last of the four prototypes is the family at the least productive level of functioning. Because this family, which has unresolved family-of-origin conflicts, functions at a chronic level of anxiety, the reaction to even minor stressors is likely to be extreme, and certainly the presence of extraordinary stressors may have catastrophic consequences. The family's ability to make any purposeful change is negligible, since it views its entrenched pattern of behavior as the only way. Major and even minor life stressors are seldom, if ever, resolved; the problems of twenty years ago are as anxiety-producing as current difficulties.

FAMILY MAPS: FROM TYPOLOGY TO TOPOLOGY

As we have seen, past family has an enormous impact on the present family. If, for example, two persons from relatively closed families marry, they will likely create a new family system that is also closed. The events of the past are also usually recycled in the present, and the unresolved relationship issues in the family of origin will reappear in a new system created through marriage. Any tool that aids those who work with families in identifying these patterns and predicting them accurately would be enormously helpful. Such a tool does exist: it is the genogram, or family tree, which serves as a typologic map of the family. The genogram can be used to identify a family's type through its multiple generations.

All families go through certain predictable events as they move from one stage of their lives to another. Some stages tend to draw family members closer together, and others, by necessity, force them to separate. Families are most vulnerable at transition points in their lives. The ups and downs, hills and valleys, of family life can be broadly anticipated by tracing the family through a topologic map called the "life cycle."

The Genogram: A Map Across the Generations

The genogram serves three functions: it is a map of family structure; it provides information about the family through its history; and it outlines the nature of relationships within the family. The reader who wishes to learn more about the use and application of genograms is referred to the definitive text on this subject, McGoldrick and Gerson's *Genograms in Family Assessment*. The authors define a genogram in these words:

"A genogram is a format for drawing a family tree that records information about family members and their relationships over at least three generations. Genograms display family information graphically in a way that provides a quick gestalt of complex family patterns and a rich source of hypotheses about how a clinical problem may be connected to the family context and the evolution of both problem and context over time."[6]

Each chapter in the present book includes a genogram in the opening case study. You have already been introduced to two family genograms—those for the Bergs in Chapter One and the Marshes in this chapter. These genograms can be used as a guide to the following description of genogram construction. It should be noted that clinicians who use genograms are not bound by universal rules for their construction. The more one uses genograms, the more a personal style develops in creating them.

Six basic rules guide construction of genograms:

1. Men are represented by squares, women by circles.

2. People related by marriage or a similar relationship are connected by a horizontal line (a broken line if it is not a formal marriage). Offspring of the relationship are represented by vertical lines extending from that horizontal line. On the horizontal plane, men are on the left, women on the right; offspring are depicted from the oldest on the left to the youngest on the right; miscarriages are represented by small triangles. (For example, in Figure 2.1, Richard and Char Marsh are joined by an unbroken horizontal line with Richard on the left. The children extend from that line, and Richie appears on the left since he is the elder child.)

3. A death is indicated by an X within the square or circle. Separation and divorce are represented by slashes on the marriage line—one slash for separation and a double slash for divorce. Dates of death, divorce, and separation are included. (In Figure 1.1, Alice Berg's divorce is represented by the double slash and the date. Each of the many deaths is identified with an X.)

4. People who live together in a single household are encircled by dotted lines.

5. Other family information is recorded whenever possible, particularly when it has a direct bearing on the present condition. (In the Marsh genogram, Peter's hospitalization for schizophrenia is noted. In the Berg genogram, the moves from Germany and London are indicated.)

6. Close relationships are illustrated by solid double lines between the people (for example, Richard and Char Marsh). Conflictual relationships are indicated by zigzag lines (for example, Catarina and Carmen in Figure 5.1). Close but conflictual relationships are shown by a combination of double lines and zigzag lines (for example, the relationships between all three Berg women). Emotional cutoffs between family members are depicted by gaps in the line (for example, Richard Marsh and his brother Peter).

In this admittedly limited description, I have given only a general guide to plotting an intergenerational family map. Most families are quite complex, and genograms of multiple marriages, blended families, or the like require more sophistication. But even in its most rudimentary form, the genogram is a helpful tool for looking at a family's structure, history, and relationships. A further exploration of the use of genograms in working with families facing death will be found in Chapter Six.

The Life Cycle: The Family's Road Map

Throughout this chapter, I have alluded to the family life cycle, which is a sort of road map that charts the course all families travel. When I refer in this book to the life cycle, I am speaking of the road map of the traditional nuclear family.[7] However, there are many exceptions to the traditional family and, thus, to the life cycle. Some people choose not to marry, and many of those who do marry choose not to have children. Other families are reconstituted from the remnants of several families. There are families with one parent, families with no resident parent, homosexual families, and collective families. A family may live together through only one or two stages of the life cycle. Because the limits of this text prevent consideration of all the variations of the family life cycle, I will, for illustrative purposes, examine a fairly traditional family and its road map (see Table 2.2).

The life cycle of adulthood begins when the unattached young adult is separating from his or her family of origin and developing intimate relationships with peers. The goals of the unattached young adult between families are to individuate, to become self-

Table 2.2. The Family Life Cycle.

Stage	Goals
1. Single young adult between families	• Achieving emotional and financial independence • Accepting parent-offspring separation
2. Newly married couple; joining of two families	• Forming a new marital system • Realigning relationships with family and friends
3. Family with young children	• Adapting to parenting roles • Making room for children in marital system • Managing relationships with family of origin
4. Family with adolescents	• Adjusting to children leaving family • Focusing on midlife marital issues
5. Family launching children and moving on	• Reestablishing marital dyad • Managing relationships with children and grandchildren • Dealing with aging and disability of selves and previous generation
6. Family in later life	• Facing physical decline and disability • Dealing with multiple losses • Facing mortality

sufficient, to establish an appropriate place in the work world, and—usually—to find a mate.

When the young adult marries, the second stage of the family life cycle begins: the creation of a new family. In fact, it is more correct to define this period as the joining of two families rather than the creation of a new one, although few newly married couples would support this view. In this stage, both spouses expect their mate to shift allegiance from the family of origin to the new family and its attendant network of friends.

When children are born, whether this occurs one year or ten years after the marriage, the family enters the third stage of its life cycle. In this newly defined family, husband and wife become father and mother. Priorities change to include children as significant members of the family system, and adults see themselves in new roles.

In the fourth stage of the life cycle, the family with adolescents, separation becomes the primary challenge of family life, as heretofore dependent children strive for independence. Parents must begin refocusing their attention from the children, who have been dominant in their lives, to their spouse and their own plans for the future. Adolescence can be a difficult phase of the family life cycle, primarily because the family system needs to undergo drastic change.

The fifth stage of the life cycle is the launching period, when children are sent forth from the family into the world. The family configuration changes radically as children leave home—or try to—and parents and their offspring begin to relate to each other as adults. At this time in a family's life, the parents' own elderly parents are likely to demand attention because of failing health, and they take on greater significance in the emotional makeup of the family system. This stage epitomizes the basic circularity of the family life cycle, for as children are launched and form new families, the life cycle recapitulates itself.

In the final stage of the life cycle, the family in its later years, major reorganization occurs as illness and death alter the family construct. The parents who started the life cycle many years ago as unattached young adults are now the older generation. While they come to grips with death and loss as a natural part of life, they simultaneously participate in a new family system that includes new life—their grandchildren.

Notes

1. Homeostasis is a rich and complex concept. For a more in-depth discussion of how families operate to achieve homeostasis, see Lynn Hoffman, *Foundations of Family Therapy* (New York: Basic Books, 1981), especially chap. 10; and M. S. Palazzoli, G. Cecchin, G. Prata, and L. Boscolo, *Paradox and Counterparadox* (Northvale, N.J.: Aronson, 1978). The latter is the work of the well-known "Milan School" of family therapy.

2. The concept of boundaries and family emotional functioning was originally presented by a pioneer of family therapy, Salvador Minuchin. See his seminal work, *Families and Family Therapy* (Cambridge, Mass.: Harvard University Press, 1974), from which many of these ideas are derived.

3. Gender roles and the relative places of men and women in families are important dimensions for understanding how families function. Unfortunately, an in-depth examination of these issues is beyond the scope of this book. I refer the reader to two excellent books on the subject: M. Walters, B. Carter, P. Papp, and O. Silverstein, *The Invisible Web* (New York: Guilford Press, 1988); and M. McGoldrick, C. Anderson, and F. Walsh (eds.), *Women in Families* (New York: Norton, 1989).

4. These interviews are edited in *Jackie: A Family Faces Death,* part of a series of videotapes that I use in my teaching. Even professional audiences are often surprised by the degree of candor and openness that families are able to express when dealing with the prospect of death or with their grief.

5. A more detailed discussion of the concept of differentiation of self, originally developed by Murray Bowen, can be found in Michael Kerr and Murray Bowen, *Family Evaluation: An Approach Based on Bowen Theory* (New York: Norton, 1988); and Daniel V. Papero, *Bowen Family Systems Therapy* (Needham Heights, Mass.: Allyn & Bacon, 1990).

6. Monica McGoldrick and Randy Gerson, *Genograms in Family Assessment* (New York: Norton, 1985), p. 1. This work is not only an excellent text for the clinician who wishes to learn nearly all there is to know about genograms, but it is also highly entertaining for the lay reader, plotting the family trees of such diverse families as the Freuds, the Fondas, and the Kennedys.

7. In discussion of the family life cycle here and in Chapter Three, I am indebted to the work of Betty Carter and Monica McGoldrick. Their text *The Changing Family Life Cycle: A Framework for Family Therapy* (Lake Worth, Fla.: Gardner Press, 1988) is a classic in the field of family therapy, but a highly accessible book for any interested reader. I strongly recommend it.

3

Loss and the Life Cycle

For he who lives more lives than one
More deaths than one must die.

Oscar Wilde
The Ballad of Reading Gaol

Betsy Scapella, age fifty-one, has begun to wonder about what her recently deceased father used to say: "Betsy's one lucky girl. She'll always land on her feet." Lately she feels as though her world is collapsing around her. Gene, her youngest, has left for college; her husband, Mike, suffered a serious heart attack eight months ago at age fifty-two and was hospitalized for nearly two months, and his full recovery remains doubtful; her father, who had been caring for her mother in an advanced stage of Alzheimer's disease, died a few months ago; within the last month, she has had no choice but to place her mother in a nursing home; and her father-in-law, who lives close by, recently had a fourth heart attack and does not seem to be recovering. When I first met her, she was feeling anything but lucky.

The Scapellas are an upper-middle-class family who reside in a prosperous suburb of New York City. As illustrated in Figure 3.1, Mike, a lawyer, is a first-generation Italian-American, the first person in his family to attend college and enter a profession. He has two unmarried elder brothers, who with their father built a successful landscaping business and together supported "little Mikey" as he

Figure 3.1. Genogram of the Scapella Family, 1997.

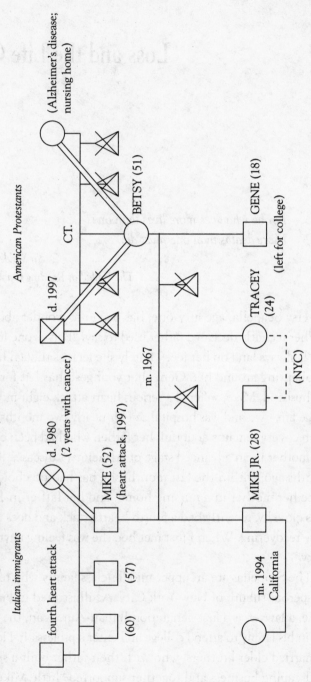

Italian immigrants

American Protestants

fourth heart attack

d. 1980
(2 years with cancer)

MIKE (52)
(heart attack, 1997)

(60)

(57)

MIKE JR. (28)

m. 1994
California

m. 1967

CT.

d. 1997

(Alzheimer's disease;
nursing home)

BETSY (51)

GENE (18)
(left for college)

TRACEY
(24)

(NYC)

made his way through school. When Mike married Betsy, the only child of a wealthy old-line Connecticut family, none of the four parents was pleased with the match, but over the years Mike and Betsy have each come to be regarded as the favorite in the other's family. The only time Betsy worked outside the home was during the first year of her marriage, when she taught school. Then she started to raise a family. The Scapellas have three children: Mike Jr., twenty-eight (a married stockbroker living in California); Tracey, twenty-four (who is in her last year of law school and lives with her boyfriend in Manhattan); and Gene, eighteen. Between each viable pregnancy, Betsy suffered a miscarriage late in the third trimester.

Soon after Gene was born, Mike's mother was diagnosed with cancer. Betsy was expected to care for her mother-in-law, even though she had a new baby and two school-age children. She was her mother-in-law's primary caretaker for nearly two years, until her death. When her own mother began to deteriorate, her father expected her to be available, and she was. Even after Mike's heart attack, Betsy traveled forty minutes to her parents' home two or three times a week and spent most of the day with them. After her father's death, her mother came to stay with her and Mike, but she had deteriorated to an almost infantile state and needed constant care, more than Betsy felt able to provide. Nursing home placement was unavoidable.

Mike's cardiologist referred the Scapellas to me. The couple agreed that it might be helpful to talk with an objective person about the changes in their lives during the past year, but Mike was emphatic about not getting into any "touchy-feely business." The major concern Betsy expressed was how depressed she had felt since Gene had left for college. All the rest of the problems—her husband's heart attack, the death of her father, the need to put her mother in a nursing home, and her father-in-law's precarious health—she perceived as the normal stresses and strains of life, and she was sure she could handle them. But in "losing" her last child, she had nothing meaningful left in life, and she was not sure what to do. Her father-in-law had full-time, live-in help, and Mike did not want her "hovering over him." He was impatient with Betsy's constant worry about everyone and expressed his own philosophy as *que sera, sera* (whatever will be, will be). The only thing that bothered him, Mike said, was that he wasn't getting his strength back as quickly as he had hoped; when he looked at his father, he had forebodings for his own future.

During the three months I worked with the Scapellas, the couple gradually began to speak more openly about their lives, reviewing the past and planning for a future that both feared would not include Mike. Much time was spent discussing the many losses they had undergone in a short period. Mike's loss of his physical vitality and the questionable hope for the future had made him depressed and irritable. He admitted that he was feeling very empty with all three children gone, especially as he was not working at the office very much. He felt uncomfortable, even lonely, whenever Betsy left the house. Betsy, in turn, was able to tell her husband how responsible she felt for the entire family, including Mike's father and brothers. When he resisted her attempts to help him or dismissed her expressions of concern, she was left feeling very empty. It was helpful for both of them to talk about the meaning of the loss of their children and their parents. Mike confessed that he was convinced—and quite scared—that he wouldn't live much longer, and he could not bear the idea of leaving Betsy alone. This uncharacteristic and poignant verbalizing of his feelings allowed Betsy to confess that putting her mother in the nursing home had been, in her mind, the first major failure of her life.

It was only when the couple were able to speak about their losses that Mike's depression and Betsy's anxiety were lessened. Aside from the psychological benefits derived from these discussions, practical matters related to Mike's medical condition, his father's care, and Betsy's future plans were now more open for examination. Acknowledgment of their pain had made both of them more secure about raising issues that they deemed painful to the other. In one meeting, Mike demanded that Betsy listen to him without inter-rupting, and he spoke about wanting to die if he did not regain adequate strength to live a physically active life. With my encour-agement, Betsy was able to ask her husband's "permission" to dis-engage from the constant care of his father. After she invited her father's family for a memorial gathering, she found herself able to cut back on her visits to her mother, from twice a day to two or three times a week.

Mike encouraged Betsy to begin looking for work outside the home, something that he had resisted whenever the subject had been raised in the past. The couple planned to orchestrate their lives so that each of them could begin adjusting to their present sit-uation. Betsy could not abandon the caretaking role she felt was such an important part of her life, but she was beginning to appre-ciate the necessity of establishing an identity distinct from her pre-vious roles as wife, mother, daughter, and daughter-in-law. Mike needed to feel that, despite his diminished strength, he could con-tinue to make decisions and not be relegated to invalid status. He undertook the ambitious project of supervising construction of a new guest wing in their home. Happy with his new role, he was more easily able to relinquish to Betsy certain responsibilities that had been in his domain.

About eighteen months after I first met with the Scapellas, Betsy phoned to tell me that Mike had died. She had begun work as an assistant coordinator of volunteers at a community hospital and was planning a vacation in California to see her new grandson, Michael III. Betsy reported that her father-in-law had died a few months be-fore Mike. Her mother continued to survive in a vegetative state, and Betsy permitted herself to visit no more than once a week. The most extraordinary news of all, she said, was that Mike's eldest brother had just married, at age sixty-two. In keeping with her care-taking role, Betsy had played matchmaker and introduced her brother-in-law to a widowed coworker whom she had met in her new job.

Experiencing losses on many fronts simultaneously is a common phenomenon. Some losses, such as the departure of adult children from the family home or the death of an elderly parent, are more or less expected. These losses are "life-cycle-continuous," in that they are part of the normal flow of life. Other losses are discontinuous with the life cycle—that is, they are not expected at the time they occur.[1] The near-fatal heart attack suffered by Mike Scapella at age fifty-two, the loss of his vitality, and his subsequent death fit into this category. His father's illness and ultimate death, on the other hand, are continuous with life cycle expectations.

Although the loss of a loved one has emotional repercussions regardless of the stage of the family's life cycle, discontinuous loss may devastate families and cripple them emotionally. For example, parents are supposed to raise their children through adolescence and then launch them into the world outside. But the death of a young parent leaves the spouse without a partner, which diminishes the efficiency with which the family operates and also destroys the surviving mate's expectations of a future after the children have gone. Romantic notions of "growing old together" are shattered, and the survivor's future is shrouded in enormous uncertainty. The death of a young parent is not only disruptive to the path normally followed by children and spouses, it is also discontinuous with the life cycle of the family of origin. When parents outlive their child, they have a changed relationship with their child's spouse and with their grandchildren. Both they and the surviving spouse's parents may become more involved in the family's life at a time when the normal life cycle calls for less involvement with young people.

The untimely death of a young parent illustrates another dimension of the life cycle: few individuals, except perhaps children, find themselves at any time in only one stage of the family life cycle. Each person exists simultaneously in more than one stage, because he or she is a participant in the life cycle of each generation of the family. Thus, at the time of death of the young parent, this family is at stage three of its life cycle and will soon move on to become a family with adolescents (stage four), and then a family launching children (stage five). However, the surviving spouse is also a part of his or her family of origin, which is in the last stage of its life cycle. In some sense, as Oscar Wilde suggests, each person lives more lives than one—child, spouse, and parent—and each participates in the overlapping life cycles of the multigenerational family. As Murray Bowen, regarded as the "granddaddy" of family systems theory, has suggested, one death will have an ever-repeating effect as it resonates across generations, creating an emotional shock wave.[2]

A Note on Family Terminology

Family systems literature is replete with terminology to describe the family at various stages of development. The term *family of origin* is used to describe the family in which an individual grows up—the family of childhood, in other words. The more common term *nuclear family,* used to describe the traditional "daddy-mommy-kids" grouping, is somewhat limiting. For the family of the second generation, some family therapy literature uses the term *family of procreation,* but that has obvious limitations because many people do not become parents. The term we will use instead is *family of adulthood.* Although not a perfect designation, it comes closest to describing the family in the generation after the family of origin.

THE PUSH-PULL OF THE FAMILY LIFE CYCLE: CENTRIFUGAL AND CENTRIPETAL FORCES

The family life cycle includes periods during which the natural tendency is to draw together and other periods when the family is in the process of thrusting members out. Certain life cycle tasks, by their very nature, push members away from the family of origin. An example of such a centrifugal life cycle stage is the latter period of adolescence, when the teenager develops a growing self-identity and makes efforts to move away from parents and siblings. At other stages of the family life cycle, the tasks are the very opposite in nature, and the effect in the family is centripetal. In these periods when the family is pulling inward, such as when children are young, the family focuses on solidifying itself as a unit and staying together.

At every stage of the family life cycle, both centrifugal and centripetal forces are at work, although one side or the other of the push-pull dichotomy does tend to dominate. These two forces operate more or less simultaneously in the fifth stage of the family life cycle, the period when parents launch their children and move on. The very word *launch* connotes a centrifugal force that propels children out from the family. Yet the parents, as they seek to reestablish a two-person household, are affected by a centripetal force.

A crisis in the family produces a powerful centripetal force, regardless of the stage of the family's life cycle. Families have a natural tendency to draw together at times of difficulties, often blocking the entrance of outsiders. Although pulling together may allow the family to manage the crisis, this is not always the case. Frequently, the inward pull that takes place in response to danger is not in the family's best interests. A barricade effect can result, closing up the family system and making external and internal boundaries rigid. This effect prohibits resources from reaching the family from the outside and prevents family members from helping each other.

The centripetal effect triggered by the crisis may impede the family's ability to progress efficiently through the necessary stages of its life cycle. For example, more than a year after James Hart died suddenly, his wife was still crying constantly. She was short-tempered and angry with her children and resisted offers of assistance from friends and family. Jessica, nine years old, remained sullen and withdrawn and stopped playing with her friends; her seven-year-old sister, Samantha, began wetting her bed and refused to let Mommy out of her sight. The Hart family was at a primarily centripetal stage of the life cycle when James died. The interplay of two centripetal forces—the natural tendency at this stage of the life cycle and the reactive pulling inward in response to crisis—had an additive effect. The family became arrested in its development and regressed symptomatically.

Similar problems can occur when the centripetal reaction to crisis occurs at a centrifugal stage of the family life cycle. When Janice McNeely was diagnosed with amyotrophic lateral sclerosis, she and her husband, Bill, had recently sent their second child to college. Bill, a diabetic who had habitually eaten himself into a diabetic crisis at times of stress, was panicked at the prospect that the strain of Janice's illness would cause him to begin eating uncontrollably, a behavior which he had managed to contain for about ten years. The McNeely children—Walter, who was in graduate school, and Meg, who was a college sophomore—feared that Dad would also become ill. Although constantly reassured by Janice's sister that she would provide whatever care their mother needed and also look after Bill, both children decided to transfer to schools nearer home, over their mother's and aunt's objections. Shortly afterward, Walter dropped out of school, and Meg was considering quitting college. Although Bill McNeely did remain faithful to his diet, he was in open conflict with his sister-in-law and was constantly angry with his children for "getting in the way."

The boundaries of the family system may be violated as individuals in overlapping life cycle stages each try to play significant roles. Such was the case when Margo Herman, a newlywed, learned she had cancer. In the few months of their marriage before Margo became ill, she and her husband, Tom, had performed the typical structure-building tasks of the newly married couple. They had settled into their new apartment, established routines that they saw as the beginning of their family traditions, created appropriate boundaries with their families of origin, and worked at creating a new image as a family. But the diagnosis of life-threatening illness changed everything. Margo's father, a physician, and her mother called or came to visit constantly. Although Margo's family of origin had entered a centrifugal, launching stage, the serious illness was exerting a more powerful centripetal force. Meanwhile, tension was mounting between Margo and Tom. He felt excluded from offering his new wife support during this crisis, and the couple came to see me. I explained that at this critical time, when Margo was naturally drawn toward her parents for support, she needed access to them but also had to maintain marital boundaries. I encouraged the couple to establish definite boundaries that her parents would have to respect and to ask them to assume new roles: her father would arrange contacts in the medical community and provide information about the disease and treatment, whereas her mother would be with her for support when Tom was unavailable. Margo told her parents that they could not come by unannounced and that they would have to limit their phone calls. Both she and Tom worked at reaffirming his role as husband and hers as wife in their newly established family.

DEATH, LOSS, AND DISRUPTION OF THE FAMILY SYSTEM

A variety of factors combine to affect how a family faces illness and death: the family's values and beliefs, the nature of the illness, whether the loss is sudden or expected, the role played by the dying person in the family, the emotional functioning of the family before the illness, and many other factors.[3] The family life cycle can be examined as a critical variable in the adjustment to loss by looking at the impact of death on four families at various stages of the life cycle. Each of these four deaths—that of an elderly man, a middle-aged woman, a young mother, and a child—affects multiple generations of their surviving families.

Normative Death: Death of an Elderly Person

RICE, John, 82, formerly a dentist in this community, died peacefully at Brookdale Retirement Home. For fifty-one years devoted husband of Helen Pearson, he is survived also by a son, John Jr., and a daughter, Cynthia Kellogg. Loving grandfather of James Rice, Janice Rice-Martin, John Kellogg, Clare McPherson, and Sandra Kellogg. Proud great-grandfather of Christopher Rice, captain of the Montrose High School basketball team, and of Timothy and Susan McPherson. Funeral services Saturday,

11 A.M. at First Presbyterian Church. Contributions may be made to
Montrose High School Athletic Scholarship Fund.

Part of the process of maturation is the acceptance of death as a part
of life. People expect that they will die in old age, and that their
parents and other elders will die. Yet even the anticipated death,
continuous with the life cycle, has repercussions in the lives of the
survivors. The effects of the loss are variable, depending on the stage
in the life cycle of the surviving families.

Among the heirs of John Rice, the family at the first stage—the
unattached young adult—is represented by Sandra Kellogg. If her
mother, Cynthia, is greatly stressed by her own father's death, Sandra's position as the unmarried, youngest daughter may cause her to
put her plans aside and return home to support her mother. If Sandra is having difficulty with her movement away from the family,
her grandfather's death may provide a rationale for returning. Although the death of an elderly grandparent at this stage of the family life cycle could retard development and individuation, it could
also facilitate a prime developmental task. Sandra may begin to see
her mother not as a demanding parent from whom she needs to escape but as a human being who, like herself, feels pain and loss and
needs emotional support. The dependency roles of mother and
daughter may reverse as Cynthia begins to rely on the child who in
the past had always relied on her in times of need.

Sandra's cousin Janice is in the second stage of the family life
cycle, the newly married couple. Like Sandra, Janice may feel the
need to provide support to her parents and grandmother as they adjust to the loss. But Janice needs to balance this pull back to her
family of origin with the push to maintain her fledgling marriage.
A father may be reluctant to look to his daughter for emotional support, so the pull toward her family of origin may be tempered in
comparison with Sandra's experience.

Although Clare McPherson, like her unmarried sister, Sandra,
may feel an urge to be an emotional support for her mother, the

centripetal forces within Clare's family—at the third stage of the life cycle, with young children—are likely to be stronger. However, her position as the eldest daughter in the family of origin, with its implied caretaking function, could create tension both between her and her siblings and between her and the adult family where she has primary parenting responsibilities. In addition, at this stage of that family's life cycle, Clare has the task of explaining the death of their great-grandfather to her two young children and handling whatever upset results.

James Rice, his wife, and his teenage son, Christopher, are at the next stage of the family life cycle—adolescence—when John Rice dies. This may be the teenager's first encounter with a loss felt so personally. At a time when he needs to be separating emotionally from his family, the death of his adoring great-grandfather could be an enormous blow that draws him closer to his parents and grandparents. In addition, the death of the family elder leaves both James and Christopher acutely conscious of the mortality of their respective fathers.

The launching stage of the family life cycle is represented by the family of Cynthia Kellogg, the daughter of the deceased, whose children are embarking on their careers and beginning new families. Bereft at the death of her father and now more responsible for her elderly mother, Cynthia's struggle to loosen the emotional ties to her children is going to be tested. She may find it difficult to allow her children to continue their moving away from the family, as that movement represents another dimension of loss in her life. Although she had been looking forward to this time alone with her husband, the responsibility she now feels for her mother could prompt her to invite Helen to move into the "empty nest."

The last stage of the family life cycle is represented by the widow, Helen, who must deal with the issues that typically affect the elderly: the loss of a spouse, the increasing loss of friends as they move away or die, a growing dependence on children, and, of course, the realization that one's own days are numbered. If Helen were to accept her daughter Cynthia's invitation to move in with her, the normative flow of the family life cycle could become complicated as family boundaries lose their distinction.

Premature Death: Death of a Middle-Aged Person

COLEMAN, Tina, age 52, suddenly. Devoted wife and partner of Joel. Loving mother of Philip, Margaret Meany, and Frank. Adoring grandmother of Tracy. Beloved daughter of Mildred and the late Frank Korvan. Fond sister of Charles and supportive aunt of Josie. Winner of the 1995 American Jewelry Design Award, and owner and manager with her husband of TeeJay Jewelers, 232 Broad Street. Memorial service Tuesday at noon, at the Ethical Culture Society; interment will be private.

The death of a person in middle age brings a life story to a premature conclusion. Such a death may come at either the height of a career or at a time when the person's life work is incomplete. While the world may be deprived of more of Tina Coleman's lovely jewelry designs, her family will suffer from the suddenness of her passing at a point in the life cycle when she played many roles: a mother still closely involved in the lives of her children, a wife recently freed from child-care responsibilities, a daughter who was a mainstay of support, and an important member of an extended family system.

His mother's death occurs as Tina's younger son, Frank, begins the adult life cycle. Having recently moved to another state as part of his company's management training program, twenty-two-year-old Frank has only begun to experience independence and separation from his family of origin. As he establishes an adult identity and enters into new relationships (one of which may lead to the creation of a new family), the unexpected death of his mother creates a powerful tug to return home. A major challenge for Frank will be to continue the tasks of individuation while he sustains an emotional connection with his father that does not necessitate his physical presence in the family of origin.

Margaret, Tina's only daughter, had grown especially close to her mother when they planned her wedding together five years ago. Now in the second stage of the family life cycle, Margaret is inconsolable at the loss of her mother. "She so wanted me to get pregnant," Margaret weeps, "but I kept insisting that there was plenty of time for that." Margaret is now torn between her allegiance to her husband and her burgeoning career on the one hand and a sense of duty to her father on the other. She plans to go to his home several days a week to cook dinner for him, clean the house, and do his laundry, trying to fill the void created by her mother's death. The centripetal force that compels Margaret to care for her father is likely to be temporary, but will depend greatly on how well she has differentiated herself from her family of origin. In all likelihood, she will fill the void in her own life by beginning her own family.

Joel now spends as much time as he can at his son Philip's home, with his adored three-year-old granddaughter. Although he would like to see even more of little Tracy, he often feels like an intruder and is not sure that his daughter-in-law welcomes his presence. Tracy's confusion about where her grandmother has gone adds to his pain. Like her, Joel keeps believing that Tina will come walking through the door. At the penultimate stage of the life cycle, Joel had anticipated spending "quality time" with Tina, selling their business, buying a trailer, and traveling. All of their dreams died with her, and he now wishes that they had not launched their children so eagerly. His secret desire is that one of the three children might decide to come into the business with him. Or perhaps Frank might move back home. Or maybe Margaret will have a baby soon. After years of anticipating a life free of responsibility for his children, Joel now feels the loss of involvement in their lives almost as acutely as he suffers the loss of his wife.

There is also a family in the fourth stage of the life cycle, the one with adolescents, that is affected by Tina's sudden death. Tina's brother Charles, his wife, and daughter are very close to the Colemans. Charles's marriage has been highly conflictual, and on the several occasions when he and his wife have separated, each depended on Tina's wise counsel and support. Their sixteen-year-old daughter, Josie, was extremely close to her aunt and relied on her wisdom and sensitivity during the difficult times in her parents' marriage. Since Tina's death, Josie has become excessively withdrawn and moody. At a stage of the life cycle when her parents need to give her opportunities to feel independent, they have become more protective in response to her troubling behavior. Charles is also feeling burdened by his increased responsibility for his widowed mother now that Tina is dead. Trapped between the needs of these two families, his wife and daughter on the one hand, his mother on the other, Charles has nearly ignored his own sorrow at the loss of his sister.

Seldom a day went by when Mildred and her daughter Tina didn't talk. Now she finds herself alone with no one to talk to about her horrible fate. "A parent isn't supposed to outlive a child," sobs Mildred, and outrage at the untimely death of her daughter is justifiable. The death of a fifty-year-old child is, in many ways, no less painful than the death of a five-year-old child, in that the family's sense of itself as a nurturing, protective unit is shattered. Mildred has endured many losses through the years: the deaths of her husband and sister; the move of her brother and sister-in-law, and many of her friends, to a warmer climate; and her own deteriorating health. But the death of her daughter is more emotionally searing than all of the previous losses combined.

Cut Off in the Prime of Life: Death of the Young Adult

MEDINA, Linda, 28. Loving wife of Carlos, mother of Jonny and Amelia, daughter of Reuben and Juanita Torres, oldest sister of Juan, Michael, Carmela, and Anita, granddaughter of Pedro and Conchita Suarez and Bonita Henderson. Service Thursday, 10 A.M., at Our Lady of Perpetual Peace.

If the death of a person in middle age ends life prematurely, the death of a young adult ends life just as it has begun. The young adult has barely had the opportunity to establish a role in society separate from the family of origin and is likely to be a central figure in both the family of origin and the family of adulthood. A man or woman in the third or fourth decade of life can be simultaneously child, parent, spouse, sibling, and grandchild. Probably no death demonstrates the interrelationship of the family of origin and the family of adulthood more profoundly than does the death of the young adult. For not only does such a death confound life cycle expectations (an emotionally upsetting event in itself), but it also demands a complex reorganization of families at disparate stages of their life cycles.

Linda Medina and her family had everything to look forward to until the day her car skidded off a rain-slicked road into a lamppost. For four months she lay in a coma, and then pneumonia put an end to her life. Linda's protracted clinging to life had a powerful impact on her husband, Carlos, and their two young children—a family in the third stage of its life cycle. The loss of a spouse and the consequent responsibility of single parenthood are totally at odds with the normal life cycle at this stage. While grieving the loss of his wife, Carlos must assume total parental responsibility for Jonny and Amelia. Unaccustomed to the functional tasks of caring for two small children, Carlos doubtless will be daunted by the prospect of trying to make the adjustment. The children's lives, of course, have been irreparably disrupted, and even if Carlos remarries, they will have lost years of maternal influence at a time when they most need it.

Like most men who find themselves in such a predicament, Carlos is likely to turn to women in his family for support in caring for the children. Few men feel able to take on the tasks of primary parenthood if those tasks have been solely the domain of their wives. The emotional demands and caretaking functions performed by women throughout their lives may appear overwhelming. At a stage of the life cycle when Carlos ordinarily would be establishing clear boundaries with his family of origin, he will likely feel compelled to break down whatever boundaries have already been established with his and Linda's families. He will now call on his mother, Linda's mother, and any other available woman in the families to rescue him, and they will respond.

Deeply religious, hardworking people, Linda's parents and grandparents are nearly inconsolable over the loss of their beloved child and grandchild in the prime of life. Because Carlos's work responsibilities prevented him from spending much time at the hospital, Linda's mother, Juanita, sat for hours at the bedside of her comatose daughter, talking to her and praying for her. Reuben, her father, took command of many of the logistical needs during this period, such as transportation and shopping. Linda's maternal grandparents live in Puerto Rico, but Bonita, her father's mother, has always been a support and comfort to the family and remained so throughout the hospitalization, caring for Jonny and Amelia by day and being available to the adults at night. The loosening of boundaries between Linda's family of origin and her family of adulthood meant that Linda, Carlos, and the children would be well cared for. Linda's death leaves her family of origin grieving for its terrible loss, and also without significant tasks to perform. Even though Carlos may turn to them and his own family initially, there will surely come a time when he will desire to reestablish the boundaries, and this could result in conflict between the generations.

Boundaries are also a problem for Linda's siblings, in a transition between stages four and five in the life cycle of their family of origin. Some of her brothers and sisters are only beginning to make tentative moves away from the family, and those who are already out on their own have not yet fully established the boundaries that separate them from their parents and from each other. Linda's death—and the sudden awareness of their own mortality—will make their moves toward independence more complicated. The centripetal forces in the family of origin set into motion by her death will hamper an otherwise natural tendency to establish intimate relationships outside the family. For example, her younger brother, Michael, who only recently set up housekeeping with his girlfriend, is even more resistant to the prospect of marriage. Carmela, the sister with whom Linda was closest, now prefers to be with Jonny and Amelia than to go out with her friends, and she has begun to involve herself with the little ones to the exclusion of all other activities.

The Unthinkable Loss: Death of a Child

SECANT, Joshua, age 7. Darling son of Fred and Ellen and favorite brother of Amanda; beloved grandson of Jonathan and Estelle Secant and Harvey and Madeline Morris; nephew of Robert Secant and Karen Morris. Funeral services private.

The death of a child is no doubt the greatest tragedy any family can endure. The relationship between parent and child is life's most intimate bond, and an implicit part of that bond is that the elder will forever protect the younger. The fatal illness of a child may jeopardize all other relationships in the family, leaving each member unsure of his or her ultimate security.

No matter how old the dying son or daughter, a parent's grief will be unlike that suffered at any other time, for when a child dies, so do the hopes and dreams for the future. The shattering of a family's dreams may be particularly poignant when the child has yet to reach adulthood, for parents can only imagine what might have been. Could this child have reached beyond the parents' own achievements? The family's sense of its very future is brought into question with the loss of the next generation.[4]

Fred and Ellen Secant now face one of life's most painful tasks: to continue living without their precious child. Many parents find the task impossible and thus mourn interminably, a phenomenon that will be discussed in Chapter Five. There are no normative temporal parameters for parental grief, which is seldom, if ever, fully resolved. In speaking with a parent whose child died many years before, I am often struck by the freshness with which the child is described and the seeming immediacy of the loss. Thus it is likely that Fred and Ellen will experience the pain of Joshua's illness and death well into the future, and his short life will affect the family through several generations.

Joshua's death will have an enormously disruptive effect on the Secants, who are in the stage of the life cycle when building the family structure and raising children are paramount. The decision about whether to have another child has become clouded by an added urgency and confusion, and Fred and Ellen may be less willing to allow Amanda, their nine-year-old, to take the necessary steps toward individuation at this stage of her development. The centripetal forces naturally present at this stage are reinforced by a child's death, to the extent that the death of a child may bring normal family development to a grinding halt.

Although the loss of a child is highly disruptive to a marriage, it is not necessarily destructive. The responses in marital relationships to the death of a child are widely variable. Some marriages cannot withstand the emotional strain and fall apart into separation or divorce. At the other extreme are couples whose relationships strengthen and who draw enormous support from each other, forming a stronger marital bond than before. Most couples, including the Secants, experience both a serious shaking of the marital foundation and a strengthening of the emotional bonds.

Fred and Ellen had dealt with Joshua's illness as many parents do. Fred expressed his concern through intense contact with physicians and hospital personnel. Otherwise, however, he did not speak much about the illness, and he continued working, even harder than before. He grew impatient when he felt unable to assuage Ellen's fears or solve the family's problems. Ellen often became enraged at him, accusing him of being cold and unfeeling, and he countered by labeling her hysterical and irrational. Ellen reacted to the illness by immersing herself in Joshua's caretaking. She became particularly attuned to the child's fears and emotions, and a kind of emotional fusion developed between her and her son, often to the exclusion of her husband and daughter. This angered Fred, and they fought frequently about the effect of Joshua's illness on their marriage and family. Yet each spouse served as the other's primary support and best friend. They communicated better and more frequently than they had before, and during periods of quiescence in the illness, they found an intensity and a closeness in their relationship that surprised them both. However, scars remain on their marriage that may never be totally erased. Ellen remains skeptical of Fred's ability to be present emotionally in the face of crisis, and Fred fears Ellen's emotional "weakness" when strength and rationality are called for. But the deep commitment they have discovered has sustained them during the most painful moments of their lives.

The effect of Joshua's death on Amanda takes a variety of forms. The serious illness of a sibling threatens a child's own bodily integrity and creates fears and uncertainties about health and mortality. Amanda was only seven when Joshua was first diagnosed with a rare angiosarcoma, but she was quite aware of how ill her little brother was, and she was solicitous and helpful in caring for him. Like her parents, Amanda felt a tremendous pull toward the family and began to drift, almost imperceptibly, away from her friends. At the time of Joshua's death, Amanda had no close friends to comfort her, partly because of the forces pulling her into the center of the family and making external boundaries rigid, and partly because she was a relatively young child. An adolescent, in contrast, would probably be capable of maintaining supportive outside relationships despite the centripetal force created by a sibling's fatal condition.

Amanda's relationship with her parents has been markedly affected by Joshua's illness and death. The Secants had to focus on the demands of caring for a fatally sick child and his physical and emotional needs, leaving Amanda to fend for herself at a relatively early age. Ellen's role as homemaker and mother to both her children changed as she became Joshua's primary caretaker, and Fred, too, was preoccupied with his son's condition, although not as involved with physical tasks on a daily basis. For some time, then, Amanda had to contend not only with the illness and prospective loss of her brother but also with the loss of effectively functioning parents.

Joshua's death reached beyond his immediate family to his four grandparents. They, too, had hopes for the coming generations of the family. In the final stage of the family life cycle, the grandparents may have been anticipating the death of contemporaries and their own mortality, but no elderly person is prepared for the fatal illness of a grandchild. The grandparents now have an unexpected emotional change at this stage of their lives. Instead of celebrating a new generation and sharing, from a comfortable distance, the joys of their children's families, they will be feeling the despair and grief of the younger generations. Perhaps they will become more interwoven in their children's lives as a result.

Notes

1. The subject of loss and its impact on the family at particular stages of the life cycle is addressed by Monica McGoldrick and Froma Walsh in their book *Living Beyond Loss* (New York: Norton, 1991) and by Ester R. Shapiro in *Grief as a Family Process* (New York: Guilford Press, 1994).

2. Murray Bowen's idea of death as the source of an intergenerational emotional shock wave will be discussed more fully in Chapter Five, in examination of grief in the family system.

3. For a helpful expansion of some of these ideas, see Fredda Herz Brown, "The Impact of Death and Serious Illness on the Family Life Cycle," in B. Carter and M. McGoldrick (eds.), *The Changing Family Life Cycle: A Framework for Family Therapy* (Lake Worth, Fla.: Gardner Press, 1988), pp. 457–481.

4. For a good description of how families cope with the death of a child, see Barbara D. Rosof, *The Worst Loss: How Families Heal from the Death of a Child* (New York: Henry Holt, 1994).

4

The Family Prepares for Death

Not talking about death with the dying patient
Is like not talking about birth with a pregnant woman.
They'll probably find out in the end.
        Michael Simpson, South African oncologist and poet
                            Telling Remarks

For three weeks, the Haleys have been conducting a death watch. Ann Haley, sixty-two years old, is in the final stages of cancer, which was first diagnosed twelve years ago. She is being cared for at home, with the cooperation of the community hospice program in which her daughter-in-law, Maggie, works as a nurse. For the last few weeks, Ann has been conscious only occasionally. When she is able to talk, she apologizes for being such a bother to her family.

Ann Rourke Haley, the eldest of four children, was born in County Donegal, Ireland, and came with her parents and sister to the United States when she was seven (see Figure 4.1). Within three years, Ann's two brothers were born, and then her father was killed in an accident. His widow took a factory job to support the family, and Ann became surrogate mother to her sister and brothers for the remainder of their childhood.

By the time Ann met Andrew Haley, her siblings had all married; she was working as an executive secretary and was living with her mother. Andrew was an engaging fellow who had recently come

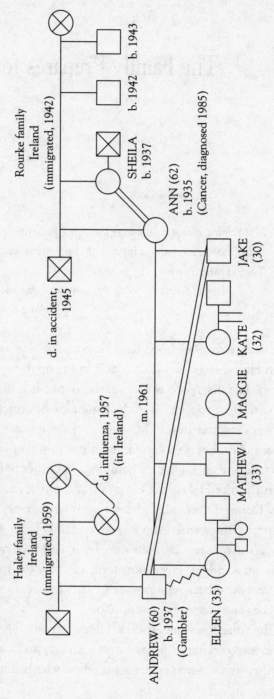

Figure 4.1. Genogram of the Haley Family, 1997.

to America with his father, after the death of his mother and sister in an influenza epidemic in Ireland. Within months, they were married, and their four children were born in their first six years together. Ann's mother lived with them and helped care for the children until she died unexpectedly of a stroke shortly after the birth of Ann's youngest child. Ann's sister, Sheila, was widowed during this same period, and she looked after the children when Ann went back to work. Andrew Haley, a compulsive gambler, had difficulty keeping a job, which made Ann the family's primary breadwinner.

The four Haley children, Ellen, Matthew, Kate, and Jake, are grown now and live close by. They are emotionally close with Ann, their Aunt Sheila, and each other, but their relationships with their father are problematic. Jake is closest to his father, and Matthew and Kate are on polite terms with him. But Ellen has barely spoken with him since he disowned her fifteen years ago, at age twenty, for marrying a Protestant. The siblings have always depended on their mother for advice and support, and even as she is dying, they do not seem to comprehend that they are losing her.

Ann had just turned fifty when she was first diagnosed with cancer. At that time, Ellen was married and at home with her two babies; Matthew had just finished college and was engaged; Kate was in her last year of nursing school; and Jake had just left for college. Ann dealt with the cancer, hysterectomy, radiation, and chemotherapy with Sheila as her only support, not even telling her children why she was having the surgery and other treatment. Andrew, who was still gambling compulsively, kept himself distant from this "female problem."

Four years later, Ann had a mastectomy and further radiation and chemotherapy. Her family was still fairly removed from the illness, even though both her daughter Kate and her daughter-in-law Maggie were nurses. Five more years passed, and Ann required a second mastectomy. During this time, Andrew joined Gamblers Anonymous, and he has now abstained from gambling for seven years.

However, he is still unable to function at more than a minimal level, moving from one menial job to another. Until she became too weak to work, Ann continued to be the major wage earner for the family.

In the final days of her life, Ann is never alone. Andrew, Sheila, her children, and their spouses have arranged a schedule to ensure that someone is always with her. Ann's physician has made a home visit, meeting Andrew for the first time in the twelve years that Ann has been his patient. A local priest has come to administer last rites. Hospice volunteers are available, but the Haleys seem to be taking care of things quite adequately.

Despite Ann's condition, her children continue to speak about Mom's toughness, saying she'll surprise everyone by making another recovery. Ellen is very angry with her father and has complained to her siblings that "he is treating Mom like she's already a corpse." Both Matthew and Jake find it difficult to spend much time in their mother's room, and they can often be found in the kitchen of their parents' home, drinking until late in the evening.

No family that has lived with a fatal illness can emerge unchanged from the ordeal. The family of the terminally ill patient will proceed through a series of systemic changes, and although the ultimate visible change is the absence of the deceased, the surviving family is inherently different in a number of other fundamental ways. As a result of the illness and loss, some families may actually function better than before; others may experience changes so destructive that recovery of normal family functioning is a long and excruciating process. Some families achieve greater levels of intimacy as they cope with illness and loss; in other cases, issues that have lain dormant for many years explode under the strain, splintering the family. Some families are able to compensate for the loss of an important member by reallocating tasks to preserve the family's integrity; other families may be irreparably crippled by the loss of a particular member.

Illness creates problems that affect the family as a systemic unit and compel the entire family organism to adapt itself to its changed condition by finding ways to sustain equilibrium. Problems or issues that affect the family as a system can be classified under four general rubrics: disorganization, anxiety, emotional lability, and turning inward.

Under most circumstances, an intrinsic organization allows families to meet the daily demands of living. Although some families function better than others, most are sufficiently organized to pass without unreasonable disturbance from one stage of the family life cycle to another. The Haleys were not necessarily the healthiest of families, and their internal organization may not have been ideal. Andrew was addicted to gambling and could not hold a job; Ann was perhaps too involved with her children, even in their adult lives, and may not have taken good care of herself; and there was friction between the children and their father. Nevertheless, all four children were able to leave home and move on in the life cycle of adulthood without too much difficulty. But coping skills that have worked adequately in the past may break down under the challenge of terminal illness. Fear, denial, and doubts result in disorganization, which is a common systemic issue for families facing loss and death. Confusion may arise in relationships with children, regardless of their ages. Thus Ann did not tell her children when she first learned she had cancer, even though they were all old enough to be supportive. And repeating the pattern from their family of origin, Ann's children did not tell their young ones that Granny was dying.

Few life experiences are more anxiety-producing than the illness of a loved one. The ways in which anxiety is manifested in the family as a whole are usually quite striking. "Systems anxiety" may be diagnosed when family members constantly interrupt each other, apologize for (or to) each other, bicker, and disagree. Anxiety may also be demonstrated on a more subtle level, as when the family regresses to previous dysfunctional behavior that is not perceived as related to the crisis at hand.

The Geddes family displayed a regressive systems anxiety reaction. When I first met them, Bob Geddes was drinking and abusing cocaine, nine-year-old Bobby was physically violent with his father and failing in school, and Millie Geddes was constantly intervening between her husband and son. When they left treatment two years later, they were doing extremely well. Bob was in Alcoholics Anonymous and had been completely alcohol- and drug-free for many months; Bobby was doing well both with his parents and in school; and Millie had gotten involved in her own work and was letting the two of them work out their problems without her. Everything went smoothly for five years, until Millie was diagnosed with systemic lupus erythematosus, which doctors were having difficulty controlling. Within three months, Bob was again using cocaine, Bobby had been expelled from school, and the interaction among the three of them was nearly a carbon copy of what I had seen seven years before. I helped them acknowledge the fears each had about the illness and find ways to deal with it to avoid recycling their anxiety.

Although not all families are equally prone to outward expressions of emotions, it is not unusual for strong feelings of anger and guilt to surface at times of illness, even in the most emotionally low-keyed families. Families with a well of unresolved issues, like the Haleys, are much more likely to react with emotional lability. The conflict between Ellen and her father, festering for years, was heightened in response to Ann's illness. Ellen's anger, though rooted in problems that began long before her mother became terminally ill, was translated into rage at her father's acceptance of the unthinkable: Ann was going to die. The emotional lability could not be contained in the conflict between Andrew and his daughter; the tension had to affect others. Matthew and Jake, for example, who initially reacted to their mother's illness by denying it, later withdrew and started drinking together. In some families, members may vie in the "Who is doing more?" competition or argue over who is hurting more. Families may maneuver to soften the hostility by demanding pseudomutuality—"we all hurt the same"—but this device, characteristic of the closed family system, usually cannot hold back the flood of emotions lurking beneath the surface.

As discussed in Chapter Three, illness and death are strong centripetal forces, and a bunker mentality often characterizes families facing death. Turning inward in the face of prospective loss is a natural response in both open and closed family systems, although it is greatly accentuated in the closed system, where the nuclear family becomes a fortress, forbidding entry even to those outsiders who could provide much-needed help. The process of turning inward also involves subtle and covert agreements among family members to avoid discussing emotionally charged issues.

Although the death watch they are keeping suggests that the Haleys may have prepared themselves intellectually for Ann's death, they have yet to accept what their life as a family might be without her. Their turning inward does not extend to denial of entry to outsiders; it is more subtle. Ideas and feelings that might upset the family's shaky equilibrium are not permitted. Anyone who does not correctly play the role in the implicit script written by the family may be thrown out of the cast.

PHASES OF FAMILY ADAPTATION

These four emotional responses of the family to the crisis of prospective loss—disorganization, anxiety, emotional liability, and turning inward—will be dramatically different at various phases in the family's adjustment to the illness. Just as a terminally ill person progresses from a state of health to moribundity to dying, a family's progress in response to a fatal illness can be roughly divided into three phases: (1) the preparatory phase, beginning when symptoms first appear and continuing through the initial diagnosis; (2) the middle phase, which can be quite lengthy, when the family lives with the reality and caretaking tasks of the fatal illness; and (3) the final stage, when the family accepts the imminent death and concludes the process of saying farewell.

The phases of family adaptation do not necessarily correlate with the physical course of the illness, although in many cases they do. In addition to the course that the illness takes, the family's response will depend on two other factors, which are not directly related to the patient's physical condition: (1) the structure of the family system before the illness—that is, openness, level of function, and the role played by the patient in that system; and (2) the family's perception of the course of the illness, which may not be synonymous with the reality of its physical course.

Phase One: The Preparatory Phase

A family actually begins to address the prospect of loss with the very first symptoms of disease. As incredible as this may seem, when any member of a family is stricken with illness, even the mildest of physical ailments, the family automatically begins a process of adaptation to preserve threatened homeostasis. For example, we are likely to be familiar with the kind of behavior set in motion in the Smith family if little Mary Smith gets the sniffles. Her parents may become overly solicitous, aware of every twitch of the youngster's nose. Mary may want to crawl into Mommy's lap, a behavior she had more or less abandoned, and Mommy will readily comply. If, instead of Mary, it is Dad who gets the cold, he may mope about, expecting to be waited on. And if Mom gets a cold, life in the Smith household could grind to a halt as long as the person responsible for daily chores is under the weather. Should this bug stay in the family for a while, all of the Smiths will make moves to continue their lives without serious disruption, aware of the need to adapt when the integrity of the system is threatened.

The process of adaptation that the Haleys began when Ann faced her first surgery set the tone for how the family would cope with her illness until her death. She may have chosen not to share the fact that she had cancer, but the rest of the family colluded in her decision. Her husband opted to remain ignorant of the significance of the surgery and did not accompany her on visits to the doctor or attempt to learn anything about her condition. Ellen, her elder daughter with two children, and Kate, who was finishing nursing school, certainly had to be aware of possible reasons for a hysterectomy. The Haleys' response in this preparatory phase illustrates the notion that a family's adaptation to the prospect of death may be quite unrelated to the physical course of the disease and is much more influenced by the family's mode of functioning prior to the illness.

The most characteristic responses in the earliest phase of life-threatening illness are fear and denial. Ann bore these emotions for the entire Haley family—as she bore most burdens for both her family of adulthood and her family of origin. The Haleys are unusual in that the rest of the family did not enter an active preparatory phase until much later in the illness, when Ann could no longer keep the reality secret. Thus, even as her mother neared death, Ellen was still denying the obvious. Fear and denial are nearly automatic responses to serious illness: "This lump can't be cancer . . . but what if it is?" "There's no way Dad can be that sick. We'll get a second opinion." In this early phase, families will often go from doctor to doctor, hoping for a benign verdict, refusing to believe a frightening diagnosis. "Sure he thinks open-heart surgery is necessary—he's a surgeon. We'll find a doctor who believes in diet and medication!" "Of course you have more than five months to live! We'll go to Mexico, where they can cure you."

Denying the seriousness of the illness or refusing to accept the prospect of death, persuasive family members may decide to withhold all information from those they consider to be vulnerable, such as children or elderly parents, who must be "protected" from upsetting news. Recall the Marshes, the family encountered in Chapter Two. The "protection" of the children from knowledge of Richard's leukemia ultimately had a totally disorganizing effect on the family and led both children to suffer unnecessary emotional distress.

In this preparatory phase of the illness—the period of initial symptoms, diagnosis, treatment plan, and prognosis—the family may be highly disorganized. In rational moments, when they accept the doctor's pronouncements, some relatives may try to imagine life as it will be and may worry about the integrity of the family with such a vital part missing. The family begins turning inward, building walls that it mistakenly believes will protect it. In fact, this initiates a destructive process by cutting off the family from sources of support and by making it impossible for family members to share their fears and sadness.

Anxiety may be higher at this time than at later periods. Emotional lability is seen in anger and hostility, which may be unusual in the family's experience. At all stages of terminal illness, families may look for scapegoats to blame for the fate that they must accept. In this early phase, the blame is often placed on "stupid doctors" who have given bad advice or on "insensitive nurses." But the patient may also be blamed for creating the condition because of real or imagined behavior, such as a poor diet, inadequate exercise, overwork, or too much worrying. And when the patient chooses treatments that are unacceptable to another family member, the entire family may become engulfed in a storm of anger and hostility, which serves as an effective distraction from the harsh reality.

Phase Two: Living with Fatal Illness

The phases of adaptation are neither time-limited nor directly correlated with the physical course of the illness; rather, they are distinguished by the emotional response of the family. When the family has made the initial adaptation to the prospect of loss, it passes from the preparatory phase and begins to live with the reality of fatal illness. This second phase can be viewed as a kind of settling-in period, during which the family adjusts to its caretaking role and anticipates the ultimate loss of its loved one. Often quite complex and sometimes protracted, this phase is differentiated from the initial preparatory phase and the final parting phase because this is the time when the patient and family live with the day-to-day challenges of symptoms, treatment, and physical care. Because fatal illness can also be chronic, the second phase may be quite long.[1]

This period may follow closely on the heels of the initial diagnosis. In some cases, the second phase is quickly shortened by death, but it may also last for years, as it did in the case of Ann Haley, whose course was marked by alternating periods of illness and remission. During this phase, the Haleys were able to manage their lives and avoid severe developmental difficulties, partly because their children were grown and more or less independent.

Such was not the case for the Borellis, a family in an earlier stage of their life cycle. When Joe Borelli suffered a heart attack that left him permanently disabled, his three children were still in elementary school. The middle phase for the Borellis lasted three years, until Joe's death, and was fraught with difficulties, both emotional and physical. At this stage of the family life cycle, the Borellis had adopted fairly traditional gender roles. With the loss of Joe as the primary wage earner, Roslyn Borelli had to go to work outside the home. Joe was left to oversee the house and children, a role that taxed him physically and for which he was emotionally unprepared. Joe resented his wife's financial support of the family, and Roslyn was finding the separation from her children difficult. The tension in the family was exacerbated by the reaction of the children to the chaos that had entered their lives: they became unmanageable and angry at home and disruptive in school. The Borellis were never able to master the demands of the second phase of Joe's illness. It was only after his death that his wife and children were able to reorganize themselves without the symptoms that had been present during the time Joe was ill.

A lessening of disorganization may indicate that the family is moving into the middle phase of adaptation and beginning to live with the reality of the situation. No longer pursuing miracle cures or doctors with more favorable opinions, the family reorganizes to assume new caretaking roles, both for the patient and for other members. Ironically, in its attempts to organize itself around caring for the patient, the family may wind up in a more disorganized state, neglecting its responsibilities to other members and to its overall health and well-being. For example, whereas mealtimes might have been a highlight of a family's day before the illness, food may now be prepared hastily and eaten on the run. Birthdays and holidays may come and go without notice. It is difficult to predict how a family is likely to react in this second phase. However, the capacity for individuals and families to rise to the challenges of potentially fatal illness is frequently related to the degree of openness in the system. Ongoing communication about the nature and course of the illness among family members tends to increase the prospect of its arriving at a calmer, more organized pace.

The anxiety in families during this middle phase is usually related to the demands of caretaking and to financial uncertainty. Family members may understandably question their ability to provide the kind of nursing care the patient requires—and, in fact, they often *are* unable to do so. Fears of harming the patient when trying to be helpful may be reinforced by the patient, whose feelings about pain can create a generalized anxiety in the family. Anxiety may also center on the type of care chosen, whether it is home care, hospitalization, or institutionalization. Care for the terminally ill during a drawn-out middle phase can be exhausting and draining, and secret wishes for the patient's quick demise may create enormous guilt and anxiety.

The costs of illness can be staggering, and realization of how much it might ultimately cost is strong in this second phase. As the bank account diminishes with each visit to the doctor, the family may justifiably worry whether the disease will outlive its financial resources. Sometimes the patient, feeling useless and a drain on the family's everyday life, will use finances as a way of maintaining some semblance of control. For example, a patient who has always been the one to oversee the family's finances may struggle to maintain that role, even when it is highly impractical.

The tedium of daily care is particularly taxing in the middle phase of illness. With protracted hospitalization or institutionalization, the logistics of visitation may create discord among family members, some feeling that others are visiting too little or too much. When the patient is being cared for in the home, some family members may feel that they are bearing too much of the responsibility. During this middle phase, when the shock of the diagnosis has receded and the family must settle into the routine of daily care, the unresolved issues of the past—both real and imagined, major and minor—rise to the surface. The daughter of a terminally ill woman thus screams at her brother, who she feels is avoiding his part in their mother's care: "You could always get out of work. How many times did I have to do the dishes when it was your turn?" Such emotional baggage from the family's past is most likely to tumble into the present when family members have not openly discussed their responsibilities for the patient and when they have glossed over the ultimate loss by focusing on the patient's physical needs.

A common coping mechanism that families employ to manage the daily stress of terminal illness is to deny any differences in temperament, emotions, and attitude among their members. The family enters into an unspoken pact: we are all in this together, and we must all act and feel the same; we shall pretend to be alike. This behavior, which family therapists term *pseudomutuality*, creates an enormous emotional drain on the system. It is most common during this second phase in the adaptation to illness, when dissension might threaten the family's belief in its ability to function adequately. Pseudomutuality is a manifestation of turning inward in response to terminal illness and is nearly synonymous with the closed system. The acknowledgment of individual differences among family members threatens the closed family system, and the centripetal forces set in motion by the illness reinforce the family's tendency to close itself off from the outside and demand allegiance from those within.

Pseudomutuality was prominent in the Gibson family, whose twenty-seven-year-old, Ralph, was dying of AIDS. The family doctor, who referred the Gibsons to me, expressed concern that they were "burning out." But each of the four caretakers—Ralph's parents, sister, and grandmother—insisted that they were doing fine. Nor would they admit to any anger or resentment toward the young man, for whom they had been caring for nearly a year. Subsequently, his sister requested a "secret" meeting without the rest of the family, and at that time she confessed that the surface cheerfulness, optimism, and good feelings that family members presented to the outside world and to each other were false. But, she said, there was no choice but to act that way; to do otherwise would be cruel to her brother. The Gibsons could tolerate no departure from the facade they had constructed, although its very existence was never openly acknowledged.

Phase Three: Final Acceptance

For nearly every family, there arrives a time when death becomes an active presence in their lives. Phase three in the family's course of adaptation is usually the shortest. Hopes for a cure or for further remission may be abandoned, although some level of denial may still be present. Despite Ann Haley's comatose state, her children continued to cling to the illusion that she might recover. Such denial is not uncommon if the family has not already adequately addressed the prospect of death. Over the years, the Haleys had responded to Ann's illness by refusing to accept its seriousness, so in this final phase, despite an intellectual awareness of her impending death, they were emotionally unprepared to accept reality.

As was the case with the Haleys, not all family members may be equally ready to accept the obvious. It is not unusual at this stage for one person to be making funeral plans while another continues to insist that the patient is looking better every day. Nevertheless, the family as a whole must undertake certain transitional tasks, which will be explored in more detail in Chapter Five. It is helpful for families to begin some of these tasks at an earlier point, but by this final phase they must be addressed.

Families that have managed to cope efficiently for months with the demands of a sick member suddenly find themselves disorganized and in shock, often because of the diminished need for active physical care toward the very end of life. No longer having important caretaking tasks to perform, family members may feel superfluous and unsure of how to act around the patient and each other. Moreover, the general anxiety level in the family may rise once again, not only in anticipation of death but also because of fear of the many demands that will undoubtedly be made. One source of anxiety for many families is that certain behavior will be expected from them after the death. As the wife of a dying man remarked: "I'm cried out. I'm afraid that people will think me callous and uncaring at his funeral. But after all this time of waiting for him to die, I feel empty. I have no emotions left."

In this final phase of adaptation, powerful emotions that were present in the early stage of illness, but that subsided during the gradual adjustment to the illness, may resurface as the family once again faces the harsh and now-immediate reality of loss. Ellen Haley and her father, for example, had managed to keep their conflict from exploding until Ann's final days. Ellen was not yet emotionally ready to accept that her mother was going to die, and the truce with her father was shattered because he was accepting his wife's death.

Centripetal forces may become stronger as family members cling together in anticipation of their loved one's death. The tendency to draw the circle tight may be reinforced at this time by the fears of abandonment that are triggered by the prospect of loss. As individual family members struggle with their own personal fears, the family as a whole prepares to absorb a crushing blow to its integrity as a system. This natural emotional response is palliative. Family members do need each other at this time, and the family can best heal itself as a unit if they anticipate this need. The tendency to draw closer is not universal, however. This final stage may set in motion a move away from the family rather than toward it. The observant and skilled professional will encourage family closeness at this time, helping family members to accept that by coming together now, they will ensure their ability to separate in a healthy way in the future.

Healthcare workers can help families with a dying relative realize that the process of healing begins long before death occurs. To provide this guidance, the health professional must acknowledge that the medical care of the patient is but one component of care. In addition, a patient's emotional and psychological well-being and the family's role in that aspect of care both need to be addressed. Directing families to appropriate resources, helping them accept their feelings, and informing them that families must pass through a series of phases and must grapple with complex issues in each of these phases are services that the professional can perform.[2]

A PROCESS OF GRIEF BEGINS

Chapter Five will examine more closely the ways in which families adjust to the death of a loved one and the specific tasks that need to be performed as families go about the process of healing. But here can be noted a process called *anticipatory grief,* which accompanies the three phases of adaptation.

The death and dying literature has, for many years, reverberated with a debate over whether grieving can begin before a loved one has died. The controversy goes even further, to question whether such a process *ought* to begin before death.[3] I will not examine this controversy in detail. Instead, I will describe some of the characteristics of families as they prepare for death and relate them to anticipatory grief.

Anticipatory grief is by no means an automatic process that is set in motion when a fatal disease is diagnosed. In fact, individuals and families often fail to begin any process of grieving before a death. As the discussion of the three phases of adaptation has emphasized, the family's perception of the meaning and seriousness of an illness does not always correspond to the physician's diagnosis of disease. Thus, after discussing with the doctor the unavailability of treatment for a fatal cancer and indicating that it understands what will happen, the family might nevertheless insist, "Well, whatever it is, we're going to lick it."

Emotional upheaval in anticipation of a loved one's death reflects the ultimate struggle between holding on and letting go, and it is present at every phase of adaptation. In the preparatory phase, each family member is likely to fantasize widely, touching on such topics as funeral arrangements, financial inheritance, and life after the individual is dead. Frequently, these fantasies are unaccompanied by emotion, and this phenomenon can be interpreted as a psychological "trying on for size." Such ideas are usually not articulated at this early phase, yet conflict can be fueled by the unspoken anxiety of anticipating the loss. This process tends to be highly individual. The family systems perspective, however, focuses on the more interactive aspects of anticipatory grief; these include specific tasks, which will be considered in Chapter Five.

The second phase of adaptation, when the family is living with the reality of the illness and is unquestionably aware of its life-threatening nature, provides the best opportunities for anticipatory grief. When fifty-seven-year-old Marty Sandman was dying of colon cancer, his family fully accepted the irreversibility of his condition and the imminence of his death. Family members spoke with the patient about his illness, met frequently as a group to ponder the future without Marty, laughed, cried, and together made plans for the funeral. Marty's death was a painful loss for the Sandmans, and they grieved for some time. However, the grief was uncomplicated by other symptoms, all members of the family resumed productive lives, and the family managed to remain functionally intact. Contrast this with the Borellis, who were unable to accept that Joe's disabling cardiac condition might cause his death. Their refusal to face this possibility prevented any process of anticipatory grief from taking place. The entire family system was left debilitated and bewildered.

In the final phase of family adaptation, the potential for anticipatory grief depends on the nature of the family system and the amount of time available. The process of anticipatory grief is most effective when it is an interactive, systems phenomenon. The Haley family's difficulty in accepting the reality of Ann's impending death, almost to the end, meant that there was inadequate time for them to participate together in a process of anticipatory grief. Their subsequent adjustment to her loss was painful, conflictual, and greatly protracted.

Contrast the Haleys in this final phase with the Stiebs, who discovered that sixty-year-old Murray's headaches were the result of an inoperable cerebral aneurysm. Informed by the neurologists that he could die at any time, Murray and Eleanor Stieb immediately contacted their four children, convened a family meeting, and unambiguously explained the situation. Together, the family members planned what to do next. They elicited Murray's own wishes for the remaining time he had and quickly planned a reunion for all their relatives and friends. One son asked his father if they could use a video camera to compile an oral history of Murray and his family of origin, which the elder Stieb was pleased to do. A number of Murray's grandchildren happened to wander in and out during the few days that this project was taking place and asked him many questions about his life. Although Murray lived for only six weeks following the diagnosis, in that short time his family was able to accept the reality of his death and mobilize itself to perform important tasks that would ensure its ultimate adjustment. To be sure, the Stiebs were in shock following the death, as a result of the swiftness of Murray's passing and the short time they had to adjust. But unlike the Haleys, who would experience severe disruption and emotional upheaval for a very long time, the Stiebs were able to continue with their lives and maintain warm connections.

The examples of the Haleys, the Stiebs, and the Sandmans present convincing evidence of the impact of anticipatory grief on family adjustment following a loss. Chapter Five will examine this factor in more detail, as well as address the process of family grieving following a death.

Notes

1. For an excellent discussion of the impact of chronic illness on the family, see John S. Rolland, *Families, Illness, and Disability* (New York: Basic Books, 1994).

2. The hospice movement has, of course, been in the forefront of helping families in this final phase of the dying process. Despite many
   new challenges and difficulties encountered in a rapidly shifting
   healthcare system, hospice continues to grow. With fewer than fifty
   thousand patients in the early 1970s, hospice now serves more than
   four hundred thousand patients each year in nearly three thousand
   hospice programs. Most of these patients are helped to die at home.
   In his book, *Hospice: Practice, Pitfalls, Promise* (Bristol, Pa.: Taylor &
   Francis, 1997), Stephen R. Connor presents the most recent trends
   in the hospice movement.

3. A fine treatment of anticipatory grief is Therese A. Rando (ed.),
   Loss and Anticipatory Grief (San Francisco: New Lexington Press,
   1986). The author comprehensively examines the historical debate
   over the concept, presents solid clinical data to support the palliative effect of anticipatory grief, and suggests ways of intervening
   with individuals and families.

5

The Grieving Family

Those who are dead have never gone away.
They are in the breast of the wife.
They are in the child's cry of dismay . . .
Birago Diap, Senegalese poet
"Breath"

While shopping for a wedding dress with her daughter Marta, fifty-five-year-old Catarina Diaz felt the first pains. In less than a year, she was dead from pancreatic cancer. A strong, vibrant woman who until then had never taken a sick day off from work, Catarina always boasted that her only vice was the coffee she drank from morning till night.

The middle daughter of a large Puerto Rican family (see Figure 5.1), Catarina left Santurce as a teenager. She made her way to New York, where she lived with an aunt, finished two years of secretarial training, and got a job in a multinational corporation. She rose through the ranks, eventually becoming executive secretary to the company's chief financial officer.

Catarina married Manuel, a Mexican-American, when she was twenty-nine. Their middle daughter, Marta, is a psychiatric social worker and had been an undergraduate student of mine. She and her husband, Nicky, met in my class. At Marta's request, I met with the entire Diaz family: Manuel and Catarina, son Sal and his wife, Cindy, Marta and Nicky, and the Diazes' younger daughter, Carmen.

Figure 5.1. Genogram of the Diaz Family, 1997.

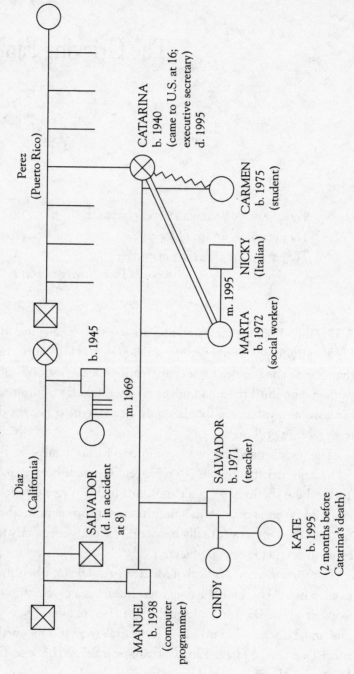

I found the Diazes to be a very close family. Catarina had always served as the strong emotional center of her family and was adored by them, as well as by her large extended family and many friends. From the perspective of the family life cycle, her illness came at an inopportune time. Marta was due to marry within a few months, and Sal and Cindy had just announced that they were expecting the family's first grandchild.

I worked with the Diaz family for eight months, the final two sessions taking place in the parents' home because Catarina was no longer able to leave her bed. Throughout this period, the Diazes spoke openly about Catarina's certain death and shared the enormous pain that all of them were feeling. Twenty-year-old Carmen's relationship with her mother was less than tranquil, and the final months were an opportunity to heal the wounds of a difficult adolescence. Unlike her sister and brother, Carmen had resented her mother's commitment to her career, because she felt it deprived her of time and attention. Marta wrestled with her anger at the pall her mother's illness was casting on her upcoming wedding. Each of the daughters discussed her feelings with her mother, both privately and in the presence of the entire family.

By nature a quiet man, Manuel had become withdrawn and nearly noncommunicative. When I met with the family, his voluble wife and children more than made up for his silence. His facial expression was nearly always sad, and he frequently wept in silence. Like his family, I found myself ignoring him and making few attempts to engage him. When I did do so, he had difficulty responding, and Catarina quickly filled the void. I soon learned that the entire family, concerned that Manuel would not survive his wife's death, preferred his silence to hearing what he might be thinking!

Manuel was devoted to his wife. This was the first time in their lives that he was unable to take care of Catarina—an unbearable thought that left him feeling helpless. Their relationship, after twenty-six years of marriage, was one of mutual dependence. She was the social planner, the family communicator, the decision maker, and the arbiter of everything from what clothes he should wear to where they should go for vacation. Yet Catarina had always depended on Manuel for her own strength. The children were astounded to learn that, just before they first met, she had been planning to return to her family in Puerto Rico, convinced that she could not make it alone. This seemingly invincible woman had, through the years, feared that if Manuel died first, she could never survive.

In the months that remained in Catarina's life, the Diazes began to discuss what life would be like without her, and Catarina demanded to play an active role in these talks. In private conversations with her husband, she encouraged him not to grieve too long and to begin a new life after she was gone, teasing him that he would never survive without a woman to take care of him.

Although Catarina was in great pain, she rallied her strength for Marta's wedding. The doctors attributed to sheer will the fact that Catarina lived long enough to hold her granddaughter and namesake, Kate.

After Catarina's death, the family grieved for many months. Each grieved in his or her own way—Marta was a great deal more expressive than her sister Carmen, and Manuel and Sal often sat quietly and reminisced together. The family created an atmosphere in which sharing of feelings was both encouraged and supported. Manuel was seldom alone on weekends; at least one of his children was always looking in on him. Marta, as the elder daughter, assumed the role of assembling the family on a fairly regular basis in the year or so following her mother's death. At the end of many Sunday afternoon gatherings, the Diazes went together to visit Catarina's grave.

About two years after Catarina died, Manuel called and asked to see me. He was, as his wife had predicted, considering marrying again but was feeling depressed and concerned that he had not waited long enough to recover from the death of his wife. Manuel mentioned in passing that he had been thinking a great deal about his brother, who had died in an accident when they were children. This had been a terrible loss from which he had never fully recovered, yet he had never acknowledged its impact. We shifted gears and spent a few months doing intensive grief work that focused on this childhood death. Feeling healed of this loss, Manuel was ready to move on, and he did indeed remarry.

I have seldom met a family that accomplished as much as the Diazes in so short a time. In many ways, this was a natural corollary to their openness and emotional closeness. Yet many open families are unable to face the prospect of catastrophic loss with such equanimity. The reasons are unique to each family. Some may be paralyzed by a history of previous losses. Other families may find the demands of physical caretaking so overwhelming that normally good patterns of functioning and communicating are disrupted. Still other families may be open and communicative when stress-free, yet crumble at times of crisis. Many of the principles of family functioning explored in Chapter Two help to explain why families behave as they do and to predict how families might act in times of crisis. Yet the only theory that is wholly dependable is that grief is an interactive, family process, as well as something that happens within each person.

The Diazes, calling on their own reservoir of inner resources as well as on professional help, underwent a process of grieving that began long before Catarina's death and continued long afterward. Their grief process enabled Catarina to die with the reassurance that her family would survive, and it also allowed the family to maintain the equilibrium necessary to continue their lives productively. Her two elder children had recently entered a centripetal period in their respective family life cycles, and they were able to continue the structure building that would solidify their new families. Carmen, her younger daughter, who was in that precarious early stage of the family life cycle when a young adult leaves the family of origin and begins a new and separate life, needed to take leave of her mother in a healing way. Manuel's resumption of a normal life after his wife's death would depend to a large extent on how well he resolved the grief over her loss. His eventual difficulty in solidifying a new relationship, which was related more to issues hanging over since the childhood death of his brother, demonstrates how grief, when unresolved, can interfere with good psychological functioning.

Recently, many observers, including myself, have begun to challenge long-held assumptions that grief must present in particularly identifiable ways.[1] For example, the notion that grieving needs to be a highly emotionally charged phenomenon in order to "work" is questionable. As I will discuss in Chapter Seven, the ethnic background of a family is a strong determinant of how it will grieve, and every culture has a different view of the process that ought to take place. Despite this caveat, it is my belief that families do need to perform certain tasks if they are to resume normal function and avoid a complicated or abnormal grief experience.

TASKS FOR THE GRIEVING FAMILY

In his 1982 book *Grief Counseling and Grief Therapy*,[2] William Worden first suggested the notion of specific tasks that grieving persons need to perform to heal the wounds caused by death. Although Worden was concerned with the emotional recovery of the individual, his prescriptions can be broadened to apply to the family as a system. In this context, the word *tasks* refers not to specific duties, such as administering medications or planning the funeral, but to psychological experiences the family must have and behavioral changes they must make in order to survive.[3] The four tasks are:

1. Shared acknowledgment of the reality of death
2. Shared experience of the pain of grief
3. Reorganization of the family system
4. Redirection of the family's relationships and goals

The family must find ways to achieve these tasks together, as doing so will potentiate healing and recovery. The tasks may be viewed as the bridge between life as it once was and life as it will be in the future. Ideally, the family will begin working on these tasks during the early stages of the patient's illness and will continue to do so through the terminal period. None of the tasks can be fully realized until after the death, however, and some may take many months or years to complete. Once they are accomplished, the survivors will be able to continue their lives successfully in a new family system.

Acknowledging the Inevitable

Ironically, it is in the face of death that people often find themselves least able to discuss the reality of death. The process of grieving requires acknowledgment that loss is final, that death is irreversible. Denial of this reality, though common at various stages of the dying process and even afterward, can be psychologically damaging to the individual and may impede the family's recovery from loss.

Mourners often search for the deceased or expect the newly departed to suddenly appear. This common grief reaction, an example of the denial of the reality of death, may actually be palliative early in the mourning process. However, the same behavior long after the loss is likely to hinder recovery.

The family's shared acknowledgment of death begins with open communication in clear, noneuphemistic terms. The word *dead* may seem final and even painful, but "gone to rest," "passed away," or "no longer with us" often connote less than full acceptance of the end of corporeal life. Needless to say, for some families, the use of such terms may not imply a denial of the finality of death but rather the belief that physical death is not equivalent to spiritual death. However, language can be a powerful psychological tool, and our ability to understand how families choose the terms they use to describe death may go far in our helping them accept reality. Thus it is important that healthcare workers use clear and direct language when speaking about death. Families that avoid use of direct terminology may be sending signals that they have not fully integrated the reality of their loss.

Rituals and rites, which are usually steeped in ethnic traditions, help families acknowledge the reality of death. In Chapter Six, I will suggest ways in which professionals can facilitate the use of rituals as an effective intervention to help families deal with death. In Chapter Seven, I will examine the role of ethnic background as a dimension of the family's adjustment to loss. For now, it will suffice to say that the avoidance of death rituals may be an indication that the family has yet to accept the reality.

When Marcus Granville was killed in an industrial accident, his wife and two children chose to have him cremated, with no funeral service or burial. They angrily refused the pleas of Marcus's mother and her pastor for some sort of religious service. The Granvilles, a traditional black family, let anger and bewilderment over the sudden death prevent them from utilizing the rituals that were part of their background. A year later, they continued to reject any ritual commemorating his death, still essentially denying the reality of their loss.

It is imperative that the entire family share in the acknowledgment of the reality of death, beginning as early in the process as possible. When Manuel Diaz related the story of his little brother's death, I was struck by how his family of origin had not collectively acknowledged its loss. Manuel's mother was grief-stricken, and her Mexican origins determined how her grief was expressed: she went to church frequently and called for the intervention of saints. For many years, she functioned minimally, until giving birth to another son. The family understood that this child was to be Salvador's replacement, although his death was a forbidden topic of discussion. Everyone acknowledged the long-term grief of the mother, yet there was little realization that Manuel and the entire family were grieving, too.[4]

Although loss should be an open issue, not all family members need to be informed of every fact immediately. In the earliest stages, for example, when a fatal diagnosis may still be uncertain, children might be spared. And if an immediate remission of the illness is likely, it might be appropriate to delay the bad news. Despite these exceptions, the tendency of families to keep the truth from children and other family members deemed "vulnerable," such as the elderly or the emotionally ill, does more harm than good. Very young children who are told, "Granny has gone on a trip" or "God took Daddy up to heaven" may become needlessly confused. Not only do children anticipate the loved one's return, assuming that death is reversible, but for them the knowledge of death is replaced with a sense of rejection and abandonment. Excluding children and other vulnerable individuals from rites such as wakes and funerals prevents the family from sharing the acknowledgment of their loss and blocks the resolution of grief. New secrets create new tensions in the family system and prevent it from moving on to a different state of equilibrium.

Sharing the Pain

Everyone hurts when a loved one dies, although some people may be more expressive of their pain. Families must understand that the loss is mutual but that the expression of emotions may be variable. A family sharing the pain of grief accepts a wide range of emotions: disappointment, helplessness, guilt, relief, and anger. Any emotion that a family member feels is OK, and no one should be judged.

Two common emotions that trouble many people are anger at the deceased for dying and guilt about feeling relieved of caretaking chores after a long and difficult illness. Family members may be reluctant to share these feelings, fearing that they would be considered unacceptable or misinterpreted as disloyal. Some people may believe that they must be strong to give others strength or to fulfill their role in the family. Thus one man explained: "I never cried publicly when my wife died. I had to be strong for the kids. Besides, they'd never seen me cry." Refusal to show pain and to share it with the family, whether for fear of censorship or to save face, retards the family's healing.

Pseudomutuality is often prominent in families in which the open expression of pain is unacceptable. Any individual expression of "deviant" emotions is forbidden when the family slogan is "We will all be strong."

Grief that is not expressed directly may become manifest in the development of symptoms. That stalwart father who chose to be strong for the children might very well begin drinking heavily once the kids are in bed. In fact, drug or alcohol abuse is a common symptomatic expression of grief. Physical illness may also be symptomatic of grief, as are depression, a tendency toward accidents, and developmental disturbances of childhood. The mourner seldom realizes that the symptoms are related to the loss. I treated one woman who listed a long litany of major and minor accidents over the previous two years. She made no connection between her accident-proneness and the death of her mother shortly before the first mishap. Manuel Diaz's bewilderment over the sudden, haunting thoughts of his long-dead brother when he expected to be grieving the death of his wife is another variation of this phenomenon.

Reorganizing the Family

When any family member dies, the relationships within the family must undergo a major realignment. The imbalance created in the family must be corrected, and the only way in which this process can take place is to allow for realignment of relationships and reallocation of roles.

The Diazes had to undergo major realignment and role reallocation because of the central role played by Catarina. She had, for example, always planned the celebration of holidays, birthdays, and anniversaries. Everyone depended on her to remember the important occasions in the family's life and to serve as their "emotional glue." In the months preceding her death, the entire Diaz family considered the need to reorganize and reallocate many of the functions performed by Catarina. However, the more subtle emotional roles for which she had been largely responsible were less amenable to realignment because, as is usually the case, they were less identifiable.

Families in which roles are rigidly fixed, such as those with traditional gender roles, often have great difficulty accomplishing the task of realignment. When thirty-one-year-old Stephanie DeMarco died suddenly of a stroke, Ralph, her thirty-three-year-old husband, found the practical demands of caring for two young children, the household, and his professional life, while simultaneously dealing with his overwhelming grief, too much to handle. Taking over another person's functional and emotional tasks is difficult enough, but it is especially complicated for young fathers in contemporary culture, because most men are not skilled in maintaining open relationships, communicating feelings, and nurturing children. Ralph had to call on his mother and sister to help him with the house and children during this difficult transition.

Families are likely to experience some breakdown in the system following a death, resulting in a short-term no-roles, no-rules atmosphere. This may not be entirely destructive. In the chaos following death, the family has the opportunity to abandon old patterns and adopt a new, more functional structure. The family that does not seize this opportunity may remain stuck in its old ways. Ben Lucas had nearly complete control of his family. In the two years of his fatal illness, his wife, Denise, nursed him at home and put up with his screaming out orders and demanding that his every need be immediately satisfied. No one dared challenge him. On Ben's death, the family was left not only with a legacy of anger and fear but also with little internal direction. The only rules they knew were the ones Ben had set. Without him to direct their lives, his wife and children were stuck in a kind of developmental arrest, unable to move forward and unsure what to do with their lives. By contrast, Catarina Diaz's willingness to allow her husband and children to begin the difficult task of role reallocation before her death shows how enlisting the dying person in the process can contribute to future family adjustment.

Another roadblock to family reorganization is the premature adoption of a replacement for the deceased. The family takes this action in an attempt to restore equilibrium. The replacement is usually a new person invited to join the family system—for example, a boyfriend or girlfriend, in-law, or new spouse. One incredible, yet real, variation on this theme was a family—a widow and four young daughters—who bought a dog a few days after the father's funeral and called the pet by the dead man's name. When I wondered aloud about the choice of name, none of the five seemed to make the connection between the deceased and the dog! Obviously, the dog, despite his name, could not replace Al. But the family was so anxious to fill the gap in their system that they irrationally looked to the dog to restore balance.

Finding New Directions

It takes at least a full year—and in many cases, more than a year—to accomplish the final task: reinvestment of a family's relationships and goals. The commonly accepted notion that four seasons need to pass makes sense, because anniversaries pose an emotional challenge. By the first anniversary of the death, the family, which has been reshaping internal relationships and reorganizing itself to move on, should be considering a new life without the physical presence of the deceased.

The task of redirecting family aspirations and relationships can be accomplished only if the family has begun to address the other three tasks. Not until the family has acknowledged the reality of death, shared the acceptance of its pain, and started to reorganize the system can it think of its future. In a real sense, then, this task is the culmination of the first three. Families can set goals for themselves and move on only if they have kept the system open, established workable boundaries, accepted individual differences, and understood the meaning of the loss to the integrity of the system.

What stands in the way of accomplishing this final task, aside from failure to do the necessary preliminary work, is the tendency in many families to idealize the deceased. As long as the ghost of the dead member remains an active part of the surviving family, they will never be able to create a new reality. When joy is diluted because "Mom isn't here to share it," when decisions are deferred because "we're not sure what Dad would want us to do," the life of the family is fixated in the past. No family is capable of reorganizing itself and setting new goals while it continues to be orchestrated by a forever-absent member. Families must learn to strike a balance between memory, which is vital to family continuity, and idealization, which prevents the family from creating a future.

Turning attention to the Diaz family, one can see how well they accomplished these four tasks. Shortly after Catarina was diagnosed as terminally ill, the family began to acknowledge that there was no cure for her disease and that she would die. They did arrange for a second opinion and sought possible treatment options, but when assured that no reasonable choices existed, they accepted that the disease was fatal. As the pain of the reality sank in, they talked with each other about what they were feeling. In their ongoing conversations, in which Catarina played an active part, the family planned how they would function without her, and they spoke about their plans for the future. Catarina's legacy to her family was an openness, warmth, and sense of optimism that made the future possible without her. Manuel was able to seek a new relationship and remarry; and some months after that, Marta called to tell me that she and Nicky were expecting their first child.

ANTICIPATORY GRIEF

It should be clear by now that the four tasks of the grieving family ought not to be postponed until the family is in mourning. As the Diazes so well illustrate, much of the work that a family must do to adjust to loss can begin before the death. Grieving while a loved one is still alive but dying is referred to as *anticipatory grief*.

Experiencing anticipatory grief by no means guarantees that the pain of loss will be any less or that it will last for a shorter period. The process of grief is not linear or defined by a strict time line, nor is it restricted to rigid stages. Grief must be measured qualitatively rather than quantitatively. The value of anticipatory grief lies in the family's ability to make the dying patient a part of the process, to tie up loose ends, to resolve interpersonal conflicts, and to say good-bye. By investing so much energy in the process of anticipatory grief, for example, the Diazes maintained the integrity of the family and created conditions in which they were later able to warmly embrace Manuel's new wife. Some other families encountered in this book failed to accept the prospect of a loved one's death or denied the pain of their grief when they were losing a member, and they had more difficult postmortem adjustments.

The tasks of grieving take on new dimensions when begun before rather than after death. As the nuclear family reaches out to inform more distant relatives of the situation, the reality of death becomes part of the family's life. Anticipatory sharing of the acknowledgment of death involves the patient in the process. Practical matters, such as financial arrangements, the writing of wills, and funeral and burial plans, can even be handled together.

As part of the early experience of the pain of grief, a family develops ways to manage the stress related to the dying person's suffering. In the anticipatory grief process, the patient and the family become aware that loss is reciprocal; just as the family is losing a loved one, the patient, too, is dealing with loss—of everyone. Families that remain open to this shared pain have an opportunity for decathexis, or letting go emotionally. Systemic decathexis is reflected in the family's ability to conceive of itself as an emotionally intact unit without the presence of the patient. Because the patient ought to remain an integral part of the family system until the moment of death, the process of anticipatory grief contains an intrinsic paradox: the family must simultaneously hold on and let go. Only in an open family system, where a wide range of feelings is acceptable, can such a process properly take place. The Diazes, of course, were an open family in many respects, and they planned for Catarina's death and the aftermath while being certain that she remained part of the emotional system of the family until the very end of her life.

One advantage of anticipatory grief is that the reorganization that must take place in the family can begin in the presence and with the input of the dying family member. It is not uncommon for the patient to set the process of anticipatory grief in motion, especially when that person has played a central emotional and functional role in the family.

Candace Kramer was such a woman. She refused all treatment after a double mastectomy, despite the pleading of her doctors and family, and was determined to do everything short of chemotherapy and radiation, which she characterized as brutal and degrading, to keep herself alive. After two years, she realized that her weakening condition meant that her time was running short. She began then to meet frequently with her daughters, sons-in-law, and grandchildren and painstakingly helped them to restructure the family so that it would remain relatively intact after her death. She and her daughters planned who would host the various holidays and celebrations, and she expressed her hopes for their keeping certain family traditions alive. In effect, Candace was granting her family permission to carry on without her, and they, in turn, were giving her permission to die. Instrumental as she was in this process, at no time did Candace feel prematurely removed from the life of her family.

This family's experience illustrates that anticipatory grief involves interactive, purposeful planning in the practical as well as the emotional spheres to ensure the future well-being of the family. The fourth task of grieving, the family's reinvestment in a future without its loved one, was achieved in the Kramer case because of the family's openness to the reality of the impending loss and its willingness to deal with the associated pain. A fascinating contrast is the story of the Millers, where a similar medical situation took a completely different turn.

Les Miller also had refused adjuvant treatment for a malignant tumor. Despite his doctor's arguments, he had convinced himself that once the tumor was removed, survival would be a matter of will. Curiously, his family accepted his unrealistic prognosis. In the few times Les and his family members met with me at their doctor's request, I was unable to help them overcome their resistance to the likelihood of his death. I endeavored to persuade them that any decisions regarding treatment were his to make, but they had to accept the implications of the choices. I did not get very far. I heard from Bea Miller eighteen months later, shortly after Les's death, and she was quite depressed. Because the family had persisted in believing that Les would, by sheer will, beat the illness, his death was a shock, even though he had been fatally ill for over two years. As she put it, her son and daughter had "disappeared from the face of the earth," and she was feeling alone and frightened. The two Miller children had not, of course, disappeared; rather, they had removed themselves from their mother and from each other, unable to share the reality of their father's death and the pain of their grief. At this point, there was no Miller family. The loss of a central family member had nearly toppled the family structure and it would take a great deal of time to rebuild. In fact, this never happened. Within a few months, Bea suffered a massive stroke and was placed in a nursing home. Her children rarely visited her, and they seldom saw each other.

Healthcare workers can encourage families facing death to take advantage of their remaining time together to perform tasks of anticipatory grief, although they need not be defined as such. Many people feel it is inappropriate to grieve for someone who is not yet dead. But in reality, nearly every aspect of a family's shared acceptance of the inevitability of loss is a dimension of anticipatory grief. Acknowledging the reality of death, either actual or anticipated, is the first step toward ultimate healing and reorganization of the family system. Hope for survival and recovery is by no means hindered by anticipatory grief, nor is there usually much danger of premature disengagement from the dying patient.

One technique that is particularly useful in facilitating anticipatory grief is called *coaching*. It is described in Chapter Six. The purpose of coaching is to guide an individual to change his or her position in the family system by addressing conflictual relationships. A problematic relationship is best dealt with when the other party to the conflict is still alive. The knowledge that death will soon end a life, but not necessarily a relationship, can spur people to take action before time runs out.

ANTICIPATED VERSUS SUDDEN DEATH

When death follows an illness or occurs in an elderly person, the family can adapt to the impending loss in the company of the fatally ill individual, passing through identifiable phases in the process. The family may begin to perform the tasks of grief early on when death is anticipated. Families that suffer a sudden, unanticipated death are deprived of these opportunities to adjust to the prospect of loss. Their adjustment will, by necessity, be accomplished posthumously. These families will be prevented from grieving in anticipation of the death, and their experience will not reflect the three phases of adaptation described in Chapter Four.

The sudden or unanticipated nature of death is only one factor that falls under the heading "timing." The stage of the family life cycle at which death occurs is also an important variable in the family's reaction to loss. As seen in Chapter Three, the family's emotional response and ultimate adjustment to loss are likely to be less complicated if the death is continuous with the life cycle. A loss that is life-cycle-discontinuous, such as the death of a child, has devastating potential. Nevertheless, even the death of a young person will have a dramatically different effect on the family if it is anticipated. A protracted illness may strain the family, but it enables loved ones to adjust over time, to part having had the opportunity to say goodbye, and to feel that they have had some impact on the patient.

Unexpected Loss: Sudden Death

When death is not preceded by illness, the family does not have the luxury of beginning its adaptation before the actual loss. One day, the family is intact; the next day, it has a gaping hole. This sudden trauma to the family system makes the process of grieving infinitely more complicated, and usually much longer.

There are three general categories of sudden, unexpected death: (1) fatal medical events, such as a sudden heart attack or stroke, or death during "routine" elective surgery; (2) accidental deaths, including random accidents as well as catastrophic events, such as airplane crashes and natural disasters; and (3) suicide.

Even if a medically related death occurs in an older person who is approaching the natural end of life, the family will be ill-prepared for the sudden loss. The family may have entered a preparatory phase of adjustment, because aging naturally implies the prospect of death. But the adaptation process is not likely to have progressed beyond the initial phase, for the acceptance of fatal illness and imminent death cannot take place without symptoms of fatality; symptoms of old age are not, in themselves, sufficient to prepare a family for loss. If a fatal medical event, such as death during routine elective surgery or a sudden stroke, occurs in a relatively young person, the family will not have entertained the notion of death, and grieving will not begin until after death.

An unexpected, medically related death is likely to create a high level of disorganization in the family system. Unable fully to accept the reality of their loss, the family may simply allow the system to grind to a halt. When thirty-five-year-old Jack Prince died from an embolism during elective arthroscopic surgery, nearly all effective family functioning ceased. I first met the Princes some six months later, and their home, their lives, and their emotions remained fixated on their loss. Bills had not been paid, social contacts had virtually stopped, the house had not been cleaned, the three children had lost all semblance of routine, and the family resembled a group at a funeral. In this closed family system, Jack had been primary breadwinner, and he also oversaw his wife's housekeeping and childrearing; indeed, few areas of family living had escaped his notice or control. Jack's family was not at all prepared for his death, and it was unable to adjust to his loss. At age thirty, Marjorie Prince, who had married when she was sixteen to flee from a chaotic family of origin, suddenly found herself with no husband, three children, and no outside supports. She was in a state of shock, unable to lead her young family into the tasks necessary for healing.

The unanticipated dimensions of the loss are the primary stumbling blocks for the family that experiences an unexpected death resulting from an accident. Such a death is often life-cycle-discontinuous, making adjustment that much more difficult. The family may also harbor anger at the deceased for being careless and causing his or her own death. The sense of shock, although of dramatically greater intensity, is similar to that felt by victims of theft, who cannot accept that what was once theirs is suddenly and inexplicably gone forever.

When an accidental death is part of a larger catastrophe, such as an airplane crash, the family struggles to extract some meaning from the event and to put the accompanying notoriety in perspective. The accident may become the quintessential event in the family's life, a historical marker as significant as universally recognizable dates such as the day Pearl Harbor was bombed or John Kennedy was assassinated. I was particularly struck by this when a family opened our first session together by stating: "Dad was killed in the plane crash in the Canary Islands." The family was surprised that I had no immediate recollection of that tragedy, which had taken place about ten years earlier.

The final category of sudden, unexpected death is suicide. Although not always totally unexpected, suicide is usually sudden and shocking. The enormous impact of suicide on the family cannot be explored within the scope of this book, but I must observe that more than any other type of loss, a suicide has the potential to alter the family system for many generations. The next section of this chapter will explore how loss creates a multigenerational emotional shock wave. Suicide, perhaps more than any other death, creates shock waves that reverberate for generations. The genogram of a family in which there has been a suicide often reveals multiple suicides, as if an ancestor's self-inflicted death gives heirs permission to end their own lives. Few other events validate the notion of the multigenerational family system more than does suicide.

The Nature of Death and Relationships: A Matrix of Adjustment

A helpful way to understand how families might react to death, both expected and unanticipated, is to examine the interplay between two seemingly unrelated factors: the timing or nature of the death and the relationship of the deceased to the surviving family. Table 5.1 shows the four possible combinations of these factors.

Like the matrix presented in Chapter Two, this two-by-two grid is an oversimplification of reality. An actual death is more likely to fall toward the middle of the grid—that is, somewhat expected and partially resolved—than in any of the extremes represented in each quadrant.

The family's adjustment to loss can be measured by the three factors indicated in each of the four quadrants: (1) the intensity of emotional response; (2) the length of time needed to resolve the issues triggered by the loss; and (3) the degree of disruption in the family system. When a close relation dies, the surviving family is likely to experience an intense emotional response; when the relationship is distant, the emotional response will be relatively mild. An intense emotional response may also occur when death cuts

Table 5.1. Factors Affecting Adjustment to Death.

Nature of Death	Family's Relationship with Deceased	
	Close and/or Resolved	Distant and/or Conflicted
	I	*II*
Unexpected and/or discontinuous with family life cycle	*Response* Intense	*Response* Mild if distant; possibly intense if conflicted
	Duration Prolonged	
		Duration Prolonged
	System Effects Mild disruption	
		System Effects Great disruption
	III	*IV*
Expected and/or continous with family life cycle	*Response* Intense	*Response* Mild if distant; possibly intense if conflicted
	Duration Short	
		Duration Short
	System Effects Very mild disruption	
		System Effects Moderate to great disruption

Family's adjustment to loss is measured on three dimensions:
  Response—intensity of emotional response
  Duration—time needed to resolve emotional issues triggered by loss
  System effects—degree of disruption in family system

short a highly conflicted relationship. Much time will be needed to resolve the emotional effects of an unexpected death or one discontinuous with the life cycle, particularly when that relationship is close. A shorter period of resolution can be anticipated when the death has been expected because of age or illness.

Despite the intense, prolonged grief that follows the unexpected death of a closely related family member, the family system will be only mildly disrupted if there is a minimum of unresolved emotional issues with the deceased (quadrant I). But when there are unresolved issues, the system will be greatly disrupted in the wake of a sudden death, and symptoms may develop in the family that appear totally unrelated to the loss (quadrant II). The system will be minimally disrupted following the anticipated death of a closely related person when issues have been resolved (quadrant III). On the other hand, in a distant or conflicted relationship, death, even when expected, can cause a fairly high level of disruption in the family (quadrant IV).

The death of Catarina Diaz would fall in the lower left-hand quadrant of this grid. Despite her relatively young age, her death was life-cycle-continuous, in that her children had been launched into their own separate lives. The family anticipated her death because of their acceptance of the diagnosis. The Diazes were a fairly close family that dealt openly with conflict and permitted the expression of a wide range of emotions. The short-term emotional reaction to Catarina's death, as would be expected, was quite intense, even though the family had spent months in anticipatory grief. Many relatives from Puerto Rico came for the funeral, and their presence raised the intensity of emotional expression, often to the embarrassment of the more subdued American family. But within a reasonably short period, the Diazes had resumed their respective lives without excessive emotional disturbance; Manuel's later depression, which will be examined more below, was a minor exception. The family reorganized and redirected itself and survived without the presence of a member who had played a central role in the previous family system.

THE EMOTIONAL SHOCK
WAVE OF DEATH

Because a family represents more than the present-generation family of adulthood, it stands to reason that death will not only affect the present survivors but also have implications for future generations. Murray Bowen has spoken of this intergenerational impact of death and loss as an emotional shock wave.[5]

Many families can point to a death in a previous generation that holds great significance in the present. All families, of course, experience some immediate shock on the death of a loved one, even if the death is life-cycle-continuous and fully expected. In most cases, the initial shock wears off as the family resumes its normal routines. But this does not necessarily prevent the death from occupying an important place in succeeding generations. When the person's role, reputation, or prominence in the family has been great, future generations will have to make a place for him or her, although they may not be fully aware of it. This legacy is most apparent at times of crisis. The first family introduced in this book—the Bergs—were living with the ghosts of at least two generations, and their case well illustrates that a family's ability to cope with a stressor in the present generation is frequently compromised by the emotional shock wave of previous generations.

When a loss or similarly profound emotional event in the family's history is either denied or felt to be irrelevant, disturbing symptoms can develop. Often the entire family is fully aware of its intergenerational baggage. But in many other families, the source of the emotional shock wave is denied, or even unknown. Such was the case with Manuel Diaz, as will be described in discussing a phenomenon called "unresolved grief."

Recognizing Abnormal Grief

The emotional shock wave caused by death is most keenly illustrated in cases of abnormal grief, a concept that is not easy to define, in either an individual or a family systems context. One helpful definition of *abnormal grief* is too little grieving immediately after a death or too much grieving long afterward. Specific time parameters, although frequently used to define grief, are based on norms that are intended to be more suggestive than absolute. Though it is not always helpful to apply a rigid temporal structure to this or any other psychological phenomenon, the notion that there are generally observed time frames for the resolution of grief can serve as a reasonable guide. One important caveat: healthcare workers need to guard against the propensity to judge a family's grief on the basis of preconceived notions of "normal" grief.

What causes families to grieve too little or too much? One answer, of course, is that they have failed to accomplish the four tasks of family grieving. The inability to grieve normally is frequently caused not by circumstances surrounding the present death but by factors associated with a death or other profound loss at an earlier stage of the family life cycle or in a previous generation. For example, if a parent dies when a child is young, the child may have difficulty integrating that loss, and separation in nearly any form thus becomes a painful event throughout life. The family of adulthood of this same person will embody this failure to have mourned adequately, and a common manifestation may be an abnormal course of grief for a present loss, without recognition of its connection to the childhood loss.

The following phenomena should alert the healthcare worker to the prospect of a complicated bereavement in families facing death:

1. The patient is either idealized or, conversely, described as a monster with a plethora of negative characteristics.

2. Members of the family seem to be confused about the illness and do not agree on what is wrong or what has caused their loved one's condition.

3. The patient is either talked about incessantly or is barely mentioned at all. In the former case, the centrality of the patient will probably never change, and he or she will become an active ghost in the family system. In the latter case, the family will cope with the loss by acting as if the deceased never existed.

4. The family complains incessantly about the poor treatment their loved one has received from an insensitive healthcare community, insisting that if the treatment had been better, the outcome would have been different.

5. Anger and resentment toward the patient defy explanation or resolution. Family members cannot explain exactly why there are

unresolved issues with the patient, but they are aware that they go back a long time.

Obviously, these are not the only advance indicators of complicated bereavement. In general, the worker should be attuned to the presence of unresolved issues among family members or allusions to unfinished business in the past. The presence of such symptoms may mean that the family will have an abnormal grief reaction.

Two distinct types of abnormal grief may be observed in families: (1) unresolved grief and (2) interminable grief. In the former case, a death in the family's history is not recognized as the cause of present symptoms, whereas in the latter case, a contemporary death is mourned without end. In neither instance is the etiology recognized as an emotional shock wave that was set in motion by a loss in the past.

Unresolved Grief

Unresolved grief is an aspect of the emotional shock wave that makes itself felt in families long after a death, even into subsequent generations. In a way, *unresolved grief* is a paradoxical label, in that it is seldom identified as grief at all. This abnormal grief reaction often stems from the failure to mourn a death at an early developmental stage. A death inadequately resolved in a previous generation is not likely to be identified as such; rather, it can be inferred from the behavior of the family. Pathologic symptoms, which often seem to be totally unrelated to a loss, may appear many years after the death.

The Kohlers were referred to me after their sixteen-year-old daughter, Wanda, had attempted suicide. This was not the first time that Wanda had made a gesture of suicide, and she had been known to school authorities for some time as a troubled and withdrawn youngster. The Kohlers were a family in great distress. The parents, Alex and Isabel, had been separated for three years but continued to occupy the same house, in separate quarters. Their two elder daughters were also unable to leave home: Ingrid, twenty-four, lived in the attic along with her three cats; Lena, twenty, was living with her boyfriend and their dog in the TV room. A fourth child, Peter, had died of leukemia at two years of age. Following Peter's death, twelve years ago, Isabel had suffered a severe depression. Eventually she appeared to have recovered, and except for being trapped in an in-house marital separation, she managed to function as a homemaker.

Both Alex and Isabel had younger sisters who had never left home but continued to live with their respective mothers. Alex's father had died when he was a youngster. Isabel's father was also dead, and only late in the treatment did she disclose that he had committed suicide and that she had discovered his body. The patterns in both Alex's and Isabel's families of origin made it difficult for them to launch their own children or to effect a separation. Further, unresolved grief was prominent for both of them. They had lost their fathers at an early age, one from a heart attack and the other from a violent suicide, and there had been no opportunity for anticipatory grief. Neither Alex nor Isabel openly acknowledged the pain of these losses, nor had they been encouraged in their families of origin to recall their fathers. They thus brought to their new family the painful legacy of loss and the fear of separation, and these problems were compounded by the death of their own child. Although Peter's death may have precipitated the marital deterioration, the seeds had been sown many years before, in another generation.

My work with the Kohlers centered on mourning these losses. I hypothesized aloud that their difficulty in separating was a means of guarding against future pain, particularly for Isabel, because the family was aware of her vulnerability to depression. I further suggested that Wanda's mental health would improve dramatically if she were freed of the burden of caring emotionally for her mother and father, which she did effectively by giving them something other than their own internal pain to focus on. After many months of family therapy, the couple was able to effect a physical separation, and the two older girls left home. Wanda, no longer bearing the burden of caring for her family, ceased to present life-threatening symptoms and resumed a reasonably healthy adolescence.

When Manuel Diaz telephoned me two years after Catarina's death and reported that he was depressed and uncomfortable with the prospect of remarriage, I initially assumed—as did he—that the source of his present problem was the death of his wife. In fact, the source was deeper: it was related to Manuel's younger brother, who had accidentally drowned when the two boys were swimming together. A child himself, Manuel did not know how to deal with his brother's death. He assumed a kind of bystander position while his parents, particularly his mother, went through paroxysms of grief. Over time, Manuel all but forgot this powerful childhood experience, but it was reactivated some two years after Catarina's death when he was considering remarriage. I suggested that perhaps his guilt and doubt about "betraying" Catarina were triggering long-dormant feelings of guilt about his brother. After Manuel did some long-overdue grief work for his brother, his anxiety about remarriage abated and he made wedding plans.

I was not surprised by Manuel's uncertainty about remarrying after he related the history of his brother's death. In fact, in my clinical work, I have discovered that the most common source of unresolved grief is the failure to mourn an early loss. However, difficulty with mourning may result from other factors as well. For example, if a family becomes engulfed in some unrelated crisis immediately following the death of a loved one, emotional energy that might have been directed toward mourning that loss is instead diverted to other pressing concerns.

A week before Gina Gabelli's father died of a sudden heart attack, her husband, Vincent, was informed that he was being transferred immediately to the Far East. Preoccupied with the multitude of tasks demanded by the move, Gina was barely able to be with her family of origin and participate with them in their grief for her father. When the Gabellis returned from overseas three years later,

Gina, who was much relieved to be back, ironically became deeply depressed. She was unable to identify any reason for her mood and found it confusing that despite her unhappiness at being posted abroad, she had not experienced such feelings in the past three years. It made no sense to her that she could be so happy to be back home yet feel so depressed. After I worked with Gina for a short time, it became clear that her depression was directly linked to her not grieving the death of her father. Once she shared her feelings of grief with her family of origin, she was able to resolve the loss, and Gina's mood reflected the joy she felt at being back home.

Another source of unresolved grief may be perinatal loss, and I will soon emphasize the importance of mourning those who have never lived at all. Frequently, perinatal death is followed immediately by a successful pregnancy, with the result that the death of the unborn child is inadequately addressed. In such cases, it is not uncommon to see perplexing symptoms, such as postpartum depression following the birth of the healthy infant.

Interminable Grief

In contrast to unresolved grief, in which a past death is often not recognized as contributing to present symptoms, in cases of interminable grief the deceased is an ever-present factor in the life of the family. Interminable grief, simply stated, is grief without end. Grief, even for a child, ought to end within a "reasonable" time, and frequently the family itself recognizes that grief has continued too long. If the details surrounding the death and the vivid experience of loss remain as intense years after the event as at the time of the tragedy, it is likely that the family is experiencing interminable grief.[6]

Although not exclusively a phenomenon observed in women, interminable grief appears to be most prevalent among mothers who have lost a child. This life-cycle-discontinuous death is so unexpected that in many ways it will be mourned forever. A child plays a central emotional role in a family, representing its very meaning and future. This makes the loss of a child among the worst tragedies a family can experience. Yet I have found that it is not the death of a beloved child alone that is responsible for an interminable grief reaction. The vast majority of parents who lose a child ultimately recover and live functional, productive lives. Many cases of interminable grief are related to an unresolved loss in a previous generation—usually the loss of a parent.

Although the intense reaction of interminable grief is experienced most acutely by one member of the family, the entire system changes as a result. Parental and spousal roles shift dramatically as the family searches for a new equilibrium. Finding it, the family may continue to function, although suboptimally, while the mourner struggles toward recovery. However hard that struggle, recovery may be impossible until both the loss that everyone acknowledges and the previous unresolved loss that initiated the emotional shock wave are grieved appropriately.

Carol and Bob Martin's daughter, Laurie, had died at age eleven in a school bus accident nearly six years earlier. Carol's grief was presently as intense as it had been when Laurie was killed. She felt hopelessly depressed and out of touch with her husband and two other children. Carol spent most of her time either in bed or performing robotlike, routine tasks. Bob was devoting much energy to work and to their two living children, who looked to him for most of their needs and spoke little of their dead sister. He remained frustrated and angry at Carol for "not letting Laurie go." The dead child's bedroom remained untouched, and the Martins had severed most of their social contacts because of Carol's depression.

The second time I met with Carol, she reported dreams in which she saw "an older, motherly woman." She made the connection between this woman and her own mother, who had died of cancer when she was five. Although Carol was initially angry at my attempts to encourage discussion about her mother, she went without prompting to visit the cemetery where her mother was buried. Treatment subsequently centered on resolution of this early loss, despite Carol's repeated protests that her mother's death was not important and had nothing to do with Laurie. Not surprisingly, though, Carol's grieving for Laurie and her taking emotional leave of her daughter were greatly hastened by her grieving for her mother. Approximately eight months after I began to work with her, Carol was ready to "put Laurie to rest" and return to an active life with her husband and surviving children.

SOCIALLY UNSANCTIONED GRIEF

Because society generally recognizes the need for time to grieve, mourning periods have been institutionally sanctioned. For example, many businesses give a certain number of days as official funeral leave on the death of a spouse, child, parent, or sibling. Absence for a day to attend a funeral might be permitted on the death of a more distant relative, and most businesses would allow a few hours to attend the funeral of a close friend but would expect the employee to return to work soon after the rite. Implicit in such regulations is a societal judgment on the relative importance of relationships and on how much—or how little—one is expected to grieve. Society's arbitrary measure of the significance of a relationship may, of course, bear little relation to the impact of a death on the survivors.

Because society has the power to sanction grief, both formally and informally, many individuals and families find themselves denied the entitlement to grieve. Reasons may be that a relationship is not acknowledged, a loss is not recognized as genuine, or the mourner is not perceived as capable of grieving, as might be the case with a young child, an elderly adult, or a mentally impaired person. Grief that is not recognized as valid is called *disenfranchised grief.*[7]

Disenfranchised grief due to absence of societal supports is more likely to be identified in an individual than in a family as a whole. Typical scenarios include the death of a friend, a distant family member, an ex-spouse, a pet, a secret lover, a coworker, a patient, or even a public figure to whom one feels emotionally connected. But a loss experienced by the entire family may also fail to be acknowledged as valid or as one that ought to be grieved. Two prime examples are perinatal death—the death of the not-yet-born through miscarriage or stillbirth, or the loss of a newborn in the first few weeks of life—and AIDS-related death. In the latter case, the social stigma may be so overwhelming that the family and loved ones feel unentitled to grieve publicly.[8]

Perinatal Death

A seldom addressed area of family grief is the loss of the not-yet-born and of infants who die shortly after birth. If a child has never drawn breath or has lived for only a few hours or days, it is presumed that the impact of the loss will be minimal. However, frequently the opposite is true, and healthcare professionals need to be attuned to this grief so that it is not disenfranchised.

Like the death of a child at any age, perinatal death means not only the loss of human life but also the shattering of hopes and dreams for the family's future. Perinatal death evokes strong feelings of guilt about what might or should have been done to prevent the loss. But unlike the death of a child who has been an active presence in the family, perinatal death is often perceived by outsiders as a nonevent, raising doubts in the family's mind about whether they ought to be feeling as they do and whether they can expect social sanction for their grief. Given the difficulty of grieving perinatal death, such a loss has a great capacity for remaining unresolved and affecting the family's emotional adjustment at future times of crisis or stress.

When a family history is taken, perinatal deaths should be approached as a significant part of the overall picture. The genogram of the Scapella family (Figure 3.1) is an example. Betsy Scapella experienced two miscarriages, and her mother had four. These losses had long-range effects on their families, particularly affecting the parenting attitudes of the women.

Perinatal losses invariably occur at a stage of the family life cycle when husband and wife are reinforcing their identity as a family. If the couple is presently childless, perinatal loss threatens this new family identity. If there are other young children, the parents' need to grieve, and the absence of social sanctions for the grief, as well as the other children's inability to understand the meaning of death, may strain parenting abilities and threaten family equilibrium. Additionally, the extended family is often not informed of losses before birth, so that otherwise available emotional support is lacking. If the extended family is made aware of the loss but does not deem it worthy of grieving, the family may feel particularly isolated and alienated.

Jessica and Craig Nevins came to see me because they were experiencing marital difficulty. They were arguing constantly, and each was angrily threatening divorce. Their arguments seemed "garden variety" for a young couple in the first few years of marriage. Craig was angry at Jessica's lack of interest in sex, and Jessica accused her husband of being insensitive and uncommunicative. Their problems had begun seven months previously, shortly after their first child, a preterm male baby, had died within a few hours of delivery. In the first few days following the loss, Craig stayed close to his wife, and Jessica felt secure and cared for. Her parents, who lived across the country, were kind and supportive on the telephone, and her mother, said Jessica, "made a halfhearted offer to come," which she turned down. After a few weeks, the loss of the baby was no longer mentioned in their biweekly phone calls. Nearly all the couple's friends had begun their families, and although Jessica's friends were sympathetic, they were quite busy with their own children. Craig could not understand his wife's continuing "obsession" with the loss, believing that they simply needed to "get to work" on beginning a new family. Jessica remained impervious to Craig's advice and shunned his sexual advances.

My work with this couple was not, as they had anticipated, marriage counseling to help them communicate better and resolve their arguments. Rather, I focused on helping them to grieve the death of their infant. At my urging, the Nevinses again shared their feelings about the death of the baby. They informed their families that they had not yet recovered from the loss and that they continued to grieve, although silently. Their fears about whether they could ever have a family, their guilt about what they might have done to cause the death, the disappointment each felt for the other's loss, their anger that no one took the death seriously enough—all of these feelings and many others were addressed.

Finally, after careful planning, the Nevinses arranged a belated funeral service for the infant. Although the hospital social worker had suggested a funeral when the infant died, neither Craig nor Jessica had wanted a burial at that time. The hospital in which Jessica gave birth, attuned to the significance of perinatal loss, had given the Nevinses a small package that contained a blanket in which the dead child had been wrapped, some pictures taken of the baby in the delivery room, and a lock of the child's hair. This package, which they had placed in the back of a closet, was what they buried during the belated service, to which they invited their respective families and a few close friends. Everyone actively participated in the service, and then the entire group retired to the Nevins home for a meal. This ritual was effective in bringing to a close a seven-month disenfranchised grief. Within six months, Jessica became pregnant and ultimately gave birth to a healthy baby girl.

AIDS and Disenfranchised Grief

The circumstances surrounding certain deaths alienate the mourners and disenfranchise them from public support and resolution of their grief. In our contemporary society, no death better illustrates this phenomenon than death from AIDS. The social stigma associated with the disease isolates both the patient and the family, and after death, the survivors are not automatically welcomed back into society. In fact, they frequently find the mourning process a solitary experience, removed from the support of extended family and friends who might otherwise have been present.

The grief of AIDS survivors may more closely approximate a pathologic reaction than normal grief. Rage, fear, and shame are typical and may be greatly exacerbated by the reactions of others. Without social sanctions for the right to mourn, grief is likely to take on symptomatic manifestations. Thus unresolved grief is common, and parents whose offspring die of AIDS are at high risk for developing interminable grief. Even when the grieving process is not pathologic, it surely is more painful without the genuine support and understanding of family and friends.[8]

Marion Cermak felt spurned by her friends and extended family after her drug-abusing daughter, Louise, died of AIDS. Although she received many expressions of sympathy, they were often accompanied by veiled suggestions that her daughter had gotten what she deserved. "Louise was nothing but trouble. She caused you much grief, and you're better off without her," said one of her closest friends. With such "support," Marion grew increasingly more isolated and depressed. She became convinced that she was a horrible mother who had somehow caused her daughter to die, and this conviction made her feel unentitled to mourn for Louise.

Families frequently shroud their children's aberrant lifestyles in secrecy. A family that cannot reveal to friends and extended family members that a son or daughter is using drugs or is homosexual cannot later share the diagnosis of AIDS and the pain of the inevitable death. The distance that the family creates around this shameful truth while the child is alive leads to disenfranchisement after death. Thus the lack of social sanction for grief and support after death may partly originate in the family's inability to acknowledge what they perceive as the shame of their child's behavior.

Disenfranchisement is more the rule than the exception for the survivors of AIDS patients and is almost a given for the partners who are not related by blood or marriage. Because they do not constitute "family" in the socially sanctioned sense of the word, they will almost certainly be denied the right to grieve. However, enti-

tling one group of mourners to grieve should not automatically disenfranchise another, as is often the case when a patient's family
disapproves of or rejects the patient's chosen family.

When Martin Corey was dying of AIDS, he returned to his family home in the suburbs, where he was cared for by his parents and
sister. His lover, Sean, frequently visited from the city, and the
Coreys tolerated these visits only because "it's important to Martin." After Martin's death, the family no longer felt they had to put
up with Sean. They refused to allow him to attend the wake or funeral and would not admit him to their home. Sean was denied a
few of Martin's belongings, which had no material value but were
of great sentimental worth to him. Before long, Sean became clinically depressed and seriously considered suicide. His fear for his own
survival, coupled with his disenfranchised grieving, combined to create a precarious emotional state. Not until he joined a bereavement
group for AIDS survivors did he find a valid avenue for grieving.

The opening case of the next chapter describes the final months
in the life of a young man dying of AIDS. Before his illness, he had
already grown apart from the support of his family, and tension
flared between his father and brother on the one hand and his gay
lover on the other. This is not an uncommon portrait of the dying
AIDS patient. But in this case, the intervention of a hospice team
prevented disenfranchised grief and enabled the family to heal.

Notes

1. In their groundbreaking article "The Myths of Coping with Loss"
(*Journal of Consulting and Clinical Psychology*, 1989, 57, 349–357),
Camille Wortman and Roxanne Cohen Silver challenged many
long-held assumptions about grief and mourning. Their notion that
there is great variability in how people express their grief has, at this
point, become an accepted principle in the field. The idea can be
explored further in D. Klass, P. R. Silverman, and S. Nickman, *Continuing Bonds: New Understandings of Grief* (Bristol, Pa.: Taylor &
Francis, 1996).

2. Worden updated some of his earlier thinking in the second edition of his book: William Worden, *Grief Counseling and Grief Therapy* (New York: Springer, 1991).

3. Froma Walsh and Monica McGoldrick first suggested the adaptation of Worden's four tasks to the larger family system. See their "Loss and the Family Life Cycle," in C. J. Falicov (ed.), *Family Transitions* (New York: Guilford Press, 1988).

4. In a text devoted to helping children with the grieving process, I discuss at length the ways in which family interventions can facilitate recovery: "The Family as a Healing Resource," in C. A. Coor and D. M. Coor (eds.), *Handbook of Childhood Death and Bereavement* (New York: Springer, 1996).

5. Murray Bowen, "Family Reaction to Death," in P. Guerin (ed.), *Family Therapy: Theory and Practice* (Lake Worth, Fla.: Gardner Press, 1976).

6. This phenomenon is discussed in greater detail in my "Family Therapy in Cases of Interminable Grief for the Loss of a Child," *Omega: Journal of Death and Dying,* 1988, *19*(3), 187–202.

7. A comprehensive treatment of the phenomenon of disenfranchised grief can be found in Kenneth Doka (ed.), *Disenfranchised Grief* (San Francisco: New Lexington Press, 1989).

8. See my "Hospice Work with AIDS-Related Disenfranchised Grief," in *Disenfranchised Grief,* cited in note 7.

6

Helping Families Face Death

I'll get by with a little help from my friends.
John Lennon and Paul McCartney
"With a Little Help from My Friends"

Mark Weinberg is thirty-four years old, a Phi Beta Kappa Yale alumnus, and a graduate of Harvard Law School. A partner in a prestigious Boston law firm, he is also a championship golfer and an accomplished violinist. As he told me the first time I met him, "It's a hell of a time to be dying of AIDS."

In these final months of life, Mark has returned to his family's home in a New York City suburb. Suffering recurring bouts of pneumocystis pneumonia, Mark is being cared for by his father and a community hospice team with which I work. His elder brother and sister are both married and live nearby with their families, although they are not actively involved in caring for Mark. His partner, Bjorn, with whom he has lived for four years, is commuting every weekend to the Weinberg home from Boston (see Figure 6.1).

The Weinbergs are a middle-class Jewish family who have lived in the same town for over forty years. Jules and Lilian Weinberg took great pride in their elder son, Jason, and their daughter, Lisa, but the apple of their eye and the undisputed star of the family has been Mark. From earliest childhood, the youngest Weinberg child demonstrated intelligence and creativity that promised a bright future. Mark was state champion in golf, a concert violinist from the

Figure 6.1. Genogram of the Weinberg Family, 1997.

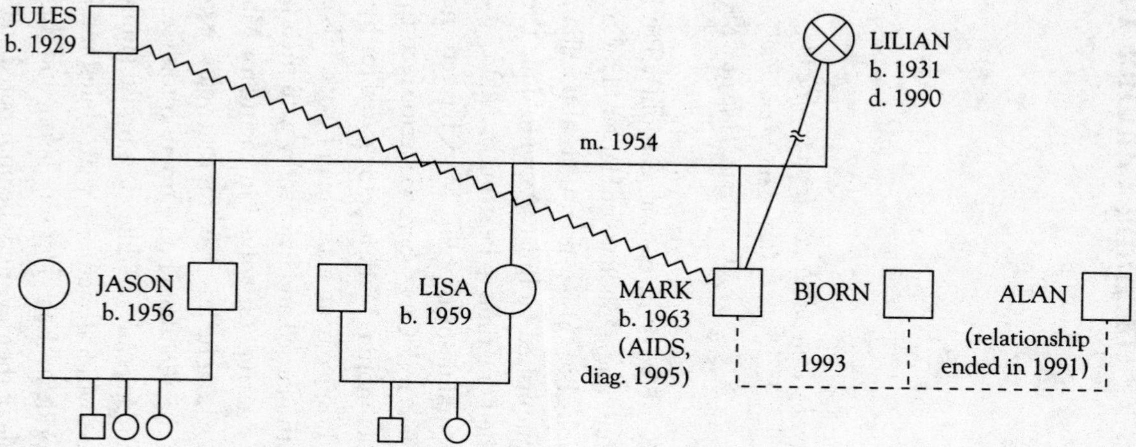

time he was twelve years old, and a straight-A student. Then, three weeks before he graduated from Yale, Mark came home, convened a family meeting, and announced that he was homosexual. The family's first reaction was to refuse to believe this shocking news; later, they would not discuss the subject or acknowledge to anyone that Mark was gay.

When Mark moved to Boston to attend law school, he entered a relationship with Alan, a fellow student, that lasted five years. Although his parents never explicitly said so, he understood that bringing his partner home would not be acceptable.

During this time, Lilian was diagnosed with cancer. Mark came home to see her periodically, but they were never reconciled. When she died seven years ago, Mark informed Jules that he was coming to the funeral with Alan. Jules emphatically replied that he was either to come home alone or to stay in Boston. The extended family was both bewildered and outraged that Mark did not attend the funeral. Although they had known there was some tension between Mark and his mother, the reasons were never made clear. The family continues to harbor angry feelings toward Mark for not going to his mother's funeral.

A year after Lilian's death, Mark ended his relationship with Alan. Two years later, he entered his present relationship with Bjorn. Since Lilian's death, Jules has come to accept that his son is gay. Lisa and her family have welcomed Mark and Bjorn as a couple, but Jason has been less accepting. Although there has been some warming in the nuclear family, Jules has insisted that Mark's "situation" not be discussed with the extended family. Although many seemed to have guessed the truth about Mark's life, his illness came as a surprise. Many extended family members live in the vicinity, but having received no overt sign from Jules or his family as to what to do, they have generally stayed away from the house.

Mark is having difficulty adjusting to his severe symptoms and increasing infirmity. But his greatest agony is feeling like a pariah.

As his condition worsens, the pain of rejection by his extended family and the coldness of his elder brother have become unbearable.

In addition to the sophisticated plan of home healthcare already in place, Mark and his family were in need of comprehensive psychosocial intervention designed to open up the family system, resolve conflicts that remained active in the nuclear and extended family, and enable the Weinbergs to begin a process of grieving. The family's openness to the hospice team encouraged us to devise a plan that would include team members from a number of professional disciplines, as well as volunteers.

Diana, a middle-aged volunteer whose thirty-year-old son had died of cancer a few years before, became the mainstay of the hospice team's intervention plan. A neighbor of Lisa's, Diana related easily to Jules and formed an instant bond with Mark. Their mutual cynicism and biting humor made them a formidable pair. Diana came to visit for an hour nearly every day, and after the first few weeks, she began putting the hospice team's plan into effect. Diana's role was to help Mark reconnect with the large family network. She encouraged him to make phone calls and write to his aunts, uncles, and cousins. The plan worked. Family members began to visit, and although it was frequently exhausting for Mark, it was comforting to see the breaches in the family healed. Indeed, after his son's death, Jules remarked that one blessing of this tragedy was that the family had come together again.

The two hospice team nurses, who visited Mark at least every other day, had the dual task of attending to his specific medical and physical needs and providing impetus for his self-care. They stressed the notion of hope, warning Mark that at every visit they would be asking him what he was hoping for—"and you'd better have a good answer!" The nurses cajoled, encouraged, and supported Mark so that he would continue caring for himself and not become dependent on others. Long self-reliant and independent, Mark's solid self-esteem became an important lever in his care. The two nurses also provided the family with a model for Mark's physical care, which made it seem less daunting.

The hospice team social worker worked with the nuclear family to help them begin the process of anticipatory grieving while Mark was still with them. To begin with, the family needed to address the unfinished business in their lives. One of their first assignments was a family visit to the cemetery with their rabbi. This was the first time that they had participated in any memorial ritual for Lilian that included Mark. Of course, the visit to the cemetery had further implications, because Mark would soon be buried there, too.

Jason, Mark's older brother, had been emotionally distant from him for many years. The social worker told Jason that she was concerned about how his children would deal with the social stigma of AIDS, both in their present lives and with their families in the future. Perhaps, she suggested to Jason, personal contact with Mark would allow his children to experience their uncle as a human being rather than as some ghoulish apparition that was kept hidden from them.

It was important to Mark that his partner, Bjorn, be accepted by his family. This became an additional area of intervention for the social worker. Bjorn was presently healthy, but whether he was HIV-positive had not been determined because he refused to be tested. Thus, along with the prospect of losing his lover of four years, his own mortality was in question. Jules was initially hostile to Bjorn, but the social worker encouraged the father to reach out to the lover, pointing out that they shared the prospect of the inevitable loss of one they both loved. Although the two men did not achieve an emotional closeness, they did maintain a cordiality which made Mark's final months less painful.

Mark was cared for in his father's home for seven months. About two months before he died, Jules—at the urging of Diana, the hospice volunteer—invited the extended family and friends to celebrate Mark's thirty-fourth birthday. Everyone who attended knew that this was Mark's last birthday. Jules asked the guests to bring as a birthday present at least one memory of their lives with Mark. Despite his condition, Mark was able to enjoy this final celebration, and he managed to offer a final toast to his family and friends.

Mark's physical deterioration was relentless. In the last few weeks of his life, he was blind and nearly totally paralyzed. However, he remained lucid to the very end. When he died, his father, sister, two nephews, and Bjorn were at his bedside; Jason, though having made some efforts toward reconciling with his brother, was not present.

The very first life on this planet ended in death, as has every life since, and as will every life in the future. If death is a natural, inevitable event, is it not appropriate to allow families to cope and grieve without the meddling of outsiders? Why is any intervention necessary to help families facing death?

This question can best be answered by viewing death in its contemporary context. Not only has the arena in which dying and death take place changed dramatically in the past decades, but as will be seen in Chapter Seven, ethnic influences have also undergone significant transformation. In an earlier and simpler time, the process of dying and the rituals that helped families to adjust to the void in their lives were an intrinsic part of the communities in which they lived. The absence of advanced medical technology, a dramatically shorter life expectancy, the frequency of neonatal and infant death, and limits on social mobility made death a more common and participatory experience. In addition, a family's subsequent adjustment took place within the context of a familiar environment, in which people were knowledgeable of the rituals and more intimate with the participants. Families were supported throughout the usually shorter period of illness and ushered into the subsequent phases of adjustment.

A process that once took place within the context of a stable community aware of the part death played in the flow of life has now been relegated to an institution—the funeral home. The framework that determines modern management of death and the grief process is no longer shaped by family or communal tradition but by the dictates of a business generally more concerned with profits and efficiency than with healing and support. In contemporary society, where individuals are generally far removed from traditional supports, many families find themselves overwhelmed by life-threatening illness and see nothing "natural" about the process of dying. The adjustments that need to be made to care for a dying family member and to cope with the loss are no longer part of most families' spontaneous repertoire.

Nevertheless, despite the complexity of death and dying in society, most families will naturally begin a grieving process and will recover from the loss of a family member without professional intervention. The sympathetic ears and supportive hands of family and friends will likely prove adequate. But for other families, such as the Weinbergs, more systematic and systemic intervention may be appropriate.

The Weinbergs, a textbook case of a closed family harboring toxic issues and marred by emotional cutoffs, suffered multiple threats to their well-being. The family's refusal to acknowledge Mark's homosexuality, their resistance to Bjorn as an important person in Mark's life, and the continuing resentments that were set in motion by Lilian's death continued to fester when I first met them. The stigma associated with the diagnosis of AIDS compounded the family's adjustment difficulties. Because very little was discussed openly in this family, it was apparent that the tasks necessary for healing—acknowledging the reality of Mark's death, sharing the grief, reorganizing, and redirecting relationships and goals—were not going to take place without outside help. The Weinbergs cried out in silence for intervention from the interdisciplinary hospice team.

Acceptance of the reality of death includes an awareness that time is passing swiftly and that unfinished family business must be addressed. The cutoffs between Mark and his family had been initiated during Lilian's illness and had intensified after her death, so that the physical loss of Lilian was compounded by the emotional loss of Mark. His return to the family at this critical moment in his life was not in itself sufficient to repair the damage done seven years earlier. In addition, a rich network of extended family to whom Jules had generally looked for support was not readily available because of anger at Mark. The hesitancy of these extended family members to become involved with Jules and his children would likely remain an obstacle to the family's adjustment after Mark's death.

Diana, the hospice volunteer, had an objective in working with Mark: to encourage him to reach out to his nuclear family, as well as to the extended family, to heal the breaches that had developed. Diana spent many afternoons with Mark, going through family picture albums, scrapbooks, and home movies, and reviewing his life with him. They spoke often about his mother and, relating her own experience with loss, Diana was able to guide Mark toward an appreciation of his mother's sadness about the direction his life had taken. When Mark began to speak about the pain of "losing everybody," Diana seized this opportunity to encourage him to talk with his father, siblings, and extended family members about his life—something he had not done since he had left for college seventeen years before.

Diana's efforts were part of a larger plan; the social worker was simultaneously working with Jules and Jason, encouraging them to make peace with Mark. The social worker, understanding the transmission of themes in families across generations, discussed Jules's family history with him and discovered that, as a result of a business conflict, he had experienced a cutoff with his father and brother when he was a young man. Although he and his brother later reconciled, his father died before they had resolved their differences, and Jules admitted that he was still assailed by feelings of guilt and remorse. The social worker used a different approach with Jason: she talked about the implications of his brother's death from AIDS for his three children, and pointed out that their response would be colored by their father's relationship with his brother. Ironically, Jason found that he could make peace with Mark by finally expressing his anger at his brother, despite the fact that he was terminally ill. Mark was not entirely pleased with his brother's feelings, but Jules played an important role as intermediary between his two sons. Helping the brothers to achieve harmony gave Jules the opportunity to relive the history of reconciliation in his family of origin and emphasized the urgency of his own rapprochement with Mark.

In cases such as the Weinbergs, it is necessary to expand the concept of family to include a less traditional configuration. Bjorn's place in the family had to be defined so that he would not be disenfranchised from the processes of caring and grieving for Mark. The social worker spent time with Bjorn and Jules together, encouraging cooperation between them. In addition, the nurses attempted to relate to Bjorn as they would to any patient's spouse. This was not an easy task, because Bjorn was present mostly on weekends and was not entirely comfortable with his position in the Weinberg home.

The hospice nurses also needed to ensure that Mark would retain his self-esteem as his physical condition deteriorated. Demanding that he assume responsibility for his physical care as long as this was possible gave Mark a sense of autonomy, which could easily have been lost as a result of his presence in his father's home after so many years away. The nurses urged Jules to allow his son to do more, despite his weakening condition. This delicate balance of care was closely monitored by the two primary nurses assigned to the family, and even subtle shifts in Mark's condition were discussed with the entire team, in order to identify each point at which Mark needed more care from others.[1]

Not all families facing death demand the high level of intervention required by the Weinbergs. Many families, although deeply pained by terminal illness and death, naturally meet the needs of a loved one and spontaneously embark on an appropriate path of mourning and healing without any external guidance. For example, the hospice volunteer, Diana, had lost her thirty-year-old son, Sean, fifteen months after he had been diagnosed with a pineal gland tumor. Unaware of available community resources, Diana and her husband, Henry, simply assumed that the family would have to provide whatever care was necessary for Sean. Diana and Henry rearranged their schedules, Diana's mother made herself available, and their two married daughters spent as much time as they could with their brother.

From the moment of diagnosis, the family spoke openly about Sean's prognosis. Family members discussed their feelings about losing him, shared their grief at his imminent death, and unselfconsciously expressed whatever emotions they felt. Sean's parents and sisters offered each other respite from the intensity of caretaking and freely reached out to friends and extended family members for help and support. Of course, despite all the supportiveness, there were times during Sean's illness when the family's coping skills were tested to their limits. Sean was not always an easy patient, and at moments his parents feared that they would not be able to see him through. There were angry confrontations, as well as times when family members were emotionally removed from each other. But overall, the family was able to adjust to this crisis and perform the tasks necessary for their survival.

Diana and Henry describe Sean lovingly and feel good that they were able to help him have a "good death." They visit the cemetery regularly, often with their daughters and their families. The family has established a scholarship fund in Sean's memory, and his parents and sisters display pictures of Sean in their homes. When asked how many children she has, Diana responds easily that she has two living daughters and that her third child, Sean, has died. Henry and Diana are attuned to each other's moods and are respectful of each other's sadness. They have indeed recovered from their loss and have moved on in their lives. Diana is one of hospice's finest volunteers and although she often expresses the wish that she had known about hospice when Sean was dying, clearly her family coped adequately with its loss by calling on its own well of resources.

Other families, despite coping well in many ways, will look for outside help in areas that they personally experience as problematic. Often, families know what their strengths are and are quite specific about what they need from outside sources. A typical area of concern for many families is how they should handle children so that they are not permanently scarred; this is particularly worrying in situations of protracted illness or untimely death.

In cases of sudden or accidental death, few families are able to adjust alone without some degree of difficulty. After Don Sisler's father died suddenly on an outing with his two adoring grandsons, the boys—seven-year-old Eddie and his five-year-old brother, Denny—suffered for many months. The Sislers could not have handled the grieving any better as a family. They talked openly about their loss and went through all of the necessary rituals to acknowledge the reality of the death. But the boys were at a developmental stage where the sudden death of a close relative, particularly because it occurred in their presence, was likely to be problematic. I suggested to the Sislers that it might be helpful for the youngsters to join a group for children who had experienced a death. Fortuitously, such a group had recently been formed at a local mental health agency, and Eddie and Denny were welcomed in. At a follow-up visit about six months later, their parents reported that the boys were doing well; their nightmares had ceased, and they seemed to be back to their old selves.

Other families, of course, do not adjust well after a death, nor do they reach out for help. Even if a family does not request assistance from the professional community, though, it can still be helped. My involvement with hospice volunteers has taught me that an advanced degree is not necessary to practice many of the commonsense interventions that can benefit families facing death. Often, sensitive and insightful family members or friends can provide the necessary assistance. A friend insists that the family visit the cemetery; an aunt voices the forbidden words that a loved one is going to die; an acquaintance remarks how it helped him to speak to his dying father about the early years; a child innocently suggests that the whole family say goodbye to grandpa. Families may respond to such "natural interventions" and help themselves to heal.

One of the beliefs that guides me in my work with families facing death is the idea that everyone who interacts with the family, regardless of professional discipline, has the capability of providing help and guidance. I must emphasize, however, that those who do intervene must beware not to exceed their level of expertise. Nonprofessional caregivers should seek the advice and guidance of psychosocial professionals when working with families facing death. For example, when Ruth, the hospice volunteer encountered in Chapter One, became frustrated with the hostile environment in the Berg family and was unable to make peace among the three women, she wisely sought the counsel of the hospice team. As a consultant to that team, I suggested an intervention based on the three-generational dynamic in the family. Although the volunteer implemented the plan, the idea of writing the carefully worded letter was beyond her expertise.

This experience illustrates a useful guiding principle for intervention. Although one's instincts may often be on target, unilateral, spontaneous intervention is usually not the ideal. Psychosocial planning should be treated much like medical planning. Intervention should be orchestrated by a team of professionals working together, even though only one person might make the actual contact with the family. An interdisciplinary hospice team is perhaps the best example of this concept, but similar opportunities for cooperative psychosocial planning can be found in other settings as well.

So far in this chapter, I have purposely used the term *intervention* without defining it. This is because I want to avoid a "cookbook" approach to working with families facing death. As I have indicated, many interventions are common sense, and thus the possibilities are vast. However, interventions can be especially successful if they are related to the family systems model. A few such specialized approaches to intervention, though not necessarily techniques themselves, will be explored in the remainder of this chapter.

THE GENOGRAM:
A ROAD MAP FOR ACTION

By this time, you will be familiar with genograms, which have accompanied the opening case report in each chapter of this book. Brief instructions for constructing a genogram appeared in Chapter Two, and more zealous readers may have already begun using genograms to gather information about families in treatment, or even their own families.

In the clinical setting, the genogram is an enormously useful information-gathering tool. An organized means of taking a family history, the genogram can also be helpful in making psychosocial assessments. Using the genogram, the clinician can track the history of illnesses, previous losses, toxic issues, emotional cutoffs between family members, relationships between specific family members, and dates of critical events. The unique value of the genogram lies in its uniformity and easily readable schematic presentation. The rudiments of the genogram are relatively easy to learn, and its application is not beyond anyone's grasp.

Use of this "harmless" schematic can dispel the discomfort and suspicion that many people experience in relation to psychological issues. Describing the genogram as a "kind of family tree" immediately removes the threat of a psychosocial assessment in cases where a family might feel that strangers are probing their deepest secrets.

The complex tapestry of family life can be more easily understood when illustrated in concrete terms. Depicting family relationships across generations, the genogram can provide a key to behavioral patterns that might otherwise be only abstract. Understanding of complex psychic phenomena is simplified when these are viewed against the background of their historical antecedents, and family members may be comforted to have a context that suggests why people behave as they do.

For example, when the oncology social worker constructed a genogram of the Donnelly family, she was immediately aware of a pattern connected with paternal death in the two previous generations; after each death, at least one child had become an alcoholic and had experienced an emotional cutoff from the family. The patient, Michael Donnelly, had left home as an adolescent, never to return, after his father died of complications of alcoholism. Michael's father had begun drinking shortly after he left the old country following his own father's death; he never saw his family again once he crossed the Atlantic. Observation of the Donnelly family corroborated the social worker's suspicion that a similar pattern might be set in motion after Michael's death. He seemed to relate well to his eldest and youngest sons, but not to his middle boy, John. The family's behavior, as well as the pattern of cutoffs depicted in the genogram, suggested an intervention to the social worker. She invited the three boys and Michael to join her in reviewing their family history, as charted in the genogram. After explaining how patterns of behavior are repeated across generations, the social worker asked the Donnellys what they might predict for a family whose genogram looked like theirs. They observed that John might become the child destined to be cut off. The discussion turned to John's place in the family and his tendency toward chemical dependency. The social worker used this opening-up of the family to talk with them about how Michael wanted to take leave of his sons and how to break the pattern of cutoffs.

Unlike many other techniques of intervention, creating and analyzing a genogram is sometimes more useful as a tool for the helper than as a task to be undertaken by a family. The genogram serves as a guide to where interventions are appropriate and what types of interventions might be useful. However, the genogram can be an excellent therapeutic instrument as well as a diagnostic tool. Although the Donnelly genogram guided the social worker in taking a family history, sharing it with the family was the start of the intervention process. The multigenerational patterns of behavior suggested methods for change. Not only was Michael able to see the repetition of emotional cutoffs in his family, but he also realized that he had to change his way of relating to John if another chapter in that story was to be avoided.

The very act of constructing the genogram may open channels of communication and reveal information that is not generally known within the family. Previously forbidden subjects in the family's history may be painlessly revealed as the genogram is created. For this reason, I strongly suggest that initial family assessment based on a genogram be conducted in the presence of as many family members as possible.

The most effective use I have made of the genogram is in the training of professionals who work with families facing death. I strongly believe that those who work with families ought to have a firm sense of their own multigenerational family dynamic—in particular, of how loss has affected their own family history.

USE OF LITERARY AND CINEMATIC MATERIALS

Many works of poetry and fiction, as well as numerous movies, that explore relationships and death can serve as openers to facilitate a family's communication. Such materials are both evocative of feelings and memories and provocative of dialogue and interchange, even on forbidden subjects. Fictional material of any type is analogous to a projective test, as individuals invest their own personal meaning in what they see. There is no way to predict a family's response to a book, a poem, or a movie. Yet some reaction is certainly likely.

Books and movies are particularly useful with an emotionally closed family that has not responded to other efforts to encourage communication about prospective loss or death. With such families, it is frequently easier to use an indirect method of intervention than to directly challenge their way of operating. Families in which communication is open and where members are able to give expression to their pain and fear about the prospect of loss are likely to be able to handle the emotional impact of this material. For relatively closed families, this material may be more difficult to absorb but nevertheless of great value in raising issues in a more direct and hence safer way. However, the use of powerful emotional material might be contraindicated in certain circumstances. Once, for example, a well-meaning but untrained person suggested that a family with a schizophrenic young adult watch a movie in which extremely hostile, violent emotions were expressed. The result of this errant intervention was an unhealthy upheaval in a family that, in deference to the mentally ill son, had wisely learned to avoid such powerful expressions of emotion.

The use of evocative material takes no more outside intervention than a mere suggestion: "There's an excellent book you might find helpful" or "I think you might like this movie. Why don't you rent it and see it together this weekend?" The implementation is then left in the hands of the family. The healthcare worker does not actually participate in the process, other than inquiring in follow-up: "Did you see the movie I recommended? What did you think of it?"

Movies are likely to work well for most families. Certain ethnic groups may be especially responsive to the written word—for example, the Irish, who have a long history of respect for poets and poetry, and Jews, who value learning and intellect. Middle-class American Protestants, who tend to be task-oriented, may also respond positively to the suggestion of a book, particularly if it seems to offer an immediate practical benefit. Such a family might be pleased with a "how-to" book that provides direct advice and guidance, whereas their Irish neighbors might prefer a work of fiction that only obliquely addresses their difficulties. In neither case, however, is the family likely to discuss the contents without some prompting. Some of these ethnic differences will be examined more closely in Chapter Seven.

Books and movies may be especially useful for children. Parents who have difficulty discussing serious illness and death often find the task less onerous when it is initiated by reading a story to the children or watching a movie together. Leo Buscaglia's *Fall of Freddie the Leaf* puts death into the larger context of living and may open the door to a philosophical discussion with children about death. A more direct approach to death can be found in Alicia M. Sims's *Am I Still a Sister?* and Janice Cohn's *I Had a Friend Named Peter*. Obviously, materials must be developmentally appropriate; librarians can usually provide guidance. The Judge Baker Children's Center in Boston is a particularly good source of useful books for children. For a thoughtful explication of how parents can deal with the topic, Earl Grollman's classic text, *Explaining Death to Children*, still remains among the best.[2]

Bibliographies on the subject of death and dying, for both children and adults, can be obtained through a variety of sources. Lists of pertinent movies are harder to find, so I have included in Appendix A an annotated list of films that I find helpful for families facing death. Two superb movies that deal with parent-child relationships, of which I have made extensive use in my own work, are *I Never Sang for My Father*, written by Robert Anderson, and *The Great Santini*, by Pat Conroy. Both address the relationship between a father and a son, but they are also excellent depictions of more general family relationships. *Ordinary People*, both a movie and a book by Judith Guest, deals with the impact of the loss of a child on family relationships. James Agee's book *A Death in the Family* that chronicles the reactions of a family to the death of the father/husband. *Time Flies When You're Alive*, a short docudrama featuring the actor Paul Linke, shows how one family faced the courageous death of a young mother.[3]

I frequently suggest that families view *I Never Sang for My Father*, particularly if conflicts between parents and their adult children need to be addressed as an aspect of anticipatory grief. Anderson's movie and play relate the saga of the upper-class Garrison family and their struggle with the painful legacy of previous generations. Gene, a man in his forties whose wife had died after a long bout with cancer, has always felt distant from his father, Tom. Gene and his sister, who was banished from the home at an early age because she married outside the faith, have remained close and have supported each other against their father's anger and judgment. Their mother had always served as a buffer between the children and her husband but was largely ineffective in diverting his wrath. As the story unfolds, the mother dies, Tom begins to deteriorate both in body and in mind, and Gene struggles desperately to find some way to salvage a relationship with his father, ultimately to no avail. It is a classic story of missed opportunities and failed communication between the generations. A major theme of the family's life has been the burden that Tom felt he carried from the time his father, an alcoholic, abandoned the family when Tom was just a lad. Tom and Gene play out the family theme of father-son disconnectedness.

When I first met the Weltons, I was struck by the similarity of this family to the Garrisons. Alfred Welton, a successful businessman, was in the final months of life, suffering from prostate cancer. His wife had died suddenly, six months before I met Alfred and his two sons, who had taken on joint responsibility for his care. Neither son had followed his father into a business career. Forty-six-year old Stephen was married, had five children, and was a high school teacher; Roland, forty-one, was a freelance photographer who was unmarried and apparently homosexual, although his sexuality was not discussed directly among the three men. The relationships between the sons and their father had always been highly conflictual, and neither Stephen nor Roland felt comfortable in his father's presence for more than a few minutes. Alfred was extremely critical of both his sons and made no secret of his distaste for their "squandered opportunities." Alfred's attitude toward his own father was contemptuous; he took pride in describing how he had assumed responsibility for the family after his father—"a profligate ne'er-do-well"—left his mother, his two sisters, and him when he was sixteen. Like the father in Anderson's play, Alfred enjoyed regaling listeners with the story of his success, and he boasted about sending money to his father when he unexpectedly reappeared after many years and then paying the funeral costs when the old man died.

Alfred's physician was losing patience with him and was concerned that his exasperating behavior might lead his sons to put him in a nursing home instead of following through on their plan to let him die at home. At the physician's request, I met the Weltons for what was to be a series of only three visits. After the first two meetings with the three men, I saw clearly that any attempt to force them to deal constructively with the conflicts of four decades was destined to fail. I told them I would like to see them one more time, but in the interim I was going to leave them a movie, *I Never Sang for My Father*, that I wanted them to watch together. I asked them to call me after they had seen the film. Alfred himself called me about two weeks later. When I met with the Weltons for the last time, a palpably different mood was present in the family. Alfred seemed less on guard, and Stephen and Roland were obviously less tense. There was even some light-hearted kidding, which I had not seen on the earlier visits.

The family told me that the movie had provoked an entire evening's discussion. The sons told their father that they understood how his own father's abandonment must have affected his life. They were wise enough not to say that he risked dying alone, like Tom Garrison, but the potential was obvious to all of them. Alfred told his sons—for the first time without anger—how it pained him that they loved their mother more than him. Stephen and Roland assured Alfred that there was still time for them to love him, if he would allow them to.

I would emphasize that one reason for the success of this intervention was that the Weltons were facing death within a short period; Alfred died about four weeks later. Clinical experience has taught me that lifelong patterns are not magically reversed by any one-shot intervention, no matter how powerful. But when families are facing death imminently, short-term change is not only possible, it is also adequate. Were Alfred to have recovered miraculously and lived another ten years, I doubt that the effects of the film would have lasted. But given the Weltons' needs at the time, this intervention was appropriate.

As effective and provocative as these fictional materials and films can be with families, they can also be enormously useful in training personnel. I have seldom presented a lecture or conducted a workshop without showing some scenes from a film or from a videotape of a clinical session with a family. I strongly recommend a number of films (noted in Appendix A) as training tools for opening discussions about important issues for families and caretakers.[4]

HEALING THROUGH RITUALS

Rituals can be helpful both during periods of terminal illness and long after the mourning period presumably has ended.[5] Defining *ritual* is difficult, because the term is used differently in religion, philosophy, anthropology, sociology, and psychology. I will make no attempt to provide a comprehensive definition of the term. However, I will loosely define a family ritual as a behavior that reflects some symbolic or metaphoric meaning, has been repeated in some form multigenerationally, is generally known to the family, and is part of their collective experience. A ritual may arise from the family's religious beliefs or observance, but it is by no means restricted to religion.

I also use the term *ritual* to describe behaviors that are created anew as part of an intervention designed to help the family's healing process. In this sense, the ritual may not have a multigenerational history in the family. These newly formed rituals may also be based on some religious model, although not necessarily the family's standard practice of religion.

Regardless of the origin of the ritual, the planning and preparation are nearly always as important as the execution. As the power of the ritual usually lies in its symbolic or metaphoric meaning, the subjective meaning of the ritual further defines its function in a family. The Christmas gathering may be a significant religious rite for one family but a burdensome obligation for another, devoid of meaning and thus an "empty ritual." Regular church attendance can help to bind one family together, whereas it may create conflict in another.

Perhaps the most characteristic aspect of a ritual lies in its multi-generational repetition. Indeed, rituals may very well be the most powerful legacy that families pass on from generation to generation. In one family, the passing of a paper route from an older to a younger child at a particular age may be fraught with as much meaning as a confirmation or bar mitzvah, in that each ritual marks a passage into adulthood.

Rituals are frequently altered, and they may be newly created in response to changing family conditions. New rituals need not be entirely novel; they can be specific religious rituals, such as candle lighting; well-known cultural rituals, such as the establishment of a memorial scholarship; or more therapeutically motivated rituals, such as a life review, a memorial service, or a visit to the cemetery, which may not be part of the family's past behavior. The potential for reworking or creating rituals has significance for those who help families facing death. A family experiencing life-threatening illness, for example, may need a symbolic means to express pain or otherwise inexpressible feelings. Intimate knowledge of the family can enable helpers to create appropriate rituals.

The Crosbies were a large, wealthy Protestant family whose many children, grandchildren, and other relatives lived within fairly close proximity to each other. Milton Crosbie, seventy-one years old, had been a vibrant, active man until a sudden heart attack and subsequent complications from cardiac surgery left him weak and near death. His youngest daughter, Elena, whom I had seen with her husband for marital therapy about two years previously, asked that I meet with her father, whom she characterized as embittered, uncommunicative, and depressed.

I found Milton Crosbie engaging and voluble, but the bitterness his daughter described was quite palpable. He was burdened with guilt for "checking out on the family and leaving them nothing but money." I agreed that, indeed, he ought to feel guilty if all he left them was money. Then I told Milton about an old Jewish tradition called an ethical will, in which wise men would leave letters to their loved ones, revealing their personal thoughts and philosophy about life. Milton decided to adopt this ritual from another religion. He wrote ethical wills to his four children and their families, giving a personal life review and elaborating on his hopes for their future.

New rituals are particularly meaningful when the family itself creates them or recalls them from its past experiences. Tony and Dorrie DiPietro created a ritual from a rich part of their family history. When their son Tony died, they looked for a ceremony that would have meaning for the survivors, and they found it not far from their home. When the children were young, they used to go to a nearby woods to hike and camp. Their favorite place in the woods was a large rock, some eight feet high, which overlooked the valley where they lived. It became the touchstone of their trips, and it was common for the kids, as they grew older, to tell their closest friends, "Meet me at The Rock." Family myth has it that one of the DiPietro grandchildren was conceived on The Rock. So it seemed natural when Tony Jr. died that the last rites should take place on The Rock. All three generations gathered at The Rock; some hiked in on the several trails that led there, and the youngest and oldest family members reached the scene by car. When everyone had assembled, Tony's ashes were scattered around The Rock. The DiPietros continue to gather at The Rock to memorialize Tony, and it has become a sacred place and a natural symbol of the family's history and closeness. (Incidentally, when I observed how apt it was that this family, which prided itself on its solid, unbreakable core in the face of tragedy, had chosen a rock as a symbol and how ironic it was that their family name meant "of the rock," they were surprised; no one had made the connection.)

Most traditional rituals connected with death, including those ethnic and religious rituals that are transmitted multigenerationally, occur after death. However, rituals also help families prepare for the loss of a loved one. The McCullums, a large family spread throughout the country, had traditionally gathered every Fourth of July at the family home in Texas. After the death of the father, Jake, this ritual seemed to lose its hold on the family, even though Jake's wife, Anne, continued to organize the family gathering until she became too disabled from Alzheimer's disease. After a few years without much positive contact with her siblings, a daughter from New York, Ellen, accepted my suggestion that she plan an "old-fashioned Texas barbecue" to say goodbye to Anne, who was nearing the end of her life. My recommendation that the McCullums revive their Fourth of July get-together was not made primarily for Anne's sake. The actual goal was to begin a process of family healing and to ease the friction that had developed among the siblings since their father's death. One specific way to do this was through a ritualized series of thank-yous: family members were to thank each other for the gifts—tangible and symbolic—that they had received over the years. I also suggested that the family begin planning for the next Fourth of July to ensure that the tradition would continue.

A particularly difficult task after death is the disposal of the deceased's clothing and personal items. I have found it helpful for families to create a ritual framework within which this task can be accomplished. The ritual can be especially healing when it is planned while the patient is alive. Recall that the planning of a ritual is often as significant as its execution.

A few weeks after Milton Crosbie wrote the ethical wills to his children, he called to ask my advice about disposing of certain personal belongings, some of which had been passed down from previous generations. In his legal will, he had distributed his valuable possessions among family members, but many of these other personal items had no material value. Still, they were important to him, and he wanted a good way to pass them on to his children and grandchildren. Together we designed a ritual: Milton summoned his four children and their families and informed them that he was about to begin a tradition that he wished them to continue. He brought out three large boxes that contained, among other things, books, pictures, a pocket watch, and some jewelry. "These," he informed the assembled twenty-three family members, "are the items I treasure most in the world. I would like to tell you about them, and I would like you to tell me who should have them and why." For hours, Milton talked about how each item had been passed down in the family and what it meant to him. At various points, family members volunteered their desire to have a certain item. The four children also suggested why people other than themselves should receive certain things. It was a memorable ritual and one that will probably cement the family's bonds well into the future.

COACHING: A METHOD FOR BREAKING THROUGH "STUCK" SITUATIONS

Coaching is a family therapy technique, based on the early work of Murray Bowen and others, that emphasizes the multigenerational transmission of themes and works with an individual within a family therapy framework.[6] The person is sent back to his or her family of origin with instructions to perform specific activities that are designed to set in motion a fundamental change in the entire family system. Use of a method like coaching ought to be based on a fairly clear understanding of the family structure, which is best obtained by generating a comprehensive genogram. Although coaching is a sophisticated clinical method, used by skilled practitioners, a more down-to-earth variation on the technique of coaching can also be effective. In this context, the term *coaching* describes any attempt to encourage individuals actively to modify some "stuck" situation in the emotional life of the family as a whole or in a relationship with another person. The suggestions made to Mark Weinberg by Diana, the hospice volunteer, are examples of coaching; the purpose was to change his relationship with members of his extended and nuclear families.

When I first suggested to Ellen that the McCullum clan plan a Fourth of July barbecue, I was using the technique of coaching. The family had lost its emotional center after the death of her father and the onset of her mother's illness. A number of other difficulties beset this family, among them emotional cutoffs between some of the six McCullum siblings and tension over management of the family's finances. Because they were caretakers of the ill parents, the siblings who remained in Texas were feeling exploited by those who lived farther away, and the latter felt that the family's financial situation was being mishandled by the Texans. What had once been a warm family atmosphere had been replaced by tension and mistrust. Coaching Ellen to bring the family together socially at a traditional celebration—and proscribing any discussion of their present tensions and problems—seemed the best way to recreate some of the old warmth.

Coaching can be an excellent method of drawing a family's attention to its unfinished business. Emotional cutoffs can be addressed by having one person make contact with another in a way that changes their static interaction. An oncologist who was participating in a workshop with me told the story of a sixty-year-old patient, Bruce Walsh. He had had a bitter fight some ten years before with his father and twin brother, and they had not spoken since. He claimed that since that time, he "was never the same," and he remained depressed and withdrawn. Bruce's resignation about his illness was very much connected to the cutoff, for he straightforwardly stated, "There is nothing to live for anymore." His doctor pointed out that the quality of his remaining life would depend on how willing he was to heal old wounds. When Bruce objected that his eighty-five-year-old father and his brother would not

respond if he tried to contact them directly, a coaching intervention seemed appropriate. The specific plan was complicated: Bruce
initially contacted his nephew, and Bruce's wife wrote to her father-
in-law. At no time was Bruce asked to contact his father or brother
directly. Because he believed that such an attempt would not work,
to encourage him in this direction could have resulted in his sabo-
taging the intervention. Moreover, in situations such as this, direct
contact usually is likely to fail. According to family systems theory,
cutoffs are circular; everyone is a participant in this "no fault"
process, so a careful reconnection strategy needs to be devised.

Coaching is also effective when family members are having so
much difficulty adjusting to the prospective loss of a loved one that
they are unable not only to begin a process of anticipatory grieving
but also to provide necessary care and support to the patient and to
each other. The unexpected diagnosis of pancreatic cancer in forty-
four-year-old Janine Komisar had devastated her family. Her husband, Gerry, and her three adolescent children were unable to
absorb the meaning of the news. Although the family felt that Janine's condition had been discussed fully and openly, no one could
acknowledge that she was dying. Coaching with this family had
three primary goals: (1) to open the system and to allow for clear
communication about how sick Janine was; (2) to help the family
accept that her condition demanded a reallocation of family roles
before her death; and (3) to include all family members in preliminary planning for her funeral and the subsequent period of mourning. Each family member was assigned at least one task, all of them
connected to the goals of treatment. Gerry was asked to speak with
his wife's doctor and find out specifically what treatment was available, what the likelihood was of remission, and how much time remained. The children were asked to perform a variety of tasks, most
of which were possible only with their mother's cooperation and
were intended to involve them in the running of the household. Janine herself was encouraged to talk about her fear of the unknown
next few months. In the last few weeks of Janine's life, the family
managed to make plans for the funeral with her participation.

Coaching is an effective vehicle for helping families to resolve previous losses that continue to have impact in the present. In addition to death, other losses, such as separation, divorce, chronic illness, bankruptcy, and separation of siblings, can have enormous influence on future generations.

When Alice Graham was dying of cancer, her forty-one-year-old son, Albert, became her primary caretaker. Another son, Martin, age fifty, visited his mother infrequently, because (I was told) he had severe emphysema and an uncooperative wife. Despite all evidence that Alice was in a terminal stage of illness, the Grahams seemed to deny the gravity of her condition. Alice's concern about Albert's welfare after her death appeared to account in part for the denial process in the family. Whenever she spoke of her illness or alluded to the possibility that she might die, Albert left the room.

My initial information was that the three Grahams constituted the entire family. The father had died some twenty-five years before, shortly after the Grahams divorced. However, on further investigation, I learned about a third son, Eugene, who had had no contact with the family since he left home many years previously, after accusing his mother of throwing his father out of the house. Apparently, Alice had never ceased mourning the loss of her son. Albert's role in this family drama had been to remain at home, providing his mother with a caretaker who would never leave her.

The unresolved cutoff with Eugene provided an opportunity for coaching the Grahams. Any direct suggestion that the family try to contact Eugene would have been quickly deflected. Coaching, like all interventions, works best when a "frontal assault" on a family's defenses is avoided. Instead, I met with Albert and Martin without their mother, emphasizing how important it was that they strengthen their relationship as brothers so that they could better care for her. I asked them whether Eugene ought to be informed of his mother's illness. As is often the case, although no one in the nuclear family had contact with Eugene, extended family members did know where he lived. Finding acceptable ways to contact him took delicate negotiations, and I urged the sons not to tell their mother what they were doing. For even though Alice indeed wanted to see her son, the family rules and the roles played by his siblings made it impossible to express that desire directly. It made more sense to frame the task as a way in which the two men could care for their mother and to present her with a fait accompli. The brothers exchanged letters with Eugene, but Alice's condition deteriorated suddenly, and he never did get to see her. However, they spoke on the telephone before she died. Coaching the Grahams meant not only that Alice would talk to her son once more; it also provided Albert with a larger system within which to cope with his loss. Some months later, he told me that Eugene had invited him to visit in California and that he was seriously considering the trip.

Notes

1. The Weinberg case is a comprehensive illustration of an "all-out" hospice intervention with a family. In his book *Dying Well: The Prospect for Growth at the End of Life* (New York: Riverhead Books, 1997), Ira Byock, an innovative hospice physician, describes many families who grow, and are often transformed, in hospice care. I highly recommend this very moving book, as well as Dale Larson, *The Helper's Journey* (Champaign, Ill.: Research Press, 1993), which discusses the work of hospice team members with patients and families.

2. Leo Buscaglia, *The Fall of Freddie the Leaf* (Thorofare, N.J.: Holt & Slack, 1982); Alicia M. Sims, *Am I Still a Sister?* (Blue Springs, Mo.: Big A & Co., 1988); Janice Cohn, *I Had a Friend Named Peter* (New York: Morrow, 1987); and Earl Grollman, *Explaining Death to Children* (Boston: Beacon Press, 1969). Other books dealing with children and death can be found in Appendix B.

3. Judith Guest, *Ordinary People* (New York: Penguin, 1982); James Agee, *A Death in the Family* (New York: Bantam Books, 1971); Paul Linke, *Time Flies When You're Alive* (docudrama film).

4. Another source of training material of this sort is Sandra Bertman's book *Facing Death: Images, Insights, and Interventions* (Bristol, Pa.: Hemisphere, 1991).

5. A particularly helpful text that examines the use of rituals in working with families is Evan Imber-Black, Janine Roberts, and Richard
   Whiting (eds.), *Rituals in Families and Family Therapy* (New York:
   Norton, 1988). A different perspective on the use of ritual can be
   found in Carl Hammerschlag and Howard Silverman, *Healing Ceremonies* (New York: Pedigree/Putnam, 1996). This powerful book describes ways to create rituals and ceremonies ("activities that take
   place only on special occasions and that are . . . designed to produce
   beneficial effects") that evoke Native American customs of vision
   and healing. In a section titled "Creating Personal Rituals for
   Health," the authors describe rituals for healing and forgiveness
   that are likely to appeal to many families.

6. The faculty of the Family Institute of Westchester, of which I am a
   part, has produced a text on this subject: Fredda Herz Brown (ed.),
   *Reweaving the Family Tapestry: A Multigenerational Approach to Fami-
   lies* (New York: Norton, 1991). It is a pioneering effort to systemati-
   cally present the method of coaching first suggested by Murray
   Bowen. In addition, Monica McGoldrick, whose work on genograms is discussed in Chapter Two, discusses how to connect with
   family of origin using accessible methods quite similar to coaching.
   Her book *You Can Go Home Again: Reconnecting with Your Family*
   (New York: Norton, 1997) suggests many practical ways for laypersons to achieve the goals of coaching.

7

An Ethnic Perspective

If you want rules to measure
What lies beyond your own rules' decree,
Look for what is fresh and different
Find out what its rules might be!

Richard Wagner
Die Meistersinger von Nürnberg

Ibrahim Shaheed's six-year struggle with renal disease is coming to an end.[1] At his doctor's insistence, he recently permitted a community hospice program to assist with his care, and the nurses and social worker are finding this forty-four-year-old patient irascible, suspicious, and uncooperative, particularly where pain medication is concerned. The nurses have observed that although he may wince noticeably when he is moved, he does not report any discomfort and denies that he is experiencing pain. The social worker is frustrated with the patient's seeming ignorance of the impact of his illness on his wife and children.

Born in Karachi, Pakistan, Ibrahim is the eldest child of a middle-class Pathan family, an ethnic group noted for great courage and physical endurance (see Figure 7.1). His ancestors hail from northern Pakistan and for many centuries were nomadic warriors who fought against the encroachment of foreigners. Ibrahim is quite proud of his heritage and has made every effort to imbue his sons with an identity as the descendants of brave and courageous soldiers.

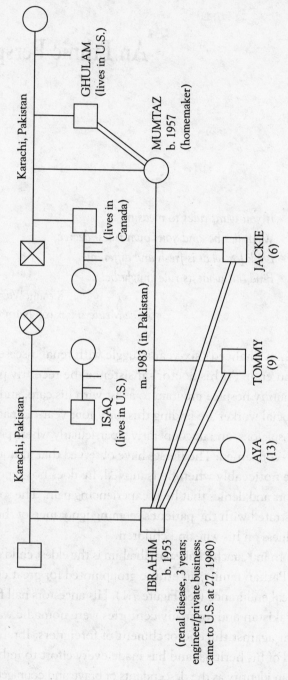

Figure 7.1. Genogram of the Shaheed Family, 1997.

His family of origin suffered in the aftermath of the partition of India in 1947 and subsequently migrated south to Karachi.

Ibrahim was trained in Pakistan as a mechanical engineer and emigrated to the United States at the age of twenty-seven. After working in a variety of jobs, he finally established himself both as an engineer with a contracting company and as owner and operator of a lucrative car-repair business, where he worked in the evenings and on weekends. During this period, he asked his family to find him a bride. He returned to Karachi to marry Mumtaz, who was six years younger, and brought her back to the United States. They have three children: a thirteen-year-old daughter, Aya, and two sons, Tamizuddin (Tommy), nine, and Iskander (Jackie), six, all American-born.

Mumtaz has never worked outside the home. Although Ibrahim has been partially disabled for the past few years, the construction company provides adequate medical insurance and disability coverage, and he has continued to keep his private business going with the help of a young cousin who recently immigrated from Pakistan. Ibrahim and Mumtaz each have a brother living in America. Ibrahim has maintained tight control over the family's finances and oversees all aspects of family life.

Subservient to her husband, Mumtaz is reluctant to speak privately with the social worker. Until hospice became involved with the Shaheeds, she was providing all his physical care. Now that the end is near, she seems overwhelmed by the prospect of her husband's death. Although the spouses seem to be respectful of each other, Ibrahim has refused to discuss with his wife any practical aspects of the family's survival after his death. He speaks openly about his illness and acknowledges that he is going to die, yet he has been resistant to taking adequate analgesia for what appears to be a high level of pain. He does not communicate easily with his daughter, but Tommy and Jackie spend long periods of time with their father.

Jim, a hospice volunteer who had been a Peace Corps worker in Afghanistan, was enlisted as part of the hospice team serving the

Shaheeds. From his Peace Corps days, Jim could manage some rusty Urdu and a few words of Pashto, the Pathan dialect, and this helped him to establish a solid rapport with Ibrahim; soon they were on an easy, first-name basis. The patient finally confessed to Jim that his back pain was excruciating and, were it not for the medication, "I would be crying right now." Jim understood that a proud Pathan's reference to pain or tears was significant, and I suggested that his first task was to encourage Ibrahim to find a way to make the taking of medicine compatible with his cultural values. He was successful in this, emphasizing to Ibrahim that it took great courage to acknowledge, particularly to women (his wife and the nurses), that the disease was creating pain. Jim characterized the pain medication as "a weapon in the battle" and added that a brave warrior would make the best use of weapons in order to be victorious in battle. This framing of pain medication as a means of courageously fighting the disease helped Ibrahim to use the medication appropriately.

The hospice team remained concerned about the family's security and well-being after Ibrahim's approaching death, which seemed increasingly imminent. The patient referred to his situation as "kismet" (the Muslim notion of fate) and seemed to accept the idea of his death stoically; however, he remained unwilling to discuss the future with his wife or to inform her of the family's financial status. The social worker made a concerted effort to speak with Mumtaz, despite the woman's reluctance, and to determine her competence in understanding and eventually conducting the affairs of her household. In fact, Mumtaz was a bright and insightful woman. She was not, however, willing to confront her husband to gain permission to assume more responsibility for running the family. His insistence that finances were "not the affairs of women" kept her fearful and ignorant of the family's financial status.

A plan was devised by which Jim would present Ibrahim with an acceptable way of ensuring the welfare of his family after his death. Mumtaz had a warm and respectful relationship with her younger brother, Ghulam, who lived nearby and was a close friend of Ibrahim. Mumtaz assured the social worker that Ghulam was "very American" and would understand that she was the person who would soon have to run the household. Jim, who was an attorney, offered to meet with Ibrahim and Ghulam to arrange a "transfer of power" that would entitle Ghulam to conduct the household's affairs after his brother-in-law's death. Without the dying man's knowledge, Mumtaz and her brother had already agreed to a second transfer of power after Ibrahim was gone. The plan worked beautifully. Ibrahim cooperated in revealing the family's financial status to Ghulam, and the transfer of power was signed just a week before the patient's death.

Jim reported: "We never fooled Ibrahim. He was a sly fox—and a proud Pathan. He knew what he had to do, but he couldn't have done it directly. What we arranged helped him to preserve his dignity. When I last saw him I told him that I admired his courage and spirit and I gave him the Muslim farewell, *Khoda Hafez* (God be with you). He thanked me for everything 'from the bottom of the heart.'"

It is impossible for us to imagine the existence of a family completely devoid of cultural roots, religious heritage, or ethnic background. If we could, we might be free of any danger of stereotyping, of making assumptions about how a particular family is likely to behave. Unfortunately, we would also be missing the richness and diversity that are part of the fabric of an open society. Yet many of us experience a certain uneasiness when we are informed that we will be working with a family labeled, say, "Hispanic," "Asian," "black," or "Polish"—particularly when our experience with such families is limited or nonexistent.

But no family profile is complete without its ethnic identity. The "vertical" stressors discussed in Chapter Two include the family's ethnic and religious background, and these components cannot be ignored. Many of the families introduced in this book have been significantly shaped by ethnic roots. To truly understand them and every other family during times of crisis, their history must be acknowledged, their beliefs explored, and their rituals understood.

Although some people are not comfortable talking about ethnic differences, inquiry into ethnic background is an important area of family history-taking. If a danger exists in considering ethnicity as an intrinsic dimension of family identity, it is the tendency to make assumptions based on superficial evidence, such as skin color or surname. These visible signs of ethnicity can be misleading. Blacks whose families have lived in this country for two hundred years are quite unlike those who have emigrated in the last decade or so from the Caribbean. Northern Italians differ in myriad ways from Sicilians, and Ashkenazic (Eastern European) Jews may have little in common with their Sephardic counterparts of Spanish descent. To assume that these blacks, Italians, or Jews are identical because of skin color, nationality, or religion can lead to erroneous conclusions.

Even when commonly held stereotypes about an ethnic group hold true—and they often do!—they do not apply to every family in that group. Although a particular tradition may be practiced by many families within an ethnic group, there may be as many variations in the way that tradition is practiced as there are families. Additionally, a multigenerational family may participate in a particular ethnic ritual, but individual branches of the family may depart from the customary pattern. Further, families that are not members of an ethnic group may nevertheless display the characteristics or behavior of that group. The foods, attitudes, beliefs, and customs of the Boston Irish, Milwaukee Germans, Minnesota Norwegians, New York Jews, Chicago Poles, and Miami Cubans, for example, have certainly taken root with their neighbors, who may pride themselves on how indistinguishable they have become from the predominant group.

The healthcare worker must not only identify a family's ethnic background but also assess how closely the family reflects its ethnic heritage. For example, the Shaheeds remained closely tied to their roots, and much of their family functioning could be understood in these terms. Not realizing this, the social worker erroneously believed that Mumtaz Shaheed was a victim of mindless sexism, and the nurses failed to understand why Ibrahim was refusing pain medication. Ibrahim's Pathan ancestry was only one factor—but an important one—that contributed to his character and to his reluctance to cooperate with the medication regimen. Efforts by the hospice team to address these behaviors within the "rules" of the Shaheeds' ethnic background made it possible for the family to achieve a good adjustment to Ibrahim's death. By identifying and understanding a family's cultural antecedents, healthcare workers can plan care that is acceptable within that family's ethnic framework.

Perhaps the most frequent disclaimer regarding ethnicity that families express is that because they do not identify with or participate in the traditions of their ancestors, they are unaffected by them. Nearly always, that is not the case. Ethnic characteristics are transmitted through the generations and are part of the historical makeup (vertical influence) of the family in the present. Even families that make an active effort to deny or disassociate themselves from their roots are undeniably and subtly influenced by their ethnic heritage.

Arthur Forman was only vaguely aware of his Italian heritage. His father, convinced that he would be unable to advance in the business world with an immigrant identity, had changed his name from Ferraro shortly after completing college, had left the Catholic church, had married a Protestant woman, and had severed nearly all relations with his family of origin, both emotionally and geographically. When Arthur was in his early twenties, his father was diagnosed with an inoperable brain tumor. In the final months of his life, the elder Forman told his son how much he regretted that he had abandoned his heritage. Arthur, who since adolescence had been bothered by a sense of rootlessness and lack of identity, asked his father for permission to change his name back to Ferraro. Arthur observed: "My father's final and dearest gift was giving me back something I never knew I had lost. I knew something was missing. I just didn't know what it was."

Families manage to pass on from generation to generation, without consciously articulating them, many beliefs and attitudes and a world view that are part of their ethnic identity. I vividly recall my first experience with this phenomenon when, in my last year of high school, a friend died in an auto accident. It was the first time that this Jewish boy had gone to a Catholic funeral, and I was shocked and unsettled by the priest's pronouncement that we should be comforted because my friend was now "in a better place." I had never given a thought to death, and I don't remember ever discussing it with my parents, but I knew instinctively that the priest was "wrong." What he was saying contradicted everything I "knew" about life and death—knowledge that I had somehow, subtly and unconsciously, received while growing up. Jewish tradition values life as lived in the world; the Catholic Church views the afterlife as an ultimate reward. That day in church, the difference was clear, but to this day, I have no idea how I first learned this part of my religious heritage.

In this chapter, it is not my intention to address all aspects of ethnicity or to present a detailed analysis of any single ethnic group. The purpose here is to increase awareness of how ethnic background makes families different from each other, creating an external boundary that distinguishes the family from the world beyond.[2]

Ethnic groups differ from each other in what they believe and in how they behave. For many families, the behaviors often continue to exist long after the belief system has been lost. Chinese families may routinely distribute hard candy with a coin inside to mourners at a funeral ("lucky money"); Jewish families may cover the mirrors in the house of mourning; Greek families may serve *koliya* (boiled wheat) to mourners. Most likely, such families would be surprised to learn that these rituals are rooted in an atavistic aspect of their ethnic heritage and are each connected to belief in demons, angels, and a complicated anthropomorphic afterlife.

Despite these interesting ceremonial vestiges, in contemporary society the distinguishing aspects of ethnic groups are more likely to be reflected in deep-seated beliefs than in ritual practice. The exigencies of our fast-paced world have homogenized many of the rituals surrounding death, resulting in fewer visible differences among ethnic groups. A permanent remnant of a family's heritage may nevertheless remain in the belief system and attitudes that direct behavior in the face of death.

Ethnic beliefs may also be at the core of unresolved family issues, and framing them in ethnic terms may help lead to resolution. For example, Italian families traditionally have erected a prodigious tombstone in honor of the deceased, even if it meant going into debt, although this practice has become less common in recent years. A conflict between Tony and Frank Bianchi regarding the size, shape, and cost of their father's gravestone threatened the relationship between their two families. Tony, who wanted a large, impressive monument, argued that Papa deserved it. He called Frank a cheapskate who did not love his father enough to honor him properly. His brother countered that a fancy stone cheapened Papa's memory and lacked dignity, and he maintained that Tony's position reflected his guilt for not visiting his father enough when he was sick. Their parents' priest, who was also a hospital chaplain and accustomed to such conflicts, helped the brothers to reach a compromise. He reframed their conflict in terms of their Italian heritage, explaining that the sons represented two trends in Italian-American families. Tony was honoring the old Italian traditions, whereas Frank was reflecting the position of Italians in modern America. The priest helped the Bianchis decide on a monument that would honor the family, without dwelling on how much each son loved his father or how much money he wanted to spend.

Five aspects of ethnicity can be explored that are important to anyone working with families facing death:

1. Attitudes toward life and death
2. Expression of pain, suffering, and grief
3. Acceptance of outside authority
4. Expectations of family responsibility
5. Gender roles

ATTITUDES TOWARD
LIFE AND DEATH

Perhaps no other area of a family belief system is more rooted in ethnic heritage than conceptions of life and death. Opinions about such matters are seldom in the forefront of thinking, so questioning a family about its views on life and death would not necessarily yield much information. The family's fundamental attitudes toward the meaning of life and death are most commonly expressed in their behavior at the time of life-threatening illness.

Some families may appear to view a mortal diagnosis dispassionately. This fatalistic attitude—Ibrahim Shaheed called his condition "kismet"—often causes conflict with doctors, nurses, and others committed to aggressive treatment. Other families, by contrast, consider life of any sort better than death, and this attitude, likely rooted in the family's ethnic heritage, causes them to cling tenaciously to life, even when it is riddled with pain and suffering. Families who view the present life as the only life may express great anger at illness and death. However, families whose religion and culture esteem life after death more than life on earth are likely to meet serious illness with a measure of resignation.

When Margaret O'Hara was diagnosed with early-stage Hodgkin's disease, her family was curiously accepting of the diagnosis. Margaret continued to go to work each day, and she, her husband, and their two adolescent sons seemed to be neither optimistic nor pessimistic about her prognosis. "If she's meant to get better, she will," explained Tom, her husband, which somewhat simplistically reflects the fatalistic view of the Irish. In one sense, this may have seemed to be a realistic attitude, yet Margaret's failure to keep her chemotherapy appointments when "something more important came up" was hampering her chances for survival.

One day, Margaret's doctor expressed his irritation with the O'Haras to his nurse, a woman of Irish descent. Her advice enabled him to change the way he approached the family. The doctor called

Tom and asked him to accompany Margaret on her next appointment, and then he spoke to Margaret and told her that he expected both of them at the next visit. When they met, the doctor repeated what he thought he had explained initially: the disease need not be fatal if the patient complies with the treatment protocol. The doctor repeatedly reinforced the notion that fate was in their hands; recovery would depend on how hard they worked at it. Margaret subsequently kept every appointment, and the disease went into remission.

The doctor's intervention was framed in three ways to accommodate traditional Irish attitudes: (1) by involving Tom, the physician made it more difficult for Margaret to assume total responsibility for her own care, a characteristic of Irish women (recall Ann Haley in Chapter Four); (2) he used the concept of fate to make the family responsible for treatment and for Margaret's destiny; and (3) he emphasized work as a component of treatment, which appealed to the Irish belief that nothing happens without hard work.

The O'Haras' fatalistic view of life was in keeping with the traditional Irish perception that life is full of suffering, but if suffering is what fate dictates, it must be accepted with stoic resignation. Jewish families are not likely to demonstrate stoic resignation. Rather, they may desperately explore any and all possibilities to defeat illness and forestall death. Thus, although the Cohen family seemed to accept that their seventy-eight-year-old mother's death from stomach cancer was imminent, they continued to talk about seeking another medical opinion or an experimental medication, and they kept urging her to eat well to keep up her strength. For many Jews such as the Cohens, the present life is the only life, a starkly different belief from the Catholic view that this life is merely a prelude to a better one beyond death. Of course, there are wide variations in people's beliefs, regardless of their affiliation with a religious tradition. However, certain beliefs, particularly in regard to death and the afterlife, are commonly shared by individuals within the same religious cohort.

Ironically, neither the O'Haras nor the Cohens were strong adherents of their respective faiths. Neither family went to church or synagogue, and neither would describe itself as particularly interested in religion or knowledgeable about its faith's position on the meaning of life and death. Yet these theological traditions survived.

Ethnic belief systems were not buried beneath the surface in the Munoz family, but they seemed incomprehensible to the hospital staff. Maria Munoz, an eighty-three-year-old Puerto Rican immigrant, had suffered a severe heart attack, and chronic emphysema and diabetes were complicating her management. The Munoz family tearfully accepted the inevitable death and were doing everything they could to ease her passage into the world beyond. The journey into the next life required all the spiritual assistance that could be mustered. The floor staff welcomed the visit by the family priest, but, losing patience with the steady stream of spiritists and faith healers, they began to enforce strict visiting rules: only four people in the room at once. Because Maria was constantly attended by two daughters and many grandchildren, this rule was an effective barrier to unwelcome visitors. But the Munoz family became distressed by the limit on nonfamily guests and begged for the spiritual assistance they so desperately wanted for their loved one. Only when the staff realized the significance of the ethnic and religious beliefs of this family did they relent and allow Maria her visitors. When she died, her family was relieved that she was at peace.

Understanding a family's attitude toward the meaning of life and death and its beliefs regarding notions such as "quality of life" can be extremely important in selecting treatment choices that are compatible with the way the family operates. Likewise, healthcare providers should be sensitive to potential sources of conflict within families. When an individual makes choices that run counter to the deep-rooted ethnic and religious beliefs of the family, tension is likely. Serious family rifts may result if these issues are not resolved.

Frieda Lebowitz had lived in a nursing home for three years. During this time, she had repeatedly told the nurses and aides who maintained the feeding apparatus that sustained her roommate, "I don't ever want to have a tube like that in my nose!" In time, Frieda began to deteriorate mentally, dawdling over meals and often forgetting why the food tray was in front of her. After she lost about twenty pounds, her family became alarmed. "She's being starved to death!" claimed her son, Ira. "Can't we get one of those feeding tubes to be sure she gets enough to eat?" asked another son, Marvin, and Ira quoted the Yiddish expression, "The worst life is better than the best death." The sons were about to get their way until a nurse's aide intervened, repeating what Frieda had told her many times about the feeding tube. They listened respectfully but repeated their belief that it would be criminal to "simply allow Mother to die." Later that week, during a period of lucidity, Frieda was told about her sons' desire to have her intubated. She asked that they be summoned immediately, and despite their pleading that she accept the feeding tube, she refused, objecting that forced feeding was degrading. She also complained that it would be an affront to her dignity to have an aide feed her. With the help of the nurse's aide, Frieda's sons arrived at a compromise: Ira, Marvin, their spouses, or one of their three daughters would stop by the nursing home each day at dinner time and assist her with the meal.

EXPRESSION OF PAIN, SUFFERING, AND GRIEF

Healthcare workers are well aware of the vast range of responses to pain. What some patients bear without complaint others will respond to with hysteria. Besides reflecting individual differences in temperament, the ways in which pain is expressed frequently reflect the background of the patient and family. What is considered painful, the level of pain tolerance, and the ways in which the experience of pain is communicated are all part of the family's belief system and mode of operating. This is not to suggest that every Muslim patient of Pathan ancestry can be expected to respond to pain stoically, as did Ibrahim Shaheed, for differences do exist among all individuals and all families. But there are family patterns in response to pain, which emanate from the shared values that are a dimension of a family's ethnic identity.

For example, healthcare workers in the Midwest who have frequent contact with Norwegian families will certainly be familiar with the concept of *kjekk*. This notion encompasses a variety of positive attitudes, including courage, strength, good humor, and hard work, and underlies an unusually high tolerance of physical pain. To be *kjekk* is a common value for Norwegian-Americans, even through the third and fourth generations. A patient from such a family who complained mightily about physical pain would undoubtedly be viewed as aberrant, or the pain would have to be taken most seriously.

Chapter Four explored the stages through which families pass in their adjustment to terminal illness, and it was noted that one dimension is the family's perception of illness, which may differ from the objective course of a disease. The distinction between illness and disease lies at the very core of our understanding the ways in which families face life-threatening illness. The notion of "disease" is embedded in the medical model, which focuses on symptomatology, treatment options, and prognosis. An "illness" paradigm is rooted in a systemic perspective on sickness, which emphasizes the interactive processes of the family and its history of loss; this, in turn, is related to its cultural roots, belief system, linguistic quirks, and cultural taboos.

The difference between illness and disease and the influence of cultural beliefs are illustrated in recent Japanese history. The late Emperor Hirohito apparently suffered with cancer for many years. However, the word *cancer*, which for the Japanese is synonymous with death, was never used to describe his condition; to do so would have been an insult to him. As he neared the end of his life, the world press regularly noted his deterioration and offered frequent interpretations of what the reports from his physicians really meant.

The entire nation prepared for his demise, yet there was never a public statement that he was dying. The rest of the world, however, was aware that Hirohito was dying of cancer.

The disparity of perception between the physical course that a disease is taking and the meaning of the illness for the family is an important dimension of ethnic differences among families. This distinction between illness and disease may create tension between the healthcare professional and the family. The former focuses on the disease entity, often ignoring the ethnic background that shapes the patient's illness. The family, in turn, may be bewildered by the physician's insistence on defining the patient's symptoms solely in terms of physical disease, for this seems too limited a definition of a loved one's suffering.

The ways in which families experience and express pain and the ways in which they perceive illness have important implications for healthcare workers, who must assess the information relayed by the patient and family in light of their ethnic background. An Italian patient may cry and moan about how much it hurts, and the family will be sympathetic and supportive, never thinking for a moment that the patient is exaggerating the discomfort. Yet an Irish or Norwegian patient with pain of equal intensity will grin and bear it, and the family may not even address the question of pain, either with the patient or with the doctor or nurses. Knowing that a family is of an ethnic group that tends to have a stoic attitude toward pain, healthcare providers will want to probe more deeply than usual to determine how much pain the patient is in. On the other hand, the vociferous complaints of the Italian patient should not necessarily send doctors or nurses running to the bedside with pain medication.

The management of pain medication should be tailored to a family's ethnic background. Portuguese and Italian families, who are more likely to demand instant relief from pain and discomfort, will cooperate with the treatment regimen if it promises quick relief. On the other hand, Jewish families may have misgivings about the long-range effects or complications from medication and may be reluctant to accept drugs unless reassured about side effects, time limitation of therapy, and the absence of alternatives. Chinese families, committed to a holistic approach to illness, may use medication if it is only one component of a treatment plan.

The physician's awareness of ethnic differences regarding the experience and control of pain, as well as his or her willingness to prescribe in accord with the patient's ethnic context, can make a big difference to the family of the terminally ill. Consider Austin Larkin and Ellen Adams, two patients of British ancestry, each of whom is suffering from end-stage disease and has been taking medication to control the constant, severe pain. Austin wishes to attend his son's wedding, and Ellen wants to spend her last Thanksgiving with her family. Both patients, not wishing their family celebrations to be clouded by drug-induced lethargy and dullness, inform their doctors that they will not take their usual pain medication while attending these special events.

Austin's physician consults with an anesthesiologist, and together they decide to prescribe a patient-controlled analgesic device that Austin can use for a few days. He is able to attend the wedding with minimal pain, and his family has happy memories of the occasion when he dies three weeks later. Ellen's doctor, on the other hand, offers her no alternative and, with some impatience, urges her to continue to take her regular medication. She refuses and abruptly ceases taking her pills the night before Thanksgiving. The next day, she dresses in her brightest clothes and puts on makeup to bring color to her wan complexion, but the cosmetic effects cannot hide her agony. Her family is greatly distressed by her suffering, and they cannot help but recall her pained expressions when they attend her funeral a month later.

Austin's doctor understood that his patient put a much greater value on his lucidity than on pain control. Ellen's doctor did not.

Just as expressions of physical pain vary among different ethnic groups, so do expressions of emotional pain. The grief process in families has been discussed more fully in Chapter Five, but here it should be reiterated that open expression of grief is encouraged in some ethnic cultures and discouraged in others. Also, some ethnic groups have highly ritualized means of expressing grief. To curtail these rituals or to refuse to participate in them can impair healing and create family rifts.

When Henry Washington died, all but one of his seven children traveled with their families to the rural Alabama town where this descendant of a slave had raised his family. There was much crying and wailing at his funeral, and the family felt that Henry had received a good send-off. But the Washington family was angry at Henry's youngest son, Thad, who did not come from New York. A musician, Thad refused his brothers' offer to pay his bus fare, saying that it wasn't only money that kept him away; he had an important gig, which could mean his break into stardom, and he could not walk out on this chance. "I'll grieve for Dad in my own way," he told his family. Three years later, Thad was still struggling for that all-important career break, he was at odds with his family, and he felt himself a failure. His absence at his father's funeral continued to plague him, and he felt estranged from his family.

The expectation of the Washingtons that the entire family take part in the funeral rite is common to many other ethnic groups, but not to all. When Beth Mathias, of British ancestry, learned that her beloved grandmother had died, she would have taken the next plane to Cleveland to be with the family had her mother, at the other end of the phone line, not insisted: "Don't be foolish, dear. Gram wouldn't want you to miss work and spend that kind of money. You'll be here Christmas, and that'll be just fine."

African Americans, Puerto Ricans, and most Mediterranean peoples are openly expressive of grief. Mourners at Puerto Rican or Iranian funerals have been known to faint from the exertion of wailing and screaming. In fact, to sit quietly at the funeral may be considered a breach of etiquette. Other ethnic groups are less likely to display their sorrow, either in public or in private. The Irish wake may seem more like a celebration than a sad farewell, and although much emotion is expressed, it is likely to be lubricated by drink, anecdotes, and humor. Tears are permitted—even encouraged—but they are likely to be suppressed quickly with a joke or reassurance. Many Asian cultures also greatly constrain the emotional expression of grief, but through a highly ritualized framework for mourning. The Japanese consider the public expression of individual feelings improper; the group (*giri*), not the individual (*ninjo*), is valued. Thus much of Japanese public life has become intricately ritualized. It would be no more proper for a Japanese mourner to display personal emotion publicly than not to take part in the public mourning ritual. This culture provides for an acceptable outlet for emotion while ensuring its culturally appropriate framework.

It may be difficult for Westerners to comprehend fully that in a culture such as Japan where overt emotional expression is proscribed, ritualized frameworks for the expression of emotion must suffice. A fascinating counterpoint to the Japanese example is the overwhelming emotional response of the British public to the death of Diana, Princess of Wales. In a society known for emotional restraint and the "stiff upper lip," the reaction to Diana's death was unprecedented in the extreme; some analysts have suggested that it was more American than British and may demonstrate the degree to which the world is becoming a "global village." This observation supports the notion that over time, cultural uniqueness gives way to homogenization when exposed to more powerful environmental forces.

Much like their traditional British forebears, members of America's White Protestant middle-class (often referred to as White Anglo-Saxon Protestant, or WASP) culture neither encourage public emotional displays nor prescribe sanctioned outlets for emotions. Families from this background need to be encouraged to express pain and grief so that repression of emotions does not result in the development of symptoms. One example is the Farnhams, introduced in Chapter Two as representative of an overfunctioning family. Roy and Marlene Farnham did not openly mourn the nearly simultaneous deaths of their parents. Their son, Ty, had no outlet for the expression of his own grief. Instead of sharing the experience of the pain of grief with his parents, he dramatically changed his model behavior in school. The young man reverted to his former self only when the family was encouraged to openly share its grief, which undoubtedly, in keeping with its ethnic background, was expressed in quiet tears and recollections in the confines of the family home.

ACCEPTANCE OF OUTSIDE AUTHORITY

The healthcare establishment, at nearly every level, represents authority. Whereas some ethnic groups readily obey and comply with the directives of authority, others traditionally question and challenge it, and still others tend to be suspicious of authority and the establishment. Some ethnic groups view authority figures simply as resources, not to be followed obediently, challenged, or mistrusted, but rather to be considered as one of many sources of help.

Ethnic differences in attitudes toward authority can be illustrated by the responses of three different families when told that the middle-aged mother had breast cancer. The Doessels, who came to this country from Germany in the 1920s, checked Martha into the hospital the day after receiving the diagnosis, and she had the radical mastectomy and adjuvant radiation and chemotherapy recommended by the doctors. The Weinsteins, a Jewish family, spent weeks reading everything they could find about treatment for Evelyn's breast cancer; they called family members and friends with connections in the medical community; they consulted two other physicians; and finally they agreed to a lumpectomy followed by radiation. The Johnsons, a rural Southern black family, first sought medical care six months after Sara discovered a lump in her breast while bathing. Reluctant to put herself at the mercy of the medical establishment, Sara and her daughter, who accompanied her to the doctor, were leery of the recommendation for surgery, but they agreed because they concluded that they had no alternative.

Certain ethnic groups relate to authority better when they feel more directly connected with that authority. Chinese families will be much more comfortable dealing with a Chinese physician, particularly a male who is respectful of the family hierarchy and takes a holistic view of health. The family's perception of the physician will ultimately determine the degree of its cooperation. The Lees, a second-generation Chinese-American family, summarily dismissed their physician, ironically a young man of Chinese extraction who was considered one of the brightest specialists on the hospital staff, when his perceived lack of respect for the elders of the family made it impossible for the Lees to relate to him and cooperate with the treatment. In a similar vein, the Conti family double-checked everything that they were told with their nephew, a physician in another city, whom they regularly consulted by phone. The Contis also insisted on clearing all instructions from the hospice team caring for seventy-five-year-old Vincent with their family doctor, a semiretired physician whom they had been seeing for decades. The family seemed dubious of both the "youngsters" who were treating Vincent and the "girls" on the hospice team, except for one Italian nurse whose grandfather had done business with Mr. Conti many years before.

Another aspect of the family's attitude toward outside authority is the control the family feels it needs to exert over decision making. Some ethnic groups demand autonomy and are thus resistant to directives from the outside. Other cultural groups take the opposite position: they are content to have health professionals tell them exactly what to do and to comply with those orders.

Jewish families characteristically respect authority, particularly when they perceive it as reflecting the highest expertise, and they will expend much effort to locate the person best qualified to care for a loved one. It is not unusual for Jewish families to question a doctor's credentials, not because they are disrespectful of authority but because they must be certain that it is backed by demonstrated expertise. Despite their respect for authority, however, Jewish families are not likely to abrogate control, even to an expert, and will demand an active role in care. Irish families, in contrast, are likely to accept the physician's authority unhesitatingly and would consider it arrogant and in bad taste to question his or her credentials.

West Indian families are reluctant to admit to illness, but when they do, they are willing to accept authority unquestioningly and will comply with medical directives. Unlike Jewish families, they will be uncomfortable if expected to share in decision making. West Indians are similar to Puerto Ricans, Mexicans, and other Hispanics, in that their compliance with authority will be more comfortable and more productive if the health professional makes an effort to include a wide range of family members in a cooperative plan of care.

Providers are frequently frustrated because they have difficulty understanding the ethnically related meaning of a family's behavior. The Mutabars, a wealthy, well-educated, second-generation Iranian family, had totally exasperated the oncologist who was treating Vita, the eighty-three-year-old family matriarch. He informed the family members whom he met—and he had met nearly all of them—that although the medication he prescribed would relieve her pain and nausea, it would have no effect on her cancer, which was inexorably progressing. He was shocked some weeks later to learn that Vita had suffered a toxic drug reaction. The family had taken her to another physician and proceeded to administer both the drugs this new doctor had ordered and the medication the oncologist had prescribed previously. Despite their intellectual sophistication, the Mutabars were behaving in a manner characteristic of Iranian families, who often go from doctor to doctor seeking a more optimistic opinion and any medication that promises the hope of cure. The objective reality of Vita's advanced stomach cancer, clearly stated by the oncologist and ostensibly understood by the family, did not alter its commitment to provide its loved one with what it perceived as the best possible care.

EXPECTATIONS OF
FAMILY RESPONSIBILITY

Respect for authority is not necessarily correlated with a family's willingness to seek or to accept help at times of illness or stress. The determining factor is the boundaries that have been established between the family and the outside world. Those ethnic groups that maintain relatively rigid boundaries between family and nonfamily and insist on the family maintaining full responsibility for its members are obviously the least likely to seek outside help.

When Thomas Taylor, a forty-year-old African American, was dying of metastatic lung cancer, his wife, Cynthia, took a second job to supplement the family's diminished income, and his widowed mother moved in to look after her son and four young grandchildren. As the patient's deteriorating condition made his physical care increasingly difficult, a neighbor convinced Cynthia that hospice could provide an enormous support to her mother-in-law and to Thomas. During the last weeks of Thomas's life, the hospice program did serve the Taylors, but the team members met with constant resistance. The elder Mrs. Taylor believed that the nurses did not understand her son's needs, and she clearly felt her space was being violated when they were in the home. Members of the hospice team were often frustrated with her uncooperativeness and tried to avoid dealing with her by speaking directly with Thomas or Cynthia. After the patient's death, the family expressed no interest in follow-up by the hospice bereavement team.

The explanation for the elder Mrs. Taylor's behavior lies partly in ethnic heritage. African Americans tend to have strong suspicions of "the system," especially when it purports to be offering help free of charge. More important, black families have traditionally relied on the kinship network—particularly embodied in women—to provide physical and emotional support in times of distress. Any suggestion that the family cannot take care of its own may be perceived as an insult. Society has long viewed black women as the bedrock of the family, and not surprisingly, they tend to view themselves that way as well. Their identity as mothers and caretakers is of great importance, and any impugning of their ability or infringement on their efforts to care for their own, no matter how well intentioned, will be met with resistance.

A similar difficulty was encountered when a physician finally convinced the Dimopolos family to accept the services of a visiting nurse in the care of seventy-six-year-old Joseph. The nurse found the family cordial enough, but she soon learned that the only help they wanted from her was with specific medical procedures; any "extraneous" advice she offered was politely ignored. Mrs. Dimopolos made it clear that she, her daughter, and her sister could take care of the patient quite adequately. Greeks honor the family as something sacrosanct and are extremely reluctant to look to outside sources for help. In fact, traditional Greek families will refuse all outside help if any female family members are available. If a woman were to fall ill and she had no daughters to care for her, the family might be willing to accept assistance, but only with great reluctance.

The discomfort experienced in certain families when help is offered may, in other ethnic groups, border on a sense of indignity. In most Asian cultures, turning to outsiders for assistance is viewed as a humiliation and a blot on the family's honor. The Kim family, first-generation Korean-Americans, handled the complicated physical care of a dying matriarch and flatly refused to allow any health-care workers to enter the home. Instead, extended family members moved in and became part of the household. In her final months, the patient was surrounded by innumerable relatives, who provided round-the-clock care and constant attention. Equally reluctant to accept strangers into their home, the Chins, a second-generation Chinese-American family, found it more acceptable to hospitalize the elderly Mr. Chin than to allow their family honor to be violated by the presence of outsiders.

For certain ethnic families, such as the Kims, the definition of *family* may be broadened, when necessary, to encompass people related in any way, no matter how distant the relationship. This is common among Asians and may also be observed in many Hispanic cultures and among Native Americans. Thus care of an ill or dying member may become the responsibility not only of the nuclear family but of the extended family—and perhaps even of those whose kinship is ill defined but who belong to the same ethnic group.

Not all ethnic groups are so rigid in their attitude toward the family's responsibilities. Some groups are more willing to accept care from institutions or unrelated individuals. Mainline Protestants may actually prefer that care of the ill or dying be turned over to health professionals and facilities. Although such families stress self-reliance, this virtue is more applicable to the individual than to the family as a unit.

One family's stubborn insistence on attending to all the patient's needs or another family's abrogation of all responsibility for care may prove frustrating. Rather than confront these families, health-care workers would be wise to consider interventions that acknowledge ethnic differences and accommodate a family's style. Respect for a family's autonomy and ability to decide what is best for the patient is appropriate, but many families benefit from clearer directives and more active involvement from professionals. Thus, when intervening with families facing death, one needs to be attuned to the degree to which the family desires the presence of outsiders and who might be appropriate.

Certain families are likely to be more comfortable with professional helpers who are of the same ethnic group. Some families might be more amenable to the intervention of a male rather than a female. Some groups are particularly concerned with knowing a provider's credentials. Some cultures are comfortable with a strictly medical approach, whereas others are traditionally more holistically oriented. When ethnic factors are not considered, professionals and others are likely to confront resistance and noncompliance.

Finally, many factors determine the choices made for care of a loved one in the final stages of life, and a family's perception of its own responsibility, which is transmitted multigenerationally and rooted in ethnic heritage, is one of those factors. Recognizing the danger of generalization, consider the likely outcomes if breast cancer had metastasized in the three women discussed earlier—Martha Doessel, Evelyn Weinstein, and Sara Johnson—and they were now in the last few weeks of their lives. Martha Doessel would probably be in the hospital, where professional caretakers would attend to her final needs. The Weinstein family might be using a variety of services to care for Evelyn, including home health personnel and periodic hospitalization. And Sara Johnson would undoubtedly be cared for at home, attended by family members, both close and extended, and with limited involvement from outside personnel.

GENDER ROLES

This chapter has emphasized the major role ethnicity plays in shaping the differences among families. Now attention can be turned to one way in which nearly all ethnic groups are similar: in virtually every ethnic group, women are expected to be the primary caretakers. The role of women as the administrants of care, both on a routine basis and in times of crisis, differs among ethnic groups only in relative terms; some cultures view this role as nearly absolute, whereas others demonstrate some flexibility. However, in more flexible cultures, where men do assume some traditional female roles, they seldom do so without the supervision or substantial assistance of women. On the whole, women, regardless of ethnic background, have been socialized to assume second-order, caretaking roles. This phenomenon has been wholly congruent with the social fabric of American life.

Of course, each ethnic culture has its own views of the specific duties and position of women. Before the hospice team became involved in Ibrahim's care, Mumtaz Shaheed was providing nearly all physical support for her husband. But she was not privy to any "higher-order" family matters, such as decision making or finances.

The expectation that she serve and obey her husband also meant that she was not to be a companion in the Western sense, nor would she be allowed to discuss his condition. Compare this position with the female role in most Mediterranean cultures, where women are expected not so much to serve and obey as to nourish and nurture. The Italian wife may not be "friends" with her husband, but she is expected to be a strong support, and her functions include an emphasis on food and a commitment to the care of her husband's family of origin as well as her own. In times of stress or illness, the Italian woman's role as the emotional center and primary nurturer of the family, as provider of nearly all care, may emerge quite clearly.

I once saw a graphic demonstration of the central role played by an Italian woman in nurturing and caring for the family—a role that allowed the family to continue to function even when she could no longer actively participate in family life. I was asked by the hospice team to visit the Palumbos and make an assessment that would help the nurses and social worker understand why they were having so much difficulty working with this family. Frances, the fifty-five-year-old wife and mother, was suffering from amyotrophic lateral sclerosis. Once a vibrant, active woman, she was now completely paralyzed and unable to move or communicate, save by slight movements of her head or by blinking her eyes. During my visit to the family home, Frances, her husband Al, their two daughters, and I were talking in the den while Annette, Frances's younger sister, was in the kitchen making dinner. Our conversation was constantly punctuated by Annette's shouts from the kitchen: "Fran, how much basil in the sauce?" "Fran, where do you keep the large frying pan?" "Fran, should I put bread crumbs in the meatballs?" Each question brought our conversation to a halt, as Frances methodically blinked out an answer. Even though barely functional, this woman continued to oversee the task of preparing the family's dinner!

Considering all of the families presented in this book, one cannot fail to notice that, regardless of ethnic identity, a woman nearly always assumed primary caring responsibilities. Whether she was the wife, daughter, daughter-in-law, mother, sister, granddaughter—and even when she was the patient—her active presence was vital to family functioning. Her duties might be primarily the concrete tasks of physical caretaking or housekeeping, or the intangible tasks of providing emotional support and management of the family's psychological well-being. Whether (like Mumtaz Shaheed) the woman primarily provides physical caretaking or (like Ann Haley) provides the family's emotional and psychological support, the family's well-being will depend greatly on how she is able to perform these tasks.

Healthcare personnel, the majority of whom are women, must respect the role of women as primary caretakers in nearly all families. They should also be aware that women must be protected from the burden of total responsibility for patient care, just as at times some women, like Mumtaz Shaheed, need to be enfranchised to take responsibility in areas previously closed to them. The Taylors, the African American family described earlier in this chapter, might have had an easier time if healthcare workers had been more sensitive to the elder Mrs. Taylor's ethnically defined role. She was determined to carry out her duty as primary caretaker for her son and his family. There was little the hospice team was able to do to relieve her of this burden; in fact, she did not view it as a burden. The hospice team erred by going over her head and talking with her son and daughter-in-law to achieve some leverage. This tactic was doomed to fail, because it did not take into account the role played by the matriarchal figure in the black family. This experience can be contrasted with that of the team working with the Shaheeds. Mumtaz was able to take over the financial affairs of the family after Ibrahim's death because the hospice team developed a strategy that involved another male in the family who was open to change.

This is not to suggest that healthcare workers in all disciplines do not need to be sensitized to the potential exploitation of women in families, particularly when the family is in crisis. A woman's acquiescence in being relegated to a second-order role is by no means adequate justification for ignoring that she is in that role, regardless of the fact that the family's ethnic makeup partially determines her place. The possibilities for change need to be explored, albeit carefully enough so as not to exacerbate the crisis being coped with in the family. However, it seems perfectly reasonable to address the family's belief system about the relative position of men and women, particularly when those roles become rigidified, creating obstacles to quality care and good family function.

Notes

1. I am indebted to Fred Davis, a talented and dedicated hospice volunteer, for his guidance in understanding and presenting the Shaheeds.

2. The most useful and comprehensive book available on the subject of ethnicity and families is M. McGoldrick, J. Giordano, and J. K. Pearce (eds.), *Ethnicity and Family Therapy*, 2nd ed. (New York: Guilford Press, 1996). For many of the ideas contained in this chapter, I owe a large debt of gratitude to my coauthors of that text. Another source on ethnic differences is D. P. Irish, K. F. Lundquist, and V. J. Nelsen, *Ethnic Variations in Dying, Death, and Grief: Diversity in Universality* (Bristol, Pa.: Taylor & Francis, 1993).

8

Ethical Dilemmas

If there were a sympathy in choice,
War, death, or sickness did lay siege to it.

William Shakespeare
A Midsummer Night's Dream (1.1)

The Costellas are an affluent family with deep ties to their community and their extended family (see Figure 8.1). Both AnnMarie and her husband, Carl, are third-generation Americans whose grandparents immigrated from northern Italy in the early part of the century. Both of their families placed high value on education and self-reliance—Carl's and AnnMarie's parents were all high school graduates, and all of their siblings are college graduates. When AnnMarie became ill with amyotrophic lateral sclerosis (ALS), the five Costella children were all adults—Carl Jr., forty; Barbara, thirty-nine; Joanne, thirty-seven; Sabrina, thirty-five; and Brian, thirty-one. All are professionals, and with the exception of Sabrina, who is divorced and lives in Chicago, they all live within a few miles of the home in which they grew up. There are six grandchildren. Carl recently retired after many years as a financial analyst; AnnMarie had taken early retirement from her position as a school administrator a few years before and was spending a great deal of her time caring for her adopted granddaughter.

I first met the Costella family in the early 1980s when I helped the family deal with some emotional problems their youngest son,

Figure 8.1. Genogram of the Costella Family, 1997.

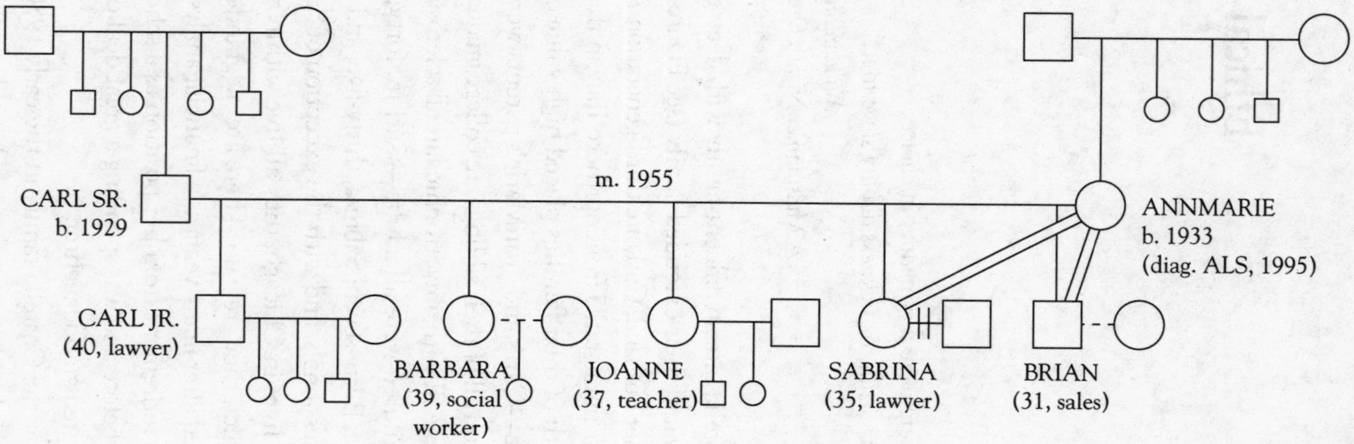

ANNMARIE
b. 1933
(diag. ALS, 1995)

BRIAN
(31, sales)

SABRINA
(35, lawyer)

JOANNE
(37, teacher)

BARBARA
(39, social
worker)

CARL JR.
(40, lawyer)

CARL SR.
b. 1929

m. 1955

Brian, was having in high school. A few years later, the Costellas called to consult me when their daughter, Barbara, "came out" as a lesbian and announced that she was living with a lover, with whom she was planning to have a family. This was a trying time for the family, whose traditional values were jeopardized by Barbara's lifestyle. However, their strong commitment to family solidarity outweighed their initial refusal to accept Barbara's orientation, and to their credit, they eventually accepted their daughter and her partner as full-fledged family members. AnnMarie sent me an annual Christmas card, and I would occasionally bump into one of the Costellas and benefit from a few minutes of "catch-up." A few years ago, after AnnMarie retired, she considered becoming a hospice volunteer and called me to discuss the possibility; she apparently never followed through, however, and years passed before I again had contact with the family.

Thus I was quite surprised to receive a message that Carl Costella had called. When we spoke, I was saddened to hear that AnnMarie was fatally ill. Diagnosed two years earlier with ALS, she was then in the hospital for testing and treatment for aspiration pneumonia; it was a short stay, and she was soon to be released. The family was in the process of contacting a hospice program and wanted to know if I would meet with them at the hospital and help them deal with "some serious complications." I arrived that evening, and given my experience with the family, it did not surprise me that everyone, including the in-law children, were present (except Sabrina, who was due to arrive the next day). Sadly, AnnMarie was a shadow of the woman I remembered, but she did greet me and managed a typically sardonic comment about how she was now the family problem. Barbara quickly teased her mother by commenting that she was *always* the family problem.

After some general discussion about AnnMarie's medical condition and the course of the illness, Brian, with tears welling in his eyes, blurted out, "And now Mom just wants to give up and die, and she wants us to help her." I asked them to tell me more, and their description was characteristic of AnnMarie's approach. After she was diagnosed, she actively pursued treatment options and learned all she could about ALS. She was a compliant but challenging patient, demanding an explanation and discussion with her doctors at every turn. As she weakened, however, she seemed resigned to the inevitability of her deterioration and death. Moreover, she had apparently concluded that the hastening of her death was now a viable option. Although she was having trouble communicating, she had managed to convey to her family that she did not wish to be resuscitated or subjected to heroic attempts to preserve her life under any circumstances. She emphasized that she no longer wished to be fed and wondered aloud whether anyone would be "kind enough" to help her die. AnnMarie seemed to be clear about what she wanted; unclear was whether her family could tolerate her choices.

I agreed to spend some time with the family after AnnMarie left the hospital. I also requested their permission to speak with her doctor, whom I knew. AnnMarie returned home two days later. Her physician confirmed her rapid deterioration and related a conversation they had had a few months before, when AnnMarie was still ambulatory. They met in his office, and she asked him directly whether he would be willing to give her a lethal dose of medication so that she could "end this horror whenever I choose to." They discussed her request at length, and he described his discomfort with participating in her plan. He refused to prescribe the medication she sought but told her that if she were truly intent on killing herself, she had the means to do so, given the various medications present in her home. He also said it was likely that eating and drinking would soon become more difficult for her and that she would certainly die if she refused food and liquid. When he suggested she might want professional help for "depression," she exploded, asking whether he might be depressed himself if he were weakening every day.

A few days after AnnMarie left the hospital, I visited with her and her family at home. It was to be my only visit. The Costellas are a voluble family, and our session was loud and long. Everyone had an opinion and felt a need to express it vehemently. An incredible range of emotions was expressed during the two hours in which the family tried to reach an accommodation with Ann-Marie's request. In only the few days since I had last seen her, she had grown weaker and was having difficulty making herself understood. Sabrina, who had long assumed a role in the family as her mother's closest confidant, "translated" for AnnMarie, and it was clearly painful for her to have to repeat her mother's requests that she be helped, or at least allowed, to die. Carl seemed resigned to his wife's choice to end her fight for survival. Brian seemed inconsolable, and Joanne and Barbara appeared united in their position that "Mom should be allowed to make her own choices." Carl Jr. expressed bewilderment that his mother, whom he had always admired as a "fighter," had decided to "give up hope."

The comment about giving up hope gave me the right opportunity to help the family consider alternative perspectives on the meaning of AnnMarie's decision to allow the disease to take its course. "Hope" can often be a powerful therapeutic tool. As described in Chapter Six, Mark Weinberg's nurses had developed a method for mobilizing his strength by constantly asking him what he hoped for. As a terminally ill AIDS patient, Mark no longer hoped that he would be cured. But demanding that he look for alternative "hopes" made it possible for him to shift his perspective from *whether* he would live to *how* he would live.[1] Similarly, my concern for the Costellas was that they not see AnnMarie's choice as giving up hope. More important was what they, as a family, could now hope for. Thus was launched a productive conversation about Mom's hopes and their own. The tone of the discussion changed: listening replaced talking, and genuinely open communication took place within this already close and loving family. I reminded them of times in the past when family members had made decisions that were diametrically opposed to the family's belief system. I did not notice that Laura, Barbara's four-year-old adopted child, was lying on the bed next to her grandmother when I made this comment, but AnnMarie made a grunting sound, and with her eyes on Laura, she smiled in agreement. Everyone understood.

We talked a bit more about hopes for the family. AnnMarie was growing tired, and everyone was emotionally spent. I promised that I would be available to visit again whenever they wished, and I took my leave. I didn't hear from them, occasionally wondered what had happened, and then, about a month later, I read in the local newspaper that AnnMarie had died. A few weeks later, I received a short note from Sabrina:

> Mom made me promise that I would let you know what happened and thank you for your help. That afternoon discussion helped a lot. We all understood that Mom could not exist without control of her body and so we had to let her go. She stopped eating and drinking and refused everything. It took about a week and the last few days she was in a coma. . . . I'm a bit worried about Brian, her "baby," but I think he'll be all right. Dad's taking it hard and I hope he'll be OK. Mom told us that her "hope" was that we would stay a *together family*. I don't think she needs to worry.

END-OF-LIFE DECISIONS

The Costellas' predicament has become an increasingly familiar one for me. In the years I have spent working with families, the decisions they face at the end of life have quite naturally affected me deeply. Their choices have become even more complicated recently, as medicine succeeds in adding not only more years but often more agony to our lives.

For two decades, the "right to die" battles, which first gained national attention when Karen Ann Quinlan's parents won the right to remove their comatose young daughter from a ventilator, have been fought in the courts and at hospital bedsides. The highly public and provocative actions of pathologist Jack Kevorkian, and the more measured debates taking place in the nation's think tanks, academies, and biomedical institutions, have exposed serious shortcomings and contradictions in how we choose, or are forced, to face our final days.

Hand in hand with new life-prolonging technologies have come increasing doubts about the appropriateness of their use in many circumstances. Families and caregivers have been thrust into a maelstrom of conflicting perspectives as end-of-life issues become part of the public conversation. Hardly a day goes by without our hearing a story that arouses anxiety about how *we* are likely to make our final journey. Many of them reinforce a growing mistrust of our doctors and the medical community. Frequent public opinion polls reflect the common fear that suffering and pain are a near certainty if we become fatally ill, and a number of studies on end-of-life care do little to reassure us.

Who's in Charge?

Particularly troubling is the SUPPORT study, sponsored by the Robert Wood Johnson Foundation, which included more than nine thousand patients and confirmed a widespread impression that the wishes of many terminally ill patients are not respected.[2] In the first phase of the study, researchers observed the care given to patients at five major medical centers and found that many of them died in moderate or severe pain and that physicians were often unaware when a request to withhold cardiopulmonary resuscitation (CPR) had been made. In the second study phase, an intervention was put in place to improve communication with the family, to emphasize pain control, and to give doctors more information about the prognosis of their patients. After two years, the intervention was formally evaluated, and researchers discovered that it had failed to produce any real change in how patients were treated. The SUPPORT study only added to fears that Americans continue to die, often alone and in pain, with little awareness of their needs on the part of healthcare workers, after being given aggressive treatments they have said they did not want—treatments their physicians knew from the outset would provide no benefit.

Unfortunately, many healthcare providers are not equipped to manage the ethical issues that arise with end-of-life decisions. In recent years, some medical and nursing schools have formally introduced the study of ethics and end-of-life decision making into their curricula, but the "doctor knows best" mentality continues to prevail. Doctors still tend to take charge and to make assumptions about the progression of steps in a patient's care without regard for the emotional needs of either patient or family. Typically, they are more comfortable with the role of aggressive decision maker than with that of patient confidant. The standard approach is "OK, we've tried this treatment and that one, here is the next thing we're going to do." Only recently have physicians begun to discuss with their terminal patients the realistic outcome of an intervention and to suggest that providing no curative treatment at all may be an appropriate option—or even to offer real choices rather than pronouncements. Physicians and other healthcare professionals have been reluctant to acknowledge that patients are dying, but ample research suggests that there is a subtle withdrawal of attention and care from those with incurable illness.

The Patient Self-Determination Act of 1990 was enacted to increase the involvement of patients in their own care and to encourage patient-doctor communication about end-of-life treatment decisions. But research and much anecdotal evidence suggest that the goals of this legislation have not been met. When physicians are asked about their patients' wishes for treatment in the final stages of fatal illness, few are able to answer accurately, yet patients believe their doctors *do* know what they want.[3]

Patients and family members share responsibility for the current climate. Many are anxious to surrender to a doctor's authority and to depend on him (or her) to make decisions in areas where he has little or no training and brings only his personal beliefs and prejudices to bear on a situation. I recently became involved in a case that was, in every way, appropriate for hospice referral. I felt strongly that the family would benefit from hospice services for a dying wife and mother, but the family physician advised against it. He told the family that caring for a dying person at home was a mistake, and that if she died there, the family would never feel comfortable in the house again. Even though this was clearly not a medical decision, the doctor's own predilections were persuasive, and I could not change the family's mind. The power of the professional caregiver—doctor or nurse—is well known but frequently ignored or denied.

Families facing death need the active and informed cooperation of healthcare professionals who are attuned to family process and the many variables that affect decision making. For example, as discussed in Chapter Seven, a family's ethnic background is a strong determinant of the degree to which it may look to professionals to make key decisions. A previous history of loss, unresolved emotional issues, or relational cutoffs are other factors that may affect the family's style of decision making. Anyone who works with families facing death—whether doctors, nurses, or other healthcare professionals—needs to be attuned to their unique patterns of communication and cautious about the degree to which they may naturally cede their autonomy to others.

It is quite common for patients who are asked to express preferences about end-of-life care to tell their doctors, "Do whatever you think is right" or "Do whatever you have to do." Although it is tempting for providers to take such comments as an invitation to assume control without further consultation, these ambiguous remarks cry out for more careful exploration. Ethical care calls not for a paternalistic approach but for a willingness on the part of providers to take on the burden of finding out what patients and their families really want.

The anxiety created by a generally ill-informed public debate on end-of-life issues has curious repercussions. For example, a sophisticated and experienced colleague of mine was describing to me the advanced illness of her aging father. A long-standing heart condition and diabetes were worsening, and according to the doctor, his failing kidneys meant he would need to begin renal dialysis in the very near future. My colleague described how sad it was to see her once-vibrant father dying.

"You know," she told me, "he really doesn't want to go on dialysis, but what can we do?"

I replied that, of course, he could say no to dialysis and be cared for at home by his family and a hospice program in the final stage of his life.

"I wish we could do that," she mused, "but isn't that illegal—for him to refuse dialysis? Isn't that euthanasia?"

When I pointed out that the choice to refuse treatment was not euthanasia, she was genuinely surprised. Moreover, her father's physician had given no indication that dialysis was a choice; rather, it was presented as the next inevitable step in his treatment. I strongly urged her to investigate the many options available to her and her family.

The Impact of Managed Care

The complications of end-of-life issues have been intensified by the sweeping changes introduced into healthcare delivery, particularly the growth of managed care. New systems for accessing and delivering care have created tension and uncertainty as healthcare professionals, hospitals, insurance companies, and patients struggle to redefine their roles and to renegotiate their relationships with one another. There is universal consensus that in this struggle, the patient's welfare has not been the top priority. Or, as one physician commented, "How can you *manage care* in a world of *managed finance?*"

One of the big concerns for terminally ill patients and their families is that changes in health insurance—which may occur when the individual who provides the family with coverage switches jobs or when an employer restructures staff benefits—will force them to sever their relationship with a trusted physician who is not affiliated with their new plan. This is a legitimate fear; patients may very likely be deprived of someone they know would respect their final wishes at the time of greatest need.

Family members also express anxiety about whether their loved ones will be offered aggressive treatment under managed care systems or will be pressured to refuse further care before termination is medically necessary or appropriate. The awareness that a disproportionate share of the healthcare budget is consumed by costs during the final months of life only heightens the pervading anxiety. One unfortunate aspect of these fears is the reluctance of some family members and patients to consider cessation of aggressive but medically futile treatment because they assume that such recommendations are cost-driven.

For example, the Greenes, an African American family, demanded to see the patient advocate in the hospital in which Betty, their sixty-eight-year-old mother, was being treated in the end stages of a three-year bout with gastric cancer. The three adult children believed that the oncologist treating their mother had decided to discontinue her expensive treatment and had suggested that she be discharged to the care of a community hospice program simply because her insurance company would refuse to pay for further aggressive medical intervention. They claimed that the decision was tantamount to a premature death sentence.

Such dilemmas are complicated by the reality that discontinuing treatment on the grounds that it is medically futile is a fundamentally subjective decision. What is *not* subjective, of course, is the cost of intensive long-term treatment with dubious medical outcomes. Thus conflicts are likely to arise among patients and their families, physicians, other healthcare providers, and insurance companies. Insurance companies legitimately claim that they need to contain costs. Physicians argue that they strive to make decisions free of cost-related influences and that patient interests prevail.

Regardless of their good intentions, however, the managed care system has not been designed primarily for patient welfare, and recent reports suggest that physicians who ignore cost issues may imperil their own livelihood. Some patients, particularly African Americans like the Greenes, see historical patterns of maltreatment and are convinced that cost-driven medical decision making will ultimately discriminate against certain segments of the population. For the Greenes, a family meeting was convened in which the physician, the patient advocate, and a medical social worker were able to allay concerns that their mother was being abandoned.

In a similar case, but with a different "twist," I was asked by a hospice social worker to convene a bioethics committee meeting to discuss the establishment of a policy for decertifying patients inappropriately maintained in hospice care by insurance companies. The precipitating case involved an elderly woman who had been misdiagnosed with a fatal disease and who had actually begun to thrive in the care of the hospice. The patient needed regular home care, but she was no longer an appropriate candidate for hospice, although her family had come to depend on the hospice team for devoted care and had formed a strong relationship with them.

On hearing that the mother was likely to be decertified by the hospice, this family complained to the insurance company representative, who suggested that the hospice maintain the patient on its roster. On the surface, this plan seemed to satisfy everyone, but there was concern that it established a care plan dictated by an insurance company rather than by the physician and the interdisciplinary team. Not surprisingly, the offer by the company had the added benefit of being less expensive than other choices. The bioethics committee suggested that a policy be instituted that patients appropriate for decertification would not receive further hospice services, regardless of an insurance carrier's preference. Ironically, while this question was being considered, the patient took a turn for the worse and died within a few weeks.

Both the cases I have described illustrate the concern that many have about the impact of managed care and the influence of cost-conscious insurance companies on end-of-life decision making. However, the whole structure is too new, and too much in flux, to permit an evaluation of the legitimacy of these fears. With providers responsible not only to their patients but to the managed care organizations that employ them, it is certainly not unreasonable to expect that economic pressures will have an impact on clinical practice. But it is worth remembering that financial incentives have always existed in American medicine. In the past, when most care was reimbursed on a per-use basis, there were surely temptations to provide unnecessary services. The challenge now is to find ways to keep patient interests at the forefront of decision making. Here, federal, state, and local legislators have important roles to play.

Along with challenges come opportunities, including the prospect of carefully negotiated contractual linkages between managed care organizations and hospice and palliative care services. Hospices are uniquely positioned to offer less medically intensive—and less costly—services, emphasizing palliative medicine and attending to the complex of emotional, spiritual, and social needs of the patient and family. Because hospice services are comprehensive and are provided in a range of settings, including homes, hospitals, clinics, and nursing care facilities, they often lower the barriers to coordinated care and ensure that services are offered by the most appropriate providers. It is also true that the hospice philosophy of "the family as the unit of care" lessens the risk of stress-related illnesses in other family members and ultimately reduces healthcare costs.

Many of us in the hospice movement emphasize that hospice practice adds a unique dimension to end-of-life care that needs to be distinguished even from palliative care. Whereas the latter focuses on patient comfort and on moderating or alleviating pain, hospice goes further, emphasizing the spiritual and psychosocial dimensions of caring for the patient *and* family. Our fear is that a profit-driven system will be reluctant to support these "soft" services unless they are demonstrated to have a measurable benefit and to be necessary to patient care.[4]

Those of us working with terminally ill patients should not necessarily despair about the new era in healthcare. Instead, we must work to see that legislation and voluntary guidelines are used to create a healthcare delivery system that is built around *both* the cost efficiencies of managed care and the ethical principles of modern medicine. Local, state, and federal regulatory bodies, legislators, institutional ethics committees, and the managed care organizations themselves must all be part of ensuring that today's delivery systems honor their obligations to the vulnerable individuals who are sick or dying. It is safe to say that ample challenges and risks lie ahead. (See Table 8.1 for guidelines that may be applied in crafting ethical decisions in a variety of settings.)

ADVANCE DIRECTIVES

Although the public-policy issues surrounding managed care will be debated for some time to come, tools have long been available to ensure that patients in the final stage of life have a voice in their own treatment. What troubles me is that they are not widely used. Two instruments, known as advance directives, are intended to be safeguards in the event that a patient loses the capacity to participate directly in decision-making processes related to care. A *living will* is a document that allows individuals to express their wishes regarding life-sustaining treatment in the event of incapacity. A *healthcare proxy* allows individuals to appoint someone else to make healthcare decisions on their behalf should they lose the capacity to do so themselves.

The Living Will

A living will provides reliable evidence of how a person feels about such issues as artificial nutrition and hydration, do-not-resuscitate

TABLE 8.1. Guidelines for Ethical Decision Making.

Principles	Questions to Be Asked
Autonomy	What are the patient's and family's wishes and values? Will treatment conflict with those values? Is the family promoting the patient's autonomy?
Beneficence	What is in the patient's best interests? Will a proposed treatment cause harm? Are benefits and burdens balanced to promote good? How are we defining "good"? What constitutes "moral duty," and how is that best promoted?
Justice	Will treatment utilize scarce health resources fairly? Is there a community consensus on fair resource allocation?
Professional integrity	What are providers' obligations to themselves and their profession? Will treatment allow professionals to act in support of those values?
Values	How do the philosophical, religious, and cultural values of the patient, the family, healthcare professionals, and the institution affect the application of bioethical principles?
The law	What impact does the law have on the understanding and application of bioethical principles?

Source: Adapted from guidelines developed at the Center for Bioethics of the Hospice of Northern Virginia in Arlington.

orders, and treatments that may extend life but will not improve it. It often eases the burdens on families facing difficult decisions, but it does not provide a guarantee that a patient's requests will be heeded. A report of The New York State Task Force on Life and the Law warns that living wills "cannot embody contemporaneous decisions . . . they do not represent an informed choice among alternatives in the immediate circumstances."[5] Partly for that reason, many hospitals and nursing homes may in some circumstances be reluctant to honor the wishes expressed in living wills.

The Masseys seriously considered bringing suit against a nursing home in which they had placed their eighty-nine-year-old matriarch, Eleanor. A few years earlier, Eleanor had signed a living will in which she indicated that she did not want to be fed artificially if she was no longer competent and refused food. However, she was becoming confused and incoherent, her physical condition was beginning to deteriorate, and her family arrived for a visit one day to discover that she was being nourished by intravenous fluids. They immediately protested to the nursing home director, who explained that it was their practice to help residents maintain good nutrition when they were experiencing difficulties eating on their own. When the family said that Eleanor had signed a living will and that it was in her medical file, the director replied that he was not aware of this and "would check into it."

A week or so later, family members returned to find that Eleanor was continuing on IV fluids. The nursing supervisor related a conversation she had had with the octogenarian in which Eleanor told her, "I don't want to starve to death." The nurse opined that she was sure her patient did not want to die. The family pressured the director to locate the living will. Eventually he did, but he pointed out that the document had been signed a long time ago, and he interpreted it to say that she did not want "forced feeding."

The family maintained a firm and unanimous position, even after each member had been asked individually why he or she "wished to see Eleanor die of starvation." Ultimately, only the threat of removing Eleanor from the institution and filing suit was adequate to bring the artificial hydration to an end.

The Healthcare Proxy

A greater confidence that one's choices will be respected can be achieved by establishing a healthcare proxy (also referred to as a durable power of attorney for healthcare decision making). In this instance, an agent is chosen whom one trusts to act as a surrogate in the event that one's mental capacity is lost. The appointed agent should be kept fully informed by the patient's physician and have access to all relevant medical information needed to make necessary choices. Obviously, a healthcare proxy presents a family with a profound challenge to deal openly with end-of-life issues, as it can be used effectively only if the appointed surrogate has full knowledge of what choices the patient would make if competent.

The issues raised by Robert Stevens's wish to appoint one of his children as his healthcare proxy were complicated and linked to many aspects of family history. Robert's most vivid memory, often described to his two children, was his mother's slow and agonizing death when he was a young boy. Stomach cancer had left her weak and in great pain, and she spent the last months of her life on the living room couch, cared for by her husband and sister. Robert remembered being awakened nightly by her screams and cries and her repeated and plaintive requests that someone help her die.

Now, at seventy, Robert, who took pride in his perfect health, has been diagnosed with a cancer likely to metastasize to his brain. Divorced for many years, Robert raised his son and daughter alone and has asked them to come and discuss his fatal illness. He wishes to appoint his son, Tom, as his healthcare proxy and makes clear that under no circumstances does he wish measures to be taken to prolong his life—or even to treat specific symptoms—if he becomes incompetent. As Robert explains his wishes, Tom, who married a deeply religious woman and regards himself as "born again," is adamant that every measure must be taken to ensure that his father does not die "until the Lord decides to take him."

Robert tries desperately to persuade his son that he has a moral obligation—"a Christian obligation"—to abide by his father's wishes, but he is unsuccessful. Robert then looks to his daughter, Judith, who agrees that her father should be allowed to die as he chooses but says she does not wish "to be the instrument" of his death. Robert is frustrated and angry, as well as frightened that he will not have the support he needs to "die with dignity."

Robert then calls on his minister, who is a member of a clergy consultation group with which I meet periodically, and asks if she will help him to enlist his children in supporting his final wishes. Beth, a dynamic young Methodist pastor, shares with the group that she feels intimidated by Robert, uncomfortable with Tom's judgmental approach, and protective of Judith. She also relates her own history, in which she lost both her parents to cancer during her adolescence and felt helpless during that time of her life. The group works sensitively and creatively with Beth and devises a plan that she feels comfortable proposing to the Stevens family.

Beth asks to meet with Robert, Tom, his wife, and Judith to explore ways of relieving Robert's anxiety about how he might die. As is often the case, Beth later reports that the family situation was not quite as Robert had described. She immediately sensed that Tom's reluctance was not solely a function of his religious beliefs but reflected a deeper hesitation to acquiesce in his father's demands. Judith, on the other hand, wished to support her father, but her previous experience with his capriciousness had taught her that she could disappoint him by inadvertently making a wrong decision.

Beth was able to guide Robert in the creation of a less threatening and more open atmosphere for discussion. She also succeeded in reframing the children's hesitation to assume the role requested of them as an expression of love and gratitude to their father, whom they wished to keep alive forever. She helped the three family members accept that Robert was going to die and that he was giving them an opportunity to offer him a great gift. Ultimately, it was Tom's wife, Chris, who became Beth's ally in the discussion and helped her to support Judith in accepting the role of surrogate for her father. Chris defined the role of healthcare proxy as a "payback" for all Robert had done for his children, and she was able to persuade Tom to promise that he would strongly support his sister. Once Judith agreed to assume the responsibility, the family was able to discuss Robert's specific wishes for treatment at the end of his life.

Unfortunately, many families never talk openly about advance directives, typically waiting until death is imminent before even considering the associated issues. The most common reason for the reluctance to sign advance directives is the belief that it means sacrificing autonomy. People have said to me that they are afraid of putting an awesome power over life and death in someone else's hands, that doing so would feel like giving away the last piece of themselves. I try to explain that the whole point of advance directives is just the opposite—that they increase the likelihood that patients will have a say in how they die. Other barriers that discourage patients from completing a living will, assigning a healthcare proxy, or even stating their wishes orally, are a family's inability to acknowledge the reality of death, long-standing impediments to communication, and unresolved interpersonal conflicts.

With professional guidance, families may be able to move past these obstructions, but unfortunately many healthcare providers are so uncomfortable with death and dying themselves that they make little effort to initiate the necessary conversations. Although legal mandates require hospitals to broach the subject of advance directives, the systems in place at most institutions do not foster candor—often, an admissions clerk or nurse's aide, who does not know the patient and has no special training, is the only individual to mention these options. The sad result is that the opportunity to learn and respect someone's final wishes is too often lost.

If the patient's feelings are unknown, the family and the patient's caregivers are left to either guess what might be right or make decisions based on their own needs. A hospice nurse told me the following story:

> Early in my career, I was involved in the case of Alma Bennett, a seventy-eight-year-old woman, suffering the aftereffects of a stroke; she had been bed-bound, mentally incompetent, and fed via a g-tube for a number of years. Her husband had introduced the feeding tube to better manage her care, had hired full-time help, and had managed to keep her condition stable, aside from a brief episode of pneumonia which was effectively treated by antibiotics. One evening, Mr. Bennett suffered a fatal heart attack and his son and daughter assumed the immediate care of their mother.
>
> Neither child lived nearby, both were uncomfortable with caring for their mother, and they questioned the validity of keeping the g-tube, given that their father had placed it in order to continue to care for her himself. This was before people talked much about advance directives, and no one knew Alma's wishes. The children consulted with the family doctor, and they agreed to cease the artificial feedings. The hospice program supported the decision and continued nursing visits to monitor the patient's dying and support the family. The patient died about ten days later.
>
> I had real difficulty with the decisions made by the children and the doctor. The patient was stable and could have lived for some time, providing the feedings were maintained. And even though her quality of life was debatable and her cognitive status low, I think there may have been moments of awareness. Her children hovered around her as she lay dying, talking to her fondly and fluffing her pillows and rearranging the stuffed

animals, as if this made a difference. I confronted the doctor and asked him how he could morally justify removing the g-tube. His reply has stayed with me ever since: "You can do whatever you want at home." Does that mean that any decision is acceptable as long as you're home and the doctor supports it?[6]

Encouraging physicians to make a greater effort to talk—and especially to listen—to their dying patients and to families needs to be a priority of our healthcare system. Questions such as "How do you understand your illness?" and "What do you think is happening to you?" help clarify the extent to which a patient has accepted the reality of approaching death. It is also very important that providers understand the hopes and fears engendered by illness so that they can respond appropriately. A patient who is terrified of dying in pain needs to understand that medication will provide relief but may also result in a partial loss of consciousness or may hasten death. Someone who most fears dying alone in an intensive care unit may be receptive to an offer of in-home hospice services. Patients who want no stone left unturned will need assurance that their advance directives will prevent a doctor from abandoning them prematurely. Only by soliciting a patient's feelings and understanding the family context within which the patient operates can a doctor present an appropriate spectrum of options—options that ensure that a patient's worst nightmares will never come true. Until such practice becomes standard, we will be left with a system that tempts all parties to pursue one fruitless treatment after another, rather than one in which a patient's wishes are determined and respected.

WITHDRAWAL OF ARTIFICIAL NUTRITION AND HYDRATION

One of the most valuable developments in medical care has been the ability to provide nutrition and hydration to patients whose capacity to eat and drink has been compromised by a medical event. Hardly a modern invention, artificial feeding has been, for many years, a common method for preserving a patient's viability while the process of healing takes place. It is generally simple, low-tech, inexpensive, and easily managed. But the use of artificial nutrition and hydration becomes much more problematic in the face of physical deterioration or fatal disease. Its continued use to keep patients alive when there is little or no likelihood that the underlying disease will remit has created a host of ethical, moral, and legal questions that plague patients, families, and their caregivers.

A number of organizations have developed medical and ethical guidelines for the withdrawal of artificial nutrition and hydration. These include the American Medical Association, the President's Commission for the Study of Ethical Problems in Medicine and Biomedical and Behavioral Research, and the Hastings Center.[7] A consistent thread among these guidelines is that the use of feeding tubes to provide nourishment constitutes medical treatment that may ethically be foregone under certain clinical circumstances. Court decisions have generally supported this finding, allowing both competent patients and the surrogates of incompetent patients to request that artificial nutrition and hydration be withheld or withdrawn.

However, for families facing the decision about whether to discontinue artificial feeding, the subject is often weighted with intense and conflicting pressures, ambivalence, and guilt. Whatever their feelings about the use of other extraordinary life-preserving measures and do-not-resuscitate orders, the perception that they are "starving" a beloved relative to death is not easily set aside. The distinction that is appropriately made between basic care—such as hygiene and patient-turning to avoid bedsores—and aggressive intervention tends to lose its sharpness when artificial nutrition is considered. The preoccupation of families and patients with eating is a striking aspect of palliative care. The dogged belief that if only Dad would eat, he would regain his strength and recover is echoed time and again. That failure to swallow, loss of appetite, and a general disinterest in food are aspects of the dying process is a difficult concept to convey to families.

My impression is that families who may be willing to accept the idea of no longer treating a relative who is dying of an incurable condition feel quite differently about making a decision they perceive as deliberately hastening death. They may not appreciate that feeding by artificial means is generally a response to the advancing deterioration of the body, when the patient can no longer survive without medical technology. An inability to acknowledge this may mean that the family is still struggling to accept the fact that the loved one is dying.

The issue of artificial nutrition is also sensitive because food and love are tightly interlocked, not only in contemporary American society but across cultures and throughout human history. Sharing a meal is often weighted with meaning—it is a way to celebrate and to preserve tradition, a means of providing comfort, even an emblem of shared humanity. Recall the Palumbo family in the previous chapter. Frances Palumbo, a patient stricken with ALS, was being fed by artificial means and had been unable to eat for some time. Yet she continued to give directions to her sister-in-law—on the making of spaghetti sauce—by blinking her eyes! Especially when so little can be done, nourishing someone who is gravely ill is seen by family members as an act of emotional nurturance and an expression of love. Withholding that cherished symbol of caring may feel like the ultimate negligence. Intensifying the emotional struggle is the fact that removing a feeding tube does not result in immediate death; family members then face the prospect of watching their loved one weaken progressively over a course of days.

Often, despite a patient's expressed wishes, family members have difficulty complying with the request not to use artificial feeding to sustain life. This was initially the case with the Costellas, but Ann-Marie remained conscious long enough to demand that her directive be honored. A case was brought to our hospice bioethics committee that raised this issue in a poignant way. Marvin Turner, a seventy-eight-year-old patient with metastasized lung cancer and advanced Alzheimer's disease, had been semicomatose and incompetent for a number of months. He was being cared for by Adele, his fifty-nine-year-old daughter, who had never left home and had run the household since her mother's death years before. For some reason, never clarified, a feeding tube had been inserted after an emergency hospital visit, before the patient was admitted to hospice. Months after his admission, it was discovered that the patient had expressed a clear wish two years previously not to be fed by artificial means. When the hospice social worker asked about this, Adele stridently replied that she knew about his request but had no intention of starving her father to death.

This case raised some very difficult issues for the ethics committee. It was clear that the g-tube had been introduced against the patient's expressed, but unknown, intent. Further, his daughter, aware of the request, had withheld the information deliberately. As the primary caregiver and the patient's only relative, she exercised her right to refuse to have the tube removed. Hospice team members were appalled that Mr. Turner was being kept alive against his specific wishes and asked for direction from the ethics committee. After a lengthy deliberation, the committee suggested that even though the tube was a clear violation of the patient's wishes, his incompetence and imminent death, as well as his daughter's insistence, made it difficult to consider removing the tube. Mercifully, Mr. Turner died shortly afterward.

Professional Ambivalence

Despite the consensus contained within formal guidelines and legal opinion, artificial nutrition tends to be distinguished from other medical procedures not only in the minds of a patient's family but among some health providers as well. Withdrawing nutrition may clash with a physician's self-image as a healer and may even be perceived as abandoning the patient. Aggressive intervention—based on a belief that any available treatment is better than none at all—

is often the only approach to caring that many doctors know. Many also believe that it is the safest one in a litigious era, and the fear of liability certainly plays a role in the reluctance to forgo or suspend artificial nutrition.

I have also known nurses and other healthcare providers who are uncomfortable caring for individuals who have refused tube feeding. Their discomfort may arise from the emotional attachment that sometimes develops with patients or from personal ethical or cultural beliefs. The latter can cause particular difficulty in institutional settings, such as nursing homes, where primary care is provided by personnel who are generally on the lower rungs of the socioeconomic ladder. These aides and primary care providers may come from ethnic groups that differ from those of their patients and families, of the personnel who supervise them, and of those who are responsible for medical decision making. When withdrawing artificial means of maintaining viability is viewed as completely appropriate by families and senior staff but tantamount to murder by the immediate caregivers, covert conflict, or even open warfare, may result. A friend described to me an incident in which he was berated unmercifully by a nursing home aide caring for his father when he observed her at meal times and asked whether she was being too aggressive about feeding, as his father did not seem to want to eat.

A Trend Against Artificial Nutrition

We cannot ignore the fact that inexpensive, low-tech nutritional support allows a comatose patient to live for years in a vegetative state, often against the wishes of both patient and family. A number of recent court cases in which families have prevailed against nursing homes that introduced tube feedings reflect a growing reluctance to submit passively to this long-standing practice. Family members can be helped to understand recent research findings that suggest terminally ill people do not suffer if they are not given food and water, and that patients can choose to allow dehydration to play a natural role in their death. Most patients, in fact, desire very little nourishment in the final months of their lives, and in some instances, may experience greater pain, swelling, nausea, or respiratory congestion if they are fed artificially. By contrast, the natural progression of disease—diminished pain, sleepiness and loss of consciousness, the gradual and peaceful "slipping away" craved by many individuals who are dying—often accompany dehydration. Some patients actually report a sense of euphoria. Studies suggest that complaints of hunger or thirst are generally transient and can be effectively relieved with simple, attentive mouth care, including cleaning or swabbing the mouth, moistening the lips and tongue with ice chips, or giving hard candy to patients able to suck on it. Though it relieves discomfort, this level of fluid intake is not sufficient to interfere with the dehydration process.

In one article that received widespread attention after it was published in the *Journal of the American Medical Association* and reprinted in the *New York Times* and elsewhere, David Eddy, a physician, described his personal experience with the terminal illness of his eighty-five-year-old mother.[8] When she asked how a decision to stop eating and drinking would affect her condition, Eddy assured his mother that it would hasten her death. With compelling resolve, she celebrated her eighty-fifth birthday by making that decision, and six days later she was dead. Of her final days, Eddy writes:

> Over the next four days, my mother greeted her visitors with the first smiles she had shown for months. She energetically reminisced about the great times she had had and about things she was proud of. . . . She also found a calming self-acceptance in describing things of which she was not proud. She slept between visits but woke up brightly whenever we touched her to share more memories and say a few more things she wanted us to know. On the fifth day, it was more difficult to wake her. When we would take her hand, she would open her eyes and smile, but she was too drowsy and weak to talk very

much. On the sixth day, we could not wake her. Her face was relaxed in her natural smile, she was breathing unevenly, but peacefully. We held her hands for another two hours, until she died.

As patients and family members struggle with the decision about whether to forgo artificial nutrition and hydration, healthcare providers should recognize the need to offer support and to communicate with tact and sensitivity. If family opinion is divided on the issue, or if other family tensions are unresolved, discussions may become heated. In any case, the family is likely to be experiencing complex and contradictory emotions. Introducing the distinction between eating and drinking as a social experience and the use of artificial, technological medical treatment to provide sustenance, which is inevitably depersonalized, may help to relieve subconscious feelings of guilt or ambivalence.

Ultimately, the extent to which a family has truly accepted that one of its members is dying often has a significant impact on decision making. The perspective with which a family approaches illness when recovery is likely, or at least considered a possibility, differs markedly from the approach taken when death is recognized as inevitable. With the ability to acknowledge a loved one's identity as a dying person—obviously a seismic shift from the individual's previous identity within the family—comes an acceptance that artificial intervention may no longer be appropriate.

PHYSICIAN-ASSISTED SUICIDE

Little has highlighted the issue of physician involvement in decision making more than the furor surrounding physician-assisted suicide. Few ethical issues stir such intense passions. In a June 1997 decision, the Supreme Court declared that there is no constitutional entitlement to assisted suicide: ". . . the asserted 'right' to assistance in committing suicide is not a fundamental liberty interest protected by the due-process clause," wrote Chief Justice William Rehnquist on behalf of the Court.

This hardly ends the debate. The issue of physician-assisted suicide will no doubt continue to be feverishly discussed in public and in hospital rooms, nursing homes, and the homes of families facing death. For doctors and other healthcare providers, the debate does more than simply raise the question of whether they are willing to participate in a patient's action to end life. It goes to the very core of what it means to be a healer and caregiver. I experienced this most powerfully when I was treating James and Celia Thornton in couples therapy. I had known them both through several professional circles. James, a psychiatrist, had been diagnosed with throat cancer, and he and his wife, a psychologist, had sought my help in managing the eight adult children in their blended family. James's illness had upset the family balance, although focusing on the children allowed them to deflect attention from James's worsening condition.

After a few sessions, I expressed my discomfort at the fact that, though James looked weaker each time I saw him, he and Celia were avoiding discussion of his illness in our sessions, focusing instead on the children. They conceded that they had been reluctant to talk to me about a very difficult issue with which they were presently grappling. A few weeks earlier, they had met with James's personal physician, a long-time friend, and asked if he would help them end James's life. His initial reaction had been anger; subsequently, he told them that he had never before been asked to involve himself in a suicide plan and had never given much thought to how to go about it. James and Celia had the answer to this, having consulted Derek Humphry's *Final Exit*, the "how-to" book on suicide. They were asking their friend to provide the appropriate medications and to be present; he was reluctant to agree and asked to think about it.

Time passed, and James's condition worsened. Barely ambulatory and no longer able to speak, he now communicated by writing feverishly in a notebook. I was visiting with the couple at home, and our sessions focused almost entirely on the planned suicide. When I asked James if it was the pain that lay at the root of his desire to die, he wrote: "Not the pain, the agony."

I was scheduled to go on vacation, and I called the Thorntons when I returned. Celia told me things were very hectic and said she would get back to me. I subsequently left a few messages, but my calls were not returned. About a month later, Celia called to inform me that James had died; she came to see me and related the story of her husband's final weeks. James had grown impatient with his physician friend and decided to take matters into his own hands. He wrote a number of prescriptions for cumulatively lethal dosages of analgesics and barbiturates and had Celia fill them at distant pharmacies. Then, on the Saturday evening before Easter, Celia mixed the medications and helped James to ingest the lethal brew.

She lay down beside him and listened to his breathing as he fell into a deep sleep. She, too, fell asleep, but stirred a few times during the night, checking his heartbeat on each occasion. When she could no longer detect one, she assumed he was dead. Early the next morning, she awakened and lay quietly next to James, thinking to herself that this was the last time she would ever be close to him. When she felt him stir, she was sure it was her imagination and chastised herself for being foolish, but after a few more minutes, she became aware that James was, in fact, alive. He looked peaceful and rested, a big smile on his face. Her first, irrational thought, she said, was that it was Easter morning, James was alive, and he was sure to conclude he was now Jesus Christ!

James became convinced that he could not end his life by himself and, by the end of that day, had become quite despondent. Celia called their friend, and when he came to visit, they spoke again about helping James to die. He finally agreed and eventually assisted Celia in administering enough intravenous narcotics to end James's life. Celia reported that she felt relieved and content that she had helped James die "the way he had chosen." As far as she knew, their physician friend was comfortable with having participated.

Mercy or Sacrilege?

Those who defend the practice of physician-assisted suicide say that it can be an act of mercy for patients who otherwise face an irreversible loss of bodily or mental function, as well as intractable pain. In a society that touts individual freedom as one of its highest values, a patient's insistence on "the right to die" may be rooted in a determined attempt to maintain control, as it was for James Thornton. Sometimes, it also reflects the fear of a painful or humiliating death, the desire not to burden family members, or a determination to escape emotional or spiritual suffering. In James's case, the motivation came from both the physical and the emotional agony of his suffering. Seldom does pain alone prompt a desire to end one's life. In fact, studies suggest that people in severe pain are less likely to consider euthanasia.

Whatever the reason, the beliefs that individuals have the moral right to decide when their lives are no longer worth living and that healthcare providers are acting responsibly when they provide the means to act on that decision, have gained a degree of public support.[9] Further, there is a growing belief among healthcare professionals that the principle of nonabandonment—committing oneself to the patient and family through the end of life, whatever the circumstances—cannot be ignored.[10]

Opponents of assisted suicide believe the practice is a violation of a doctor's sacred duty to preserve life, a desecration of the Hippocratic oath that can never be justified. A body of time-honored religious, legal, and medical codes supports that perspective. Some fear that sanctioning the right to help patients die will inevitably foster abuse and quickly spiral out of control. They ask: Who will draw the line on how elderly or disabled a patient has to be before assisted suicide is considered appropriate? Should inconvenience to the family or fears of financial ruin be factors in the decision? What role are insurance companies, concerned with the costs of end-of-life care, going to play? What message does a society that sanctions assisted suicide send about the worth of its weakest members? (This last point has also arisen in the discussion of whether extraordinary measures to maintain the life of profoundly damaged, preterm infants are justifiable.) The National Hospice Organization, representing the nation's nearly three thousand hospice programs, has gone on record as opposing the practice, affirming that it supports patient autonomy, but that "hospice care is a better choice than voluntary euthanasia and assisted suicide."[11]

Despite a handful of highly publicized cases, assisted suicide as a planned method of ending life has certainly not become commonplace. Although it is increasingly the norm to allow patients to die without intervention when additional treatment is deemed futile—a practice often referred to as "managed death"—accurate data on how often physicians or other healthcare professionals actively help patients end their lives, and under what circumstances, have been extremely difficult to collect. In the privacy of his or her own office, almost every medical professional who works with terminally ill people has been approached by someone desperate enough to ask for an end to suffering. A 1996 study found that almost one-quarter of the doctors who were asked to participate in helping to end a patient's life had prescribed the lethal doses of medication to accomplish it.[12] But such actions have, until quite recently, taken place entirely behind closed doors.

There are also data showing that nurses in intensive care units sometimes engage in the practice. A survey published in the *New England Journal of Medicine* found that of 852 nurses who worked exclusively in adult intensive care units, 16 percent reported helping a patient end his or her life; an additional 4 percent had not provided life-sustaining treatment ordered by a physician, though pretending that they had. Although some critics believe the survey was ambiguously worded, the results clearly highlight another unexamined dimension of assisted suicide.[13]

The nature of the patient-doctor relationship typically influences both a patient's willingness to raise the subject and the doctor's willingness to consider it. Many physicians say they would never assist in a suicide unless they had a long-standing relationship with a patient and complete confidence in the soundness of that person's judgment. However, as the Thorntons discovered, a relationship with the physician is not always sufficient to secure help. In some cases, families are reluctant to speak with a healthcare professional for fear of being dissuaded or reported to authorities.

For example, Luke and Chris, both in their mid-forties, would not have come to see me if Chris's sister, Delia, a colleague of mine, had not insisted. Chris's condition was worsening: he was beset with frequent bouts of pneumocystis pneumonia, Kaposi's sarcoma, and an itchy rash that appeared and disappeared without warning. Diagnosed with HIV infection in 1985, he had been relatively healthy for nine years. Although he had been dealing with a variety of AIDS-related illnesses for the previous three or four years, his disease had become resistant to any treatment only within the past nine months. Luke, his partner of ten years, was healthy but refused to be tested for the virus. The men described themselves as devoted to each other, and Chris said no one could be a better caregiver than Luke. They had recently decided that if Chris's worsening symptoms did not abate within the next few weeks, he would commit suicide.

Together, they had formulated a plan and had accumulated enough medications to ensure its success; they revealed the plan to only a few intimates, for fear that someone might prevent them from going through with it. Delia was quite upset by her brother's decision to take his life, and also feared that Luke might be prosecuted after Chris died. Although we spent a number of hours discussing the plan and Chris seemed adamant, he died from the natural course of the disease about four months after I last saw him. Delia reported that neither of the two men was able to decide on "just the right time." But she also indicated that the couple found solace and a sense of control simply in having made the plan.

It is noteworthy that there seem to be few accounts of terminally ill people of color pursuing assisted suicide, reflecting, at least in part, a historical mistrust of the medical system. The Greenes, described earlier in this chapter, illustrate the stance of many African Americans. They were skeptical of the decision to end active treatment of their mother and would probably have viewed assisted suicide as motivated by factors unrelated to her best interests. The medical undertreatment and maltreatment of poor and minority citizens have not encouraged faith in the good intentions of the system. The establishment of a legal and ethical framework in which to consider assisted suicide has lagged behind actual practice.

The Supreme Court's decision that there is no inherent constitutional "right to die" ensures that the debate will continue. Legislatures in many states have considered legalizing the practice of assisted suicide or creating some other form of legal latitude for persons who wish to be helped to die, but no explicit laws have been enacted. Oregon voters narrowly approved a ballot initiative allowing physicians to prescribe drugs in lethal doses, but that has been challenged in court and a second referendum is scheduled.[14] At the institutional level, no guidelines have been developed for considering the merits of a doctor's request to help a patient commit suicide, nor are there any universally accepted medical or psychological criteria to help determine who is an appropriate candidate. Indeed, most doctors hesitate even to engage in informal dialogue with their peers, lest they become the focus of media attention or professional recriminations.

A framework is badly needed to guide patients, families, and healthcare professionals through the maze of conflicting moral, ethical, and legal issues. Should the practice of assisted suicide be legalized, a consideration of guidelines and safeguards for patients and their families ought to be a priority for healthcare policymakers. One important question to be addressed is whether assisted suicide need necessarily mean *physician*-assisted suicide, and how much direct involvement physicians would have in the process. In addition, formal standards might require that a patient be incurably ill, although that would certainly pose a dilemma for those patients and families seeking to bring life to an end because of chronic, debilitating, or paralyzing conditions. There is also disagreement as to whether the presence of unrelenting and untreatable physical pain should be a precondition.

There seems to be a consensus that the request for assisted suicide must be made voluntarily by someone with full mental capacities, and that it must be made repeatedly. Other requirements might include counseling to ensure that the patient is not suffering from treatable depression; family participation in the decision; and some sort of institutional review. As the long-hidden practice of aid in dying comes into fuller view, it may become possible to talk frankly about the most appropriate ways to ensure a swift and painless death. Without a doubt, these decisions will be made within the context of the family. An awareness of the family environment will therefore always be a prerequisite of quality care.

The Hospice Option

Although assisted suicide certainly demands more candid discussion, my own feeling is that both opponents and supporters tend to oversimplify the issue and ignore the realities most families face. Whatever their stated beliefs, few people actually choose to end their own lives prematurely, no matter how grave the illness. And it is a rare individual who is willing to play an active role in helping a loved one to commit suicide.

For all of the recent attention to physician-assisted suicide, other problems remain unaddressed: families still fail to talk openly with one another about end-of-life decisions; an inordinate proportion of healthcare dollars is squandered to support the final, irreversible stages of life; and many healthcare providers still insistently use technology to preserve life without considering the wisdom or appropriateness of its use. In short, our continued dependence on a narrowly defined medical model of care that emphasizes aggressive treatment and cure above all other considerations has meant that we have yet to integrate a viable concept of "the dying person" into our thinking. Only when we accept the inevitability of death—and make it a part of the definition of meaning in our lives—can we begin to struggle thoughtfully with these questions.

Despite the view held strongly by many in the hospice field that all symptoms can be managed, a small percentage of patients at the end of life will suffer physical, and even psychological, pain that no palliation—save terminal sedation—will relieve. In such instances, some patients and their families will refuse the artificial induction of a comatose condition and will prefer to pursue assistance in hastening death—a choice long opposed by hospice professionals. What has become firmly established, however, is a commitment not to abandon those patients who have determined to bring an end to their lives. Although it would be unlikely for a hospice nurse or other caregiver to help a patient hasten death, hospice staff would not be inclined to actively prevent such action. Further, hospice is a setting in which open communication with families at the deepest level will reveal whether an expressed desire for aid in dying is instead a plea for something else—such as pain relief or attention to other emotional or spiritual needs.

Eventually, we will all face the death of someone we love, and our own death as well. As those times near, our choices ought not to be limited to a protracted, painful death *or* assisted suicide. The hospice option, with its emphasis on physical, spiritual, and emotional care and a dignified death, usually at home and in the company of one's family, is the appropriate choice for many people with a terminal illness. Unfortunately, hospice care is underutilized and, as discussed before, even those who eventually seek services from hospice professionals often do so too late to reap their full benefits. Hospice workers frequently observe that patients are referred for hospice care late in the dying process. Although hospice care is predicated on a prognosis of a six-month life expectancy or less, many families do not avail themselves of hospice services at all, and others wait until the last few weeks, or even days, of a patient's life. A recent study revealed that the median survival rate on hospice was only thirty-six days, with 15 percent of patients dying within the first week on a program.

Certainly, an earlier hospice referral would provide better-quality care for patients and their families, and it would reduce the costs of end-of-life care appreciably. I was recently looking through a folder of "family satisfaction questionnaires" returned to a hospice program by family members shortly after their relatives had died. Three comments are typical of what families often say: "I wish we'd known about hospice earlier." "The nurses were great. It's so sad Mom couldn't have benefited earlier." "We were wrong to think hospice would mean we gave up hope. In fact it was the best care he had and it should have started months before."

Yet in a December 1996 poll, the American Medical Association found that more than one-third of those questioned were not even familiar with the terms *hospice* and *palliative care*. We desperately need to do a better job of educating terminally ill patients, their families, and their medical providers about their options. And we need to make sure that assisted suicide is just one element in a much broader conversation about pain management, symptom control, emotional support, and the appropriate use of aggressive intervention. Unless we do, the courts and the legislatures are likely to make our most difficult and personal end-of-life decisions for us.

Notes

1. Since the publication of the first edition of *Families Facing Death*, I have expanded my keen interest in the spiritual dimensions of life-threatening illness and the family. Among the most powerful writers to influence my thinking has been Stephen Levine. His compelling book *Who Dies? An Investigation of Conscious Living and Conscious Dying* (New York: Anchor Books, 1982) eloquently presents the notion that *how* we choose to live with a terminal diagnosis is infi-

nitely more important than whether we survive one. Another valuable and practical source of information on spirituality is the *Values and Visions Circles Newsletter* (available from P.O. Box 786, Madison Square Garden, New York, NY 10159), which reviews available media sources of ceremonies and rituals.

2. "A Controlled Trial to Improve Care for Seriously Ill Hospitalized Patients. The Study to Understand Prognoses and Preferences for Outcomes and Risks of Treatments (SUPPORT)," *Journal of the American Medical Association*, 1995, *274*, 1591–1598.

3. In one study of this issue, doctors most frequently reported that they did not know their patients' wishes because "it never came up." R. M. Kaplan, L. J. Schneiderman, and J. Virmani, "Relationship of Advance Directives to Physician-Patient Communication," *Archives of Internal Medicine*, 1994, *154*, 909–913.

4. Ira Byock's book, *Dying Well*, mentioned in Chapter Six, addresses this issue straightforwardly by emphasizing the many ways in which patients and their families were helped in the final stages of life by care that went far beyond what is standard "palliation." Timothy Quill, *Midwife Through the Dying Process* (Baltimore: Johns Hopkins University Press, 1996), presents another perspective on palliation that emphasizes the physician's responsibility for care through the end of life, even when it might result in helping patients to end life.

5. New York State Task Force on Life and the Law, *Excerpts from "Life-Sustaining Treatment: Making Decisions and Appointing a Health Care Agent"* (New York: New York State Task Force on Life and the Law, 1987), p. 75. Available from the publisher at 33 West 34th Street, New York, NY 10001.

6. I am grateful to Karen McInerney, C.R.N.H., for this anecdote.

7. The guidelines of the American Medical Association were developed by the Council on Ethical and Judicial Affairs and can be found in "Decisions Near the End of Life," *Journal of the American Medical Association*, 1992, *267*, 2229–2233. The recommendations of the President's Commission for the Study of Ethical Problems in Medicine and Biomedical and Behavioral Research are available in *Decisions to Forgo Life-Sustaining Treatment* (Washington, D.C.: U.S.

Government Printing Office, 1983). The Hastings Center guidelines are in *Guidelines on the Termination of Life-Sustaining Treatment and the Care of the Dying* (Bloomington: Indiana University Press, 1987).

8. David Eddy, "A Conversation with My Mother," *Journal of the American Medical Association*, 1994, *272*, 179–181.

9. There are frequent public opinion polls in which Americans are questioned about their views of physician-assisted suicide. By substantial margins, respondents agree that it should be legal. Interestingly, in almost every poll, when respondents are asked if they themselves would avail themselves of the opportunity, the majority indicate that they would not. Gallup/*USA Today*, Jan. 5, 1997, p. B1; K. Bowman, *American Enterprise*, Jan.-Feb. 1997, p. 91; *Glamour*, May 1997, p. 199; *Washington Post*, July 27, 1996, p. 8.

10. See T. E. Quill and R. V. Brody, "'You Promised Me I Wouldn't Die Like This': A Bad Death as a Medical Emergency," *Archives of Internal Medicine*, 1995, *155*, 1250–1254.

11. National Hospice Organization, *Resolution on Assisted Suicide*, Nov. 1996.

12. For more information, see A. L. Back, J. C. Masdau, J. I. Wallace, H. E. Starks, and R. A. Pearlman, "Physician-Assisted Suicide and Euthanasia in Washington State: Patient Requests and Physician Responses," *Journal of the American Medical Association*, 1996, *275*, 919–925.

13. David Asch, "The Role of Critical Care Nurses in Euthanasia and Assisted Suicide," *New England Journal of Medicine*, 1996, *334*, 1374–1379.

14. As this book went to press, Oregon voters reaffirmed their original vote establishing a patient's right to assisted suicide. Whether this is the beginning of a trend remains to be seen.

Appendix A:
Annotated Filmography

The choice of films for use with families facing death or for the training of personnel is clearly subjective. Over the years, both families and students have suggested to me films that they have found personally helpful, and in many cases I have incorporated them into my work. This list includes not only motion pictures that deal directly with the subject of death but also films that touch on relationships in ways that can be useful to families in times of crisis.

Separate sections list films dealing with the subject of AIDS and films I have found helpful in the training of professionals and volunteers. Seven movies that are suitable for both families and trainees are included in the main list and marked with an asterisk (*).

Bang the Drum Slowly (1973)   A beautiful portrayal of friendship between two baseball players, one of whom is dying of Hodgkin's disease. The dying man is neither heroic nor particularly courageous; he is a bit dull and commonplace, and this makes the film work. Stars Robert De Niro, Michael Moriarty. Directed by John Hancock.

Brian's Song (1970)   This popular movie deals with the death of Brian Piccolo, a professional football player, and his devoted friend and teammate, Gayle Sayers. I find it excessively melodramatic, but many people have told me that it is inspirational. Stars James Caan, Billy Dee Williams. Directed by Buzz Kulik.

Cries and Whispers (1972)   This haunting and intense movie about a dying woman, her sisters, and her servant raises many of the issues that families facing death must struggle with, particularly the difficulty of forgiveness and reconciliation. As with many films that look at illness and death without euphemism, this one may not be appropriate for certain families. Stars Liv Ullman, Ingrid Thulin. Directed by Ingmar Bergman. (Swedish, with English subtitles.)

The Dead (1987)   In this James Joyce story, three women host a party during which the guests talk about their friends who have died. This film is particularly useful for Irish families, since the setting and the language reflect those of this ethnic group. Stars Anjelica Huston, Donal McCann. Directed by John Huston.

Dim Sum (1984)   This is a wonderful story about a Chinese-American family struggling with tensions between generations. The troubled mother-daughter relationship makes the film especially useful. Stars Laureen Chew, Kim Chew. Directed by Wayne Wang.

Duet for One (1986)   The impact of a chronic illness—multiple sclerosis—on a career and marriage is interestingly portrayed. The film is a bit melodramatic, but nevertheless affecting. Stars Julie Andrews, Alan Bates. Directed by Andrei Konchalovsky.

Eric (1975)   In this made-for-TV movie, a young man becomes terminally ill. The film deals with the relationship between him and his mother and his refusal to give up. Stars Mark Hamill, Patricia Neal. Directed by James Goldstone.

Family Upside Down (1978)   This is not a story about death, but about aging. An elderly couple, previously self-sufficient, become dependent on their children. The multigenerational tension is honest and surprisingly accurate in this made-for-TV movie. Stars Fred Astaire, Helen Hayes. Directed by Lowell Rich.

*The Great Santini** (1979)   This is one of the classic father-son movies. The final scenes of the father's death and the family's stoic mien are among the best. The film is adapted from Pat Conroy's novel of the same name, and I frequently recommend that book as well. Stars Robert Duvall, Blythe Danner, Michael O'Keefe. Directed by Lewis John Carlino.

*I Heard the Owl Call My Name** (1973)   Although this well-known film does not deal with family (the main character is a young priest who is sent to the wilderness to find meaning in life before he dies), it does address some important issues of life and death, and it is aesthetically moving. Stars Tom Courtenay, Dean Jagger. Directed by Daryl Duke.

*I Never Sang for My Father** (1971)   I have discussed this film at length in this book. In my mind, few better films have ever been made about troubled family relationships. Stars Melvyn Douglas, Gene Hackman. Directed by Gilbert Cates.

Ikiru (1952)   The word *ikiru* in Japanese means "to live." This little-known film looks at how spiritual death often precedes physical death. It is a beautiful testimony to the search for meaning in life by a man with terminal cancer. The film delivers an unflinching condemnation of his family for its unwillingness to understand his pain and fear. Stars Takashi Shimura, Nobuo Kaneko. Directed by Akira Kurosawa. (Japanese, with English subtitles.)

*Marvin's Room** (1996)   A moving depiction of a fragmented family that must find ways to deal with chronic, long-term illness as well as newly diagnosed terminal illness. This film raises painful issues of how families struggle with fear and insecurity about caring for each other. Stars Meryl Streep, Leonardo Di Caprio, Diane Keaton. Directed by Jerry Zaks.

My Life (1993)   This is certainly not a cinematic classic, but it is a fairly good description of how parents who have a fatal illness can do the kind of life review and leave the kind of legacy that can help their children in the future. Stars Michael Keaton, Nicole Kidman. Directed by Bruce Joel Rubin.

Nothing in Common (1986)   This is another film that addresses the conflict between father and son, but it does so in a funny, deeply felt, and surprising way. Families are not likely to feel threatened by it. Stars Tom Hanks, Jackie Gleason. Directed by Garry Marshall.

*On Golden Pond** (1981)   This popular, Academy Award–winning film is warm and humorous and will probably survive as a classic. It focuses on the relationship between father and daughter but also provides a wonderful glimpse of more general family dynamics. Stars Katharine Hepburn, Henry Fonda, Jane Fonda. Directed by Mark Rydell.

Right of Way (1984)   This is a very disturbing and provocative film about an elderly couple's decision to join in a suicide pact. Their conflict with their adult daughter over this decision raises important issues for all families. Stars Bette Davis, James Stewart. Directed by George Schaefer.

*Three Brothers** (1981)   A mother has died, and her family must deal with its loneliness and loss. This film is exceptionally real in its portrayal of the pain of grief and the family dynamics of mourning. No one who works with families facing death should fail to see it. Stars Vittorio Mezzogiorno, Philippe Noiret, Michele Placido. Directed by Francesco Rosi, Charles Varrel.

*Time Flies When You're Alive** (1991)   This extraordinary one-man show by actor Paul Linke chronicles his wife's dying of cancer and its impact on the family. Not only can this be helpful to families who are grieving but it is a "must-see" for anyone who works with families facing death. Directed by Roger Spottiswoode.

Tribute (1980)   This portrayal of father-son conflict is certainly not the best of the genre, but it does have its moments. The father's impending death spurs a reconciliation. Stars Jack Lemmon, Robby Benson. Directed by Bob Clark.

A *Trip to Bountiful* (1985)   An elderly woman goes in search of her childhood home, which no longer exists. This film is a wonderful affirmation of life and the importance of life review. Stars Geraldine Page, John Heard. Directed by Peter Masterson.

Unstrung Heroes (1995)   This quirky film introduces a quintessentially dysfunctional family and takes a very different look at the ways children call on available resources—within and without—to cope with chronic and life-threatening illness. Stars Andie MacDowell, John Turturro. Directed by Diane Keaton.

Films About AIDS

And the Band Played On (1993)   A made-for-TV docudrama based on the groundbreaking journalism of Randy Shilts. The film describes the early attempts to seek a cure for the newly discovered virus, and the political-bureaucratic foot-dragging that impeded that quest. Stars Matthew Modine, Alan Alda. Directed by Robert Spottiswoode.

As Is (1985)   This powerful drama about the effect of AIDS on a family is hard-hitting and often painful to watch. It deals directly with the need to expand the definition of "family" to include more than blood relatives. Stars Jonathan Hadary, Robert Carradine. Directed by Michael Lindsay-Hogg.

Common Threads: Stories from the Quilt (1989)   A wonderful collection of some of the many stories of families and other loved ones who contributed to the AIDS quilt. Very personal and very moving stories. Directed by Robert Epstein.

An Early Frost (1985)   One of the best movies made on the subject of AIDS and its impact on the family. The tension between mother and father concerning their son's homosexuality and illness forms the core of this excellent drama. Stars Gena Rowlands, Ben Gazzara, Aidan Quinn. Directed by John Erman.

Longtime Companion (1990)   A moving account of the death of a young man within the context of a larger "created" family—a common scenario among gay men dealing with AIDS. Stars Bruce Davison, Campbell Scott. Directed by Norman René.

Love! Valour! Compassion! (1997)   This film version of the successful stage play by Terrence McNally is a provocative and intimate look at a group of gay men—old friends who gather together for a series of weekend getaways. The revelation that one of the friends has AIDS and the overall handling of the illness as a subject create an excellent basis for discussion. Stars Jason Alexander, John Glover. Directed by Joe Mantello.

Parting Glances (1986)   A positive and upbeat treatment of homosexual relationships, this film shows the painful impact of an AIDS diagnosis. This is an unusually open and nonjudgmental portrayal of gay relationships. Stars John Bolger, Richard Ganoung. Directed by Bill Sherwood.

Philadelphia (1993)   An Academy Award–winning film about a lawyer stricken with AIDS and his fight against the ensuing discrimination he experiences in the workplace. The depiction of his family and their thorough acceptance of him, his homosexuality, and his illness is a bit unrealistic but certainly thought-provoking. Stars Tom Hanks, Denzel Washington. Directed by Jonathan Demme.

Tidy Endings (1988)   In this made-for-TV movie, a man dies of AIDS, and his lover and ex-wife meet to reconcile and grieve. Quite an affecting movie, although a bit sentimental, it is definitely worth seeing for a different perspective on AIDS grief. Stars Stockard Channing, Harvey Fierstein. Directed by Harvey Fierstein.

Films Especially Useful in Training

The Homecoming (1973)   This Harold Pinter play, adapted for the screen, portrays family tension without satisfactory resolution. It can be useful for initiating discussion about how families may try but fail to resolve their differences. Stars Vivian Merchant, Ian Holm. Directed by Peter Hall.

Interiors (1978)   A nearly melodramatic portrayal of a family in crisis because of the mental illness and ultimate suicide of the mother, this film can be helpful in promoting discussion of similar family predicaments. Stars Diane Keaton, Kristin Griffith, Geraldine Page. Directed by Woody Allen.

Ordinary People (1980)   A searingly painful drama of a family torn asunder by the accidental death of the eldest son, this film should be used cautiously with grieving families. It is a very effective vehicle for opening up discussion in training situations. Stars Donald Sutherland, Mary Tyler Moore, Timothy Hutton. Directed by Robert Redford.

Promises in the Dark (1979)   This is an unrealistic, melodramatic, and even banal film about a child dying of cancer and her very caring doctor. I list it here because excerpts from such films are sometimes useful in training to point out the idealized notions of death and dying depicted in popular culture. Stars Marsha Mason, Ned Beatty. Directed by Jerome Hellman.

Terms of Endearment (1983)   A mother's death from cancer is the climax of this popular film. This is another film that should be seen for the false note it strikes about dying and families facing death. Stars Shirley MacLaine, Debra Winger, Jack Nicholson. Directed by James L. Brooks.

Whose Life Is It Anyway? (1981)   This film addresses the ultimate questions: What constitutes quality of life? And who has
a right to decide when to die? A stage play by Brian Clark
adapted for the screen, the film is ingeniously cast and beautifully acted. Caution is appropriate when considering this film
for families. Stars Richard Dreyfuss, John Cassavetes. Directed
by John Bodham.

Appendix B: Reading List

This list includes readings that are particularly relevant to issues of serious illness, death, and grieving and their effects on the family system. It is not intended as a comprehensive bibliography of the death and grief literature but rather as a compendium of readings that address these issues as they pertain to the family and its functioning in the face of illness and death.

Some of the readings are more general in nature but are included because of their particular application to families. Also included in this appendix are readings that have been used with professional and nonprofessional hospice personnel to teach them about work with families. In general, these tend to be less technical and less clinically oriented selections, and they are indicated with an asterisk (*).

*Bertman, S. L. *Facing Death: Images, Insights, and Interventions*. Bristol, Pa.: Hemisphere, 1991.

Bowen, M. "Family Reaction to Death." In P. Guerin (ed.), *Family Therapy: Theory and Practice*. Lake Worth, Fla.: Gardner Press, 1976.

Bugen, L. A. "Human Grief: A Model for Prediction and Intervention." *American Journal of Orthopsychiatry*, 1977, 479, 196–206.

*Byock, I. *Dying Well: The Prospect for Growth at the End of Life*. New York: Riverhead Books, 1997.

Carter, B., and McGoldrick, M. (eds.). *The Changing Family Life Cycle: A Framework for Family Therapy*. Lake Worth, Fla.: Gardner Press, 1988.

Cohen, P., Dizenhuz, I. M., and Winget, C. "Family Adaptation to Terminal Illness and Death of a Parent." *Social Casework*, 1977, 58(4), 223–228.

*Connor, S. R. *Hospice: Practice, Pitfalls, Promise*. Bristol, Pa.: Taylor & Francis, 1997.

Coontz, S. *The Way We Never Were: American Families and the Nostalgia Trap*. New York: Basic Books, 1992.

Doka, K. J. "Silent Sorrow: Grief and the Loss of Significant Others." *Death Studies*, 1987, *11*, 455–469.

*Doka, K. J. *Living with Life-Threatening Illness*. San Francisco: New Lexington Press, 1993.

Evans, N. S. "Mourning as a Family Secret." *Journal of the American Academy of Child Psychiatry*, 1976, *15*, 502–509.

Fulmer, R. H. "A Structural Approach to Unresolved Mourning in Single Parent Family Systems." *Journal of Marital and Family Therapy*, 1983, 8, 259–269.

Grollman, E. *Explaining Death to Children*. Boston: Beacon Press, 1969.

Hare-Mustin, R. "Family Therapy Following the Death of a Child." *Journal of Marital and Family Therapy*, 1979, 5(2), 51–59.

Helmrath, T. A., and Steinitz, G. M. "Parental Grieving and the Failure of Social Support." *Journal of Family Practice*, 1978, 6, 785–790.

*Herz Brown, F. "The Impact of Death and Serious Illness on the Family Life Cycle." In B. Carter and M. McGoldrick (eds.), *The Changing Family Life Cycle: A Framework for Family Therapy*. Lake Worth, Fla.: Gardner Press, 1988.

Herz Brown, F. (ed.). *Reweaving the Family Tapestry: A Multigenerational Approach to Families*. New York: Norton, 1991.

Imber-Black, E., Roberts, J., and Whiting, R. (eds.). *Rituals in Families and Family Therapy*. New York: Norton, 1988.

Irish, D. P., Lundquist, K. F., and Nelsen, V. J. *Ethnic Variations in Dying, Death, and Grief: Diversity in Universality*. Bristol, Pa.: Taylor & Francis, 1993.

Klass, D., Silverman, P. R., and Nickman, S. *Continuing Bonds: New Understandings of Grief*. Bristol, Pa.: Taylor & Francis, 1996.

*Kübler-Ross, E. *On Death and Dying*. Old Tappan, N.J.: Macmillan, 1969.

*Larson, D. G. *The Helper's Journey*. Champaign, Ill.: Research Press, 1993.

Levine, S. *Who Dies? An Investigation of Conscious Living and Conscious Dying*. New York: Anchor Books, 1982.

McClenahan Bradach, K., and Jordan, J. "Long-Term Effects of a Family History of Traumatic Death on Adolescent Individuation." *Death Studies*, 1995, 19(4), 315–336.

McDaniel, S., Hepworth, J., and Doherty, W. *Medical Family Therapy: A Biopsychosocial Approach to Families with Health Problems.* New York: Basic Books, 1992.

McGoldrick, M., Girodano, J., and Pearce, J. K. (eds.). *Ethnicity and Family Therapy.* (2nd ed.) New York: Guilford Press, 1996.

*McGoldrick, M., and Gerson, R. *Genograms in Family Assessment.* New York: Norton, 1985.

McGoldrick, M., and Walsh, F. (eds.). *Living Beyond Loss.* New York: Norton, 1991.

McGoldrick, M. *You Can Go Home Again: Reconnecting with Your Family.* New York: Norton, 1997.

Montalvo, B., and Elliot, M. "Assisting Terminally Ill Patients and Their Families: An Orientation Model." *Family Systems Medicine,* 1994, *12*(3), 269–279.

Mulhern, R. K., Lauer, M. E., and Hoffman, R. G. "Death of a Child at Home or the Hospital: Subsequent Psychological Adjustment of the Family." *Pediatrics,* 1983, *71,* 743–747.

*Napier, A. Y., and Whitaker, C. A. *The Family Crucible.* New York: HarperCollins, 1978.

Olson, S. L. "Transgenerational Dynamics and Hospice Care." *Hospice Journal,* 1988, *4*(2), 67–77.

Paul, N. L. "The Role of Mourning and Empathy in Conjoint Family Therapy." In G. Zuk and I. Boszormenyi-Nash (eds.), *Family Therapy and Disturbed Families.* Palo Alto, Calif.: Science and Behavior Books, 1967.

*Pincus, L. *Death and the Family: The Importance of Mourning.* New York: Pantheon Books, 1974.

Quill, T. *Midwife Through the Dying Process.* Baltimore: Johns Hopkins University Press, 1996.

Rando, T. *Loss and Anticipatory Grief.* San Francisco: New Lexington Press, 1986.

Reilly, D. M. "Death Propensity, Dying and Bereavement: A Family Systems Perspective." *Family Therapy,* 1978, *5*(1), 35–55.

Rolland, J. S. *Families, Illness, and Disability.* New York: Basic Books, 1994.

*Rosen, E. J. "Teaching Family Therapy Concepts to the Hospice Team." *American Journal of Hospice Care,* 1987, *4*(4), 39–44.

Rosen, E. J. "Family Therapy in Cases of Interminable Grief for the Loss of a Child." *Omega: Journal of Death and Dying,* 1988, *19*(3), 187–202.

*Rosen, E. J. "The Ethnic and Cultural Dimensions of Work with Hospice Families." *American Journal of Hospice Care,* 1988, *5*(4), 16–21.

Rosen, E. J. "Hospice Work with AIDS-Related Disenfranchised Grief." In K. Doka (ed.), *Disenfranchised Grief*. San Francisco: New Lexington Press, 1989.

Rosen, E. J. "Coaching with Families Facing Terminal Illness." In F. Herz Brown (ed.), *Reweaving the Family Tapestry: A Multigenerational Approach to Families*. New York: Norton, 1991.

*Rosen, E. J. "The Family as Healing Resource." In C. A. Coor and D. M. Coor (eds.), *Handbook of Childhood Death and Bereavement*. New York: Springer, 1996.

*Rosof, B. *The Worst Loss: How Families Heal from the Death of a Child*. New York: Henry Holt, 1994.

Shapiro, E. R. *Grief as a Family Process: A Developmental Approach to Clinical Practice*. New York: Guilford Press, 1994.

Sims, A. M. *Am I Still a Sister?* Blue Springs, Mo.: Big A & Co., 1988.

Solomon, M., and Hersch, L. B. "Death in the Family: Implications for Family Development." *Journal of Marriage and Family Therapy*, 1979, 5(2), 43–49.

Vess, J., Moreland, J., and Schwebel, A. I. "Understanding Family Role Allocation Following a Death: A Theoretical Framework." *Omega: Journal of Death and Dying*, 1985–86, l6(2), 115–128.

Videka-Sherman, L. "Coping with the Death of a Child: A Study over Time." *American Journal of Orthopsychiatry*, 1982, 52, 688–698.

Walker, G. "The Pact: The Caretaker-Patient/Ill-Child Coalition in Families with Chronic Illness." *Family Systems Medicine*, 1983, 1, 513–523.

Walker, G. *In the Midst of Winter: A Systemic Therapy with Families, Couples, and Individuals with AIDS Infection*. New York: Norton, 1991.

Walsh, F., and McGoldrick, M. "Loss and the Family Life Cycle." In C. J. Falicov (ed.), *Family Transitions: Continuity and Change over the Life Cycle*. New York: Guilford Press, 1988.

*Worden, W. *Grief Counseling and Grief Therapy*. (2nd ed.) New York: Springer, 1991.

Worden, W. *Children and Grief: When a Parent Dies*. New York: Guilford Press, 1996.

Wortman, C., and Silver, R. C. "The Myths of Coping with Loss." *Journal of Consulting and Clinical Psychology*, 1989, 57(2), 349–357.

Wright, L. M., and Nagy, J. "Death: The Most Troublesome Secret of All." In E. Imber-Black (ed.), *Secrets in Families and Family Therapy*. New York: Norton, 1993.

Books for Children Dealing with Death and Loss

Bratman, F. *Everything You Need to Know When a Parent Dies*. New York: Rosen, 1995.

Brown, L. K. *When Dinosaurs Die: A Guide to Understanding Death*. New York: Little, Brown, 1996.

Buscaglia, L. *The Fall of Freddie the Leaf*. Thorofare, N.J.: Holt & Stack, 1982.

Cohn, J. *I Had a Friend Named Peter*. New York: Morrow, 1987.

Gootman, M. *When a Friend Dies: A Book for Teens About Grieving and Healing*. Minneapolis: Free Spirit, 1994.

Grollman, E. *Talking About Death: A Dialogue Between Parent and Child*. Boston: Beacon Press, 1990.

Holden, D. *Gran-Gran's Best Trick*. New York: Magination Press, 1989.

Juneau, B. *Sad but OK: My Daddy Died Today*. San Bernardino, Calif.: Borgo Press, 1989.

Liss-Levinson, N. *When a Grandparent Dies: A Kid's Own Remembering Workbook for Dealing with Shiva and the Year Beyond*. Woodstock, N.Y.: Jewish Light, 1995.

Porter, B. *Grandpa and Me and the Wishing Star*. Salt Lake City: Deseret Books, 1990.

Powell, S. *Geranium Morning*. Minneapolis: Carolrhoda Books, 1990.

Randle, K. *Why Did Grandma Have to Die?* Salt Lake City: Bookcraft, 1987.

Rofes, E. *The Kids' Book About Death and Dying: By and for Kids*. New York: Little, Brown, 1985.

Scriviani, M. *I Heard Your Mommy Died*. Omaha, Neb.: Centering Corp., 1996.

Scriviani, M. *I Heard Your Daddy Died*. Omaha, Neb.: Centering Corp., 1996.

Stickney, D. *Water Bugs and Dragonflies: Explaining Death to Young Children*. Cleveland, Ohio: Pilgrim Press, 1997.

Techner, D. *A Candle for Grandpa: A Guide to the Jewish Funeral for Children and Parents*. New York: UAHC Press, 1993.

Weitzman, E. *Let's Talk About When a Parent Dies*. New York: Powerkids Press, 1996.

About the Author

Elliott J. Rosen is director of the Family Institute of Westchester in White Plains, New York, and serves as psychological consultant to Phelps Memorial Hospital Hospice in North Tarrytown, New York. A family therapist and teacher, he lives in Scarsdale, New York, where he maintains a private practice specializing in medical family therapy and consultation. He has written extensively on the issues of ethnicity and the grieving process and has published clinical research on the impact of death, loss, and interminable grief on the family system. He lectures frequently throughout the country to both lay and professional audiences.

Index

Index of Family Clinical Cases